JIM CROW WISDOM

Jim Crow Wisdom

MEMORY AND IDENTITY IN BLACK AMERICA SINCE 1940

Jonathan Scott Holloway

The University of North Carolina Press CHAPEL HILL

Publication of this book was supported in part by a generous gift from
Eric Papenfuse and Catherine Lawrence.

Lucille Clifton, "why some people be mad at me sometimes," from *The Collected Poems
of Lucille Clifton*. Copyright © 1991 by Lucille Clifton. Reprinted with the permission of
The Permissions Company, Inc., on behalf of BOA Editions Ltd., www.boaeditions.org.

"Top of the World." Words and music by John Bettis and Richard Carpenter.
Copyright © 1972 ALMO MUSIC CORP. and HAMMER AND NAILS MUSIC. Copyright
renewed. All Rights Administered by ALMO MUSIC CORP. All Rights Reserved. Used by
Permission. *Reprinted by Permission of Hal Leonard Corporation.*

"A Story Like No Other." Written by Chris Thomas King. Published by Young Blues
Rebel Music. Reprinted by permission of Chris Thomas King Tours, LLC.

Library of Congress Cataloging-in-Publication Data
Holloway, Jonathan Scott.
Jim Crow Wisdom : Memory and Identity in Black America
since 1940 / Jonathan Scott Holloway.
pages cm
Includes bibliographical references and index.
ISBN 978-1-4696-1070-2 (hardback)
ISBN 978-1-4696-2641-3 (pbk.:   )
1. Race awareness—United States. 2. African Americans—
Race identity. 3. African Americans—Psychology. 4. African Americans—
History—20th century. 5. Memory—Sociological aspects. 6. Holloway,
Jonathan Scott. I. Title.
E185.625.H64 2013
305.896'073—dc23
2013015591

*For Ellison and Emerson, the literal embodiment of my future,
and for Aisling, who made this future possible.*

*For my ancestors, whose future I came to understand and appreciate
in writing this book, but especially for my mother. If anyone in my
memory deserves a standing ovation, it is she.*

CONTENTS

Acknowledgments, xi

INTRODUCTION / The Scars of Memory, 1

1 / Editing and the Art of Forgetfulness in Social Science, 14

2 / Memory and Racial Humiliation in Popular Literature, 40

3 / The Black Body as Archive of Memory, 67

4 / Black Scholars and Memory in the Age of Black Studies, 102

5 / The Silences in a Civil Rights Narrative, 135

6 / Heritage Tourism, Museums of Horror, and the
Commerce of Memory, 174

EPILOGUE / Memory in the Diaspora, 214

Notes, 231
Bibliography, 251
Index, 269

ILLUSTRATIONS

Cartoon editorial, Gunnar Myrdal and *An American Dilemma*, 24

Kay and Wendell Holloway, newly married, 29

At the net, Lester Granger and William Trent Jr., 65

"I Been 'Buked," *Revelations*, 80

Trying to bathe the black away, *Watermelon Man*, 100

Lott Drive, Montgomery, Alabama, 139

The neighborhood kids in Montgomery, 144

Kay Holloway, my mother, 144

Lt. Col. Wendell Holloway, my father, 147

Vi Trent, my maternal grandmother, 155

Jannifer Scales, Brian Holloway, and Pam Pryor at the
  Scales family reunion, 159

John Holloway, my paternal grandfather, 167

Fannie Holloway, my paternal grandmother, 167

My Colonial Williamsburg stockade keepsake photograph, 195

Slave cabins, Evergreen Plantation, 205

Kitchen collectibles, Evergreen Plantation, 207

Tomb of the Unknown Slave, Tremé, New Orleans, 211

Fishing village, Cape Coast, Ghana, 223

ACKNOWLEDGMENTS

As I've discovered, when you write a book about memory, you can become fairly obsessed about your capacity for forgetfulness. Keeping that in mind, I need to begin my acknowledgments with an apology: I can only assume that in the paragraphs that follow I will have forgotten some people—close friends, even—who played a real role in helping this book come to fruition. I am sorry for this oversight, but I want you to know (and you know who you are) that I think of you all the time.

This book began in Harvey Kaye's living room. When I told him my plans for the next project, he said they weren't that interesting and wondered what else I had on my mind. After I rambled on for a few flustered minutes about memory and identity, he said I'd be a fool for considering anything else. I love the fact that Harvey set me straight in a way that only he can. Although the project has changed considerably since I previewed it for him, I think he will like what he sees. If not, I'm sure he'll let me know.

My first opportunity to focus on this project came during a sabbatical year at the Stanford Humanities Center (SHC). The SHC staff, in general, was phenomenal. I particularly benefited from my extended conversations with Chiyuma Elliott, Pei-pei Lin, and Elizabeth Wahl. The Humanities Center fellows were an exceptional lot as well. Numerous lunchtime conversations helped me see the project from entirely fresh perspectives.

During that same year, I benefited enormously from the camaraderie and support of key figures in Stanford's American studies and African American studies communities: Clayborne Carson, Sandra Drake, Vera Grant, John Rickford, Arnold Rampersad, Shelley Fisher Fishkin, Harry Elam, and Michele Elam. I also profited from the research assistance of Christina Knight, an SHC undergraduate fellow. The participants in the SHC-hosted Black Routes Symposium were particularly insightful: Dwight McBride, Ann duCille, Joy Ann Williamson, Martha Biondi, Leigh Raiford, and Maurice Stevens.

Closer to my home of the last fourteen years, my colleagues at Yale have been enormously helpful at every stage. I don't have room here to offer the finer details of their contributions, but without their wisdom, interruptions, encouragement, and probing questions this project would be a mere shadow of itself. For their abiding faith, I thank Elizabeth Alexander, David Blight, Jon Butler, Hazel Carby, Robert Stepto, Paul Gilroy, Jennifer Baszile, Matthew Jacobson, Joe Roach, Paige McGinley, Terri Francis, Glenda Gilmore, Caryl Phillips, Ron Eyerman, Rich Brooks, Dolores Hayden, Adom Getachew, Joshua Guild, Brandon Terry, Grace Leslie, Caitlin Casey, Erin Wood, and Jeffrey Gonda. I also suffered from an embarrassment of riches when it came to research assistance. At various points along the way Jonathan DiMaio, Emily Weissler, Sarah O'Brien, Nate Glasser, Natalie Papillion, Shira Concool, Amanda Branson Gill, and Aurora Edington gave their time, focus, and ideas. Andrew Horowitz deserves special recognition not only for his research assistance but, more importantly, for convincing me that using a first-person voice was critical to the project. Jennifer Parker, another special assistant, answered my queries, helped me wade through a thicket of false starts, and demonstrated an acute sensitivity for tone and execution. As the project moved toward production, Dave Griffin in Yale's Media and Photographic Services Group offered critical assistance.

In Yale's Offices of the President and Provost I am indebted to Rick Levin, Peter Salovey, Lloyd Suttle, Emily Bakemeier, and Joy McGrath. In the Yale College Dean's Office, Mary Miller, Joe Gordon, Mark Schenker, and Susan Cahan were consistently enthusiastic in their support. External to Yale, significant help with the project's completion came from the W. E. B. Du Bois Research Institute (with a special nod to Abby Wolfe) and the Alphonse Fletcher Sr. Fellowship.

When I was in my most intense writing mode, I learned a lot about my project from the special opportunities I had to present various of its sections at workshops. To that end, I must thank Yale's African American Studies' Endeavors Colloquium, the American Studies Symposium, the Critical Encounters Series (also housed in American Studies), and the Legal History Forum. Away from New Haven, I am in debt to my hosts at the Duke University Law Center, the Charles H. Warren Center at Harvard, the American Studies Program at Brown, the Centers for African American Studies at Princeton and Wesleyan, the Social Science Division at the University of Chicago, the African and African American Studies Department at Northwestern (specifically, the Leon Forrest Endowed Lecture series), and, most critically, the Writing History Group at Cornell. My experience at Cornell pushed me in precisely the right way at precisely the right moment. To that end, thanks go to Tina Post, Daegan Miller, Amy Kohout, Josi Ward, Laura Martin, Carmen Krol, and Brian Cuddy. Aaron Sachs, the faculty sponsor of the Cornell group and an old friend as well, deserves special acknowledgment. His close read of the manuscript at several late stages was invaluable, as was his abiding enthusiasm for the manuscript's experiment of voice and form.

Over the years, I scurried about, chasing down different ideas and trying on different methods. Guiding me along these paths—and sometimes telling me to turn around as soon as possible—were many different scholars who honored me with their time, insights, and friendship. In this regard, I must thank Renee Romano, Fitzhugh Brundage, David Chappell, Edward Ball, Evelyn Brooks-Higginbotham, Kenneth Mack, Henry Louis Gates Jr., Celeste Watkins-Hayes, Sandra Richards, Guy-Uriel Charles, Stephen Lassonde, Amia Srinivasan, Tony Badger, Andrew Fearnley, Daniel Matlin, Jim Walvin, Richard Benjamin, Matt Reonas, J. Emmanuel Raymundo, Hilton Als, George Lipsitz, Sam Popkin, and Susan Shirk.

Back at Yale, my support network often seemed without limit. Helaine Klasky was always a delightful distraction. Justin Zaremby contributed to my institutional education in innumerable ways. Caryn Carson and Liza Joyner kept track of my research finances. My extended family at Calhoun College, one of Yale's twelve residential colleges, was a constant reminder that there are larger purposes for everything. If it were manageable, I would personally thank the 1,200+ students and staff who have touched my family's life since we moved on campus and into the master's house. I hope my "Hounies" will be content in the knowledge that something of them has found its way into this book. Having said that, it is important that I recognize my assistant Angela McCray, who pulled off a few miracles in the closing weeks of manuscript prep. The other member of the Calhoun family who deserves special recognition is Leslie Woodard, the dean of the college, but more importantly, my friend. Leslie has been a phenomenal colleague and counselor during so many challenging moments as we have managed the college together. I thank her for her wisdom and unflagging encouragement.

Thinking of extended family, special thanks go to Ned and Birgit, Steve and Alicia, Mary and Vincent, Sarah and Peter, John and Eve, Idit and Eitan, and Barry and Lauren. Terry and Lisa, however, stand apart—not only for their abiding friendship but also for their exhortation (printed on the back of a t-shirt given to me at the start of my final year with the project, no less) to "Just Write The Damn Book."

When I signed the contract with the University of North Carolina Press, I felt like I was returning home. UNC Press published my first book, and I have always admired its editors' commitment to first-rate scholarship and, critical for this book, their deep reservoir of patience. Sian Hunter has known *Jim Crow Wisdom* the longest. While she is no longer part of the

UNC Press family, she believed in this project from the start, encouraged me to go exploring when I hit a crossroads early on, and (politely) refused to let me out of the contract when I was feeling stuck and hopeless. When she left UNC Press, Sian passed this project on to David Perry, who, to my great relief, similarly invested himself in the adventure and offered sage advice as he guided this work through its final stages. At the project's beginning and ending stages, both Sian and David secured remarkable readers. These scholars, still anonymous to me, offered truly valuable ideas that bolstered this project. As the manuscript entered production, Stephanie Wenzel's steady hand left me confident that every small and bedeviling detail would be addressed.

To the elders in my blood-and-bones family—Grandma Vi, Aunt Virginia, Judy, my late aunt Toni, Danny, Brian, Karen, Dad, and my late mother—I offer my endless thanks. I am indebted to them for so many things, but particularly for their commitment to keep the family histories alive, even when some stories were clearly meant to be forgotten.

And, finally, to the family I've had the honor to make: Aisling, you are my best friend and I love the fact that I am always sure of you. Emerson and Ellison, thank you for making me Dad. I owe you. In time, I hope you'll come to see this book as partial repayment.

THE SCARS OF MEMORY

they ask me to remember
but they want me to remember
their memories
and I keep on remembering
mine
— Lucille Clifton,
"why some people be mad at me sometimes"

Jonathan doesn't know his family history.
—Wendell Holloway

"Brrrrrrriiiiiiiiiiiiiiiiiiiiiinng!"

The shrill ringing of an alarm clock opens Richard Wright's explosive 1940 novel *Native Son*, deploying a new kind of language for the reading public to consider when talking about race. *Native Son* simultaneously captivated and terrified its readers with the story of Bigger Thomas's abject poverty and his subsequent slide into an impossible nightmare when he accidentally kills a wealthy white teenage girl and then rapes and murders his girlfriend to whom he has confessed the original crime.

With this book, Wright tore into the consciousness of the reading public. *Native Son* won many accolades and sold nearly a quarter of a million copies soon after being named the March selection of the Book-of-the-Month Club.[1] What was it that drew readers to Bigger's nightmare? It's unlikely they came for the mere spectacle of racial violence, since they could get something akin to that merely by opening their newspaper to the crime blotter, where "colored" really meant criminal. Instead, they came to *Native*

1

Son because they believed that it offered them a purchase on the Negro worldview. *Native Son* allowed white liberal friends of the race to see behind the veil and moan, stammer, and shout.

This was all by design, of course, and Wright said as much in his evocative essay "How 'Bigger' Was Born." He had no intention of repeating in *Native Son* the "naïve mistake" he had made in *Uncle Tom's Children*, published two years earlier. Upon reading glowing reviews of this earlier work, Wright lamented "that I had written a book which even bankers' daughters could read and weep over and feel good about. I swore to myself that if I ever wrote another book, no one would weep over it; that it would be so hard and deep that they would have to face it without the consolation of tears."[2]

In the world of black cultural expression, Wright's *Native Son* came at the end of a two-decade-long celebration of arts, letters, and music. This era, the New Negro Renaissance, was animated by a new sensibility concerning African American cultural contributions as whites raced to consume black poetry, literature, painting, sculpture, and music. It was also an era of a changing political language as blacks began to assert their claim to full citizenship more aggressively than in the past. Nationalist Marcus Garvey thrilled the black masses gathering in increasing numbers in northern and midwestern cities with his call for race pride and a black empire; intellectual and provocateur W. E. B. Du Bois warned white America that black soldiers were returning from fighting in Europe and would continue to fight for their freedoms at home; poet Claude McKay urged his audiences to "face the murderous, cowardly pack . . . Pressed to the wall, dying, but fighting back." Political organizations, not just individuals, were also fluent in this new discourse. For example, the Communist Party USA and then the Popular Front looked appealing to many blacks who had become frustrated with the Democratic and Republican Party status quo.[3]

In the fall of 1940, a mere six months after *Native Son* was published, several prominent blacks lobbied President Franklin Roosevelt, urging him to desegregate the armed forces. When labor leader A. Philip Randolph, National Association for the Advancement of Colored People (NAACP) executive secretary Walter White, and National Urban League head T. Arnold Hill were rebuffed, Randolph developed a new tactic aimed at forcing Roosevelt's hand.

As the head of the Brotherhood of Sleeping Car Porters and Maids as well as the first president of the Popular Front–era National Negro Congress, Randolph believed he could tap into a vast network of organized workers who shared his frustrations with the pace of change. In January 1941, and in response to Roosevelt's stonewalling, Randolph issued a call for blacks to march on the nation's capital to denounce segregation in the armed forces as well as rampant discrimination in the nation's defense industries.

Roosevelt sent New York mayor Fiorello La Guardia and then First Lady Eleanor Roosevelt to convince Randolph to cancel the march. Randolph did not comply and even increased the size of the planned protest. In late June, with only one week remaining before the march was scheduled to start, Roosevelt called Randolph to the Oval Office and said that he would do something to meet Randolph's demands if he would call off the march. This time, Randolph agreed, and Roosevelt signed Executive Order 8802 making discrimination in the nation's defense industries illegal and establishing the Fair Employment Practices Committee. Randolph succeeded in calling the president's bluff, and soon the March on Washington Movement, one of the earliest national civil rights organizations, was established.[4]

Randolph's meeting with Roosevelt, the signing of Executive Order 8802, and the establishment of the March on Washington Movement suggested that there was a new opportunity in America's political landscape for blacks to be more than a mere presence. Now the broader public, embodied in this moment by Book-of-the-Month Club readers and Roosevelt's executive branch apparatus, had to acknowledge an ascendant black voice.

Using this moment as a starting point, *Jim Crow Wisdom: Memory and Identity in Black America since 1940* listens to that black voice and the stories that it tells over the course of the long second half of the twentieth century.[5] More specifically, *Jim Crow Wisdom* observes how this voice is articulated through personal and public memories, academic and popular literature, dance, film, and heritage tourism, all the while examining how these ways of self-imagining are connected to a black identity that is engaged in a battle to secure full citizenship rights. Relying on so many different types of sources helps us develop a portrait of black memory work that is appropriately complex, reflecting the consistencies and contradictions embedded in the construction of the African American character.

Memory and identity have always been intertwined. Parents have always told stories about themselves, their families, or their people in order to contextualize their decisions in the present or to prepare future generations for the worlds to come. Similarly, politicians, clergy, artists, activists, and intellectuals have shared their visions of the past in order to stake claims to the present and future and to shape the collective identity of the groups they address. Speaking specifically about African America, we know that as long as enslaved people of African descent or, later, second-class citizens of African descent journeyed throughout the diaspora, many individuals have waged public and private battles to claim full citizenship rights and have done so by weaving protest and admonitions into powerful autobiographies. One only has to think of the narratives written by Frederick Douglass, Harriet Jacobs, or William Wells Brown to understand that there is a long history of claims for full human rights communicated via memoirs.[6] These kinds of narratives have been consistently popular. One reason for the popularity, historian John Blassingame argues, is that the mere act of the autobiographical claim to humanity was deeply therapeutic for the author and the reading public. For black authors, the autobiography allowed them "to express their true feelings without having them distorted by whites. It imposed some order on an irrational world." For black readers, the autobiography was a moment when a "fellow sufferer had 'attacked' their white oppressors, proved the race's moral superiority over whites, and demonstrated that the readers' failures were not due to personal shortcomings, but rather to racial discrimination."[7]

Blassingame offered this assessment in 1973, almost perfectly in the middle of the era that is the focus of this book. Blassingame was writing in the years immediately following the apparent collapse of the modern civil rights movement and at the height of the black pride era when talk within the black community of its moral superiority over whites was especially resonant. As much as Blassingame reflected that era's revolutionary sensibilities, he could not have seen that he was writing on the cusp of a radically intensifying phase of a different kind of revolution—this one related to information and technology.

When we consider the breadth, depth, and pace of technological change since the early 1940s—television saturation, twenty-four-hour news cycles, desktop publishing—we see that the scope and pace of sharing information has fundamentally changed.[8] However, even though the technological changes of the last seventy years have made sharing a personal story with a consuming public significantly easier for an individual, thus suggesting the formation of new collective memories and identities, the stories' themes, especially when they pertain to black life in America, have not changed dramatically. Indeed, as *Jim Crow Wisdom* reads black memories across time and across a broad spectrum of spaces, several phenomena abide: the traumas of racial humiliation and shame are regularly narrated, class issues hide behind the racial veil, there is a palpable anxiety about telling children the truth about race, and vexed questions about home and belonging abound. There is no doubt that black memory gets narrated in different ways over the breadth of the twentieth century, especially in light of the dramatic political, social, and economic changes since 1940, but this is largely a history of a changing same.[9]

At one level, it is easy to see why the narrative of the black past is so stable. Put simply, racism and the physical and psychological violence that accompanies it has and continues to be a key component of the American character. Reaching back to the Civil War, a moment that is undoubtedly fundamental to understanding just what this American character is, historian David Blight points to the effects violence had on how blacks narrated their past: "Mob violence and eventually lynching were so deeply embedded in black folk memory that virtually every major African American writer since emancipation has made these subjects central to his or her work in poetry and prose." Blight continues, "The sheer persistence of themes of ritualized violence in black writing indicates, as one critic has argued, that a form of 'racial memory' took hold."[10]

Violence, or the threat of it, is critical to understanding the formation of a black identity through memory. It is the literal or figurative cut, after all, that is simultaneously the original injury and the inspiration for observation and witness. It may well be, however, that the story of the resulting scar tells us more about the nuances of racial memory. The misshapen edges of the scar, its keloid surface, and the way one's fingers absentmindedly trace the original injury affect the retelling of the story that led to the cut in the first place.

THE CUT

The title of this book is taken from "The Ethics of Living Jim Crow," a short autobiographical piece Richard Wright penned in 1936. In the essay, Wright recounts a battle he and his friends engaged in with white boys who lived, quite literally, on the other side of the tracks. On an almost daily basis the black boys targeted their enemies with cinders that were thrown from the trains that passed by their back doors. One day, the white boys responded with milk bottles. Exposed in the field of battle, young Richard was hit behind his ear. A neighbor rushed him to the doctor for stitches and then left Richard sitting on his front porch, feeling angry at the injustice that accompanied the differential in the boys' weaponry and waiting for his mother to come home to console him. More than sympathy, however, he wanted his mother to tell him "exactly what to do next time."[11]

After Richard recounted the story, his mother examined his wound and then slapped him, asking him why he didn't hide, scolding him for fighting in the first place. Wright remembered, "I was outraged, and bawled. Between sobs I told her that I didn't have any trees or hedges to hide behind. There wasn't a thing I could have used as a trench. And you couldn't throw very far when you were hiding behind the brick pillars of a house. She grabbed a barrel stave, dragged me home, stripped me naked, and beat me till I had a fever of one hundred and two. She would smack my rump with the stave, and, while the skin was still smarting, impart to me gems of Jim Crow wisdom."[12]

Whether or not we agree with Mrs. Wright's pedagogical style, it is clear that she was trying to prepare her son for a world where blacks often had no recourse when engaged in disputes with whites, a world where one had to know one's place according to the dictates of racial etiquette. This was Arkansas in the 1910s, after all. But Richard's interaction with his mother and his mother's intention were not unique to that time and place.

I grew up in a situation quite unlike young Richard's: two parents in the house, upper middle class, a comfortable and fairly sheltered suburban experience. My playmates were a polyglot mix of children of scientists, patent attorneys, and first-generation personal computer developers. Although I was not blind to race, I had lived my life fairly free of its negative contingencies. This slowly began to change in the fall of my first semester of high school.

I knew something was "different" when my father told me one morning that he wanted to drive me to school. We lived only about two miles from my high school, and I normally took the bus. A pattern had been established years ago: Whenever my father wanted to bring up difficult subjects, he took me to school, figuring that he could jump straight to the point, complete his thought, and get me out of the car before I could ask too many questions. There was the introductory sex-ed ride when I was just starting junior high school (he didn't realize I had already learned the details in fifth or sixth grade); there was the follow-up ride informing me that I might be old enough to get a girl pregnant (a very awkward conversation to say the least, since I still wasn't yet interested in girls in any sort of potentially reproductive way); and then there was this particular morning's ride. As I got into the car, I wondered what the topic might be. That day's theme: fighting.

In my father's mind, I was now old enough and tall enough to know that I might be singled out by someone itching for a fight in order to prove who knows what. Having never been in a brawl myself, I was confused as to where this was coming from or going. My father pressed on. "The fact is," he said, "if someone decides to go after you for whatever reason, you have to protect yourself, but you cannot afford to swing back." He continued, "Because you are tall, people are going to think you are older than you actually are. But more importantly, because of 'the way things are,' people are going to suspect and punish you first if you ever get into a fight. It won't matter who started it, or what the reason was. People will assume you were the antagonist."

My father didn't have to tell me what he meant by "the way things are." By this point in my life I knew enough code to understand that he was talking about what we now call racial profiling. Even though fair-skinned, I am clearly black. And, because of the way things are, I was suspect.

This was one of my first race memories. I have written elsewhere about elementary school teasing about being an "Oreo" and about a racist teacher in junior high school who refused to recommend me for high school advanced placement U.S. history because he feared it would be too hard for me.[13] But this car ride with my father was the first instance I can recall when my race was involved as a threat. Because of my blackness, my right to protect myself was abridged; my presumption that I would be held innocent until proven otherwise was misplaced.

In retrospect, all of the preceding feels like a quaint memory, since I was sufficiently safe due to my temperament and the protection afforded by my privileged upper middle-class family cocoon. In time, however, I discovered that there was more to this story than a father merely preparing his son for a world of inequality.

THE SCAR

Just a few years ago, I discovered that my father's early morning admonition was the result of his own experience as a teenager when he was thrown in jail for pulling a butcher's knife on the white boys who lived on the next block. These were the same boys who beat him up every day on his way home from school, the same boys who everyone in the neighborhood knew were never up to anything good. While he was in jail for only a few hours (and was never charged with a criminal offense), the memory lingered. This was only one instance in my father's life, but I've come to understand that having to live with the presumption of guilt was a scar he wanted to keep hidden. It is a scar, moreover, that he wanted his sons to avoid acquiring. (At some point in the last decade I learned that my older brother received the same advice in a similar morning drive to school.) Fortunately for me, my father did not feel the need to beat his gems of Jim Crow wisdom into me. But the lack of the literal lashing does not mean that anything less brutal was going on. Despite my father's efforts to hide his own scars and thus protect his sons, the fact is that our morning drives were conveying their own burdens wrought of painful memories. These conversations were cuts, albeit clean ones, given all the contaminants that life presented.

This excursion into my own experiences is not the kind of momentary rupture in the historian's third-person omniscience that one typically finds in books' introductions or prefaces. Even though I fully intended to write this book with the third-person voice that is familiar to historians, the further I moved into my research, the more I realized that others' memories were similar to my own or to those of my parents before they passed them down to me. As I would discover, the consistency of particular themes in black memory overwhelmingly transcended the kinds of contextualizing particularities that would otherwise result in unique stories. Put another way, decades, class status, geography, civil rights law, and certainly temperament separated a young Richard Wright from a young Jonathan Holloway, but long memories of America's broken promises made it clear to our parents that they needed to do the same thing: prepare their children by sharing a deep knowledge of denial, even if, as was the case with my father, he was determined not to tell the actual story that motivated his actions. My father and young Richard's mother were, in Ralph Ellison's devastating formulation, giving their children a taste of the bitter medicine to come. "One of the Southern Negro family's methods of protecting the child," Ellison wrote, "is severe beatings—a homeopathic dose of the violence generated by black and white relationships."[14]

A CERTAIN KIND OF CUT, A CERTAIN KIND OF SCAR

There is a larger methodological point to the shifting perspectives that appear in *Jim Crow Wisdom*. It is my attempt to wrestle with the tension between memory and history and, in so doing, examine the very principles at the core of my training as a historian. When dealing with memory, the historian is faced with interesting challenges: What do you do when the memories of the actual participants in a specific event contradict official or archival records? What do you do when the people who are at the center of your study have been systematically denied a space in the official archive in the first place, since their lives had been deemed unremarkable and are thus "lost to history"? How reliable is the archive? How reliable is memory? What can be known? What is a fact?

Pierre Nora famously addressed aspects of these questions in his essay "Between Memory and History: *Les Lieux de Mémoire*." Nora explored how sites of memory (*lieux de mémoire*) could be used in the modern world to connect the ephemerality of memory to the institutionality of history. Memory and history, Nora argued, were in "fundamental opposition": "Memory is life, borne by living societies founded in its name. It remains in permanent evolution, open to the dialectic of remembering and forgetting, unconscious of its successive deformations, vulnerable to manipulation and appropriation, susceptible to being long dormant and periodically revived. History, on the other hand, is the reconstruction, always problematic and incomplete, of what is no longer." Because the living and the dead could not coexist in the same space, "history is perpetually suspicious of memory, and its true mission is to suppress and destroy it."[15]

In a very different context, essayist and novelist Tony Earley addressed similar challenges found in the clash between memory and history:

> On the night of July 20, 1969, my little sister and I followed our father into the backyard, where we studied the moon through a surveyor's transit owned by a neighbor. . . . When I wrote about that night almost thirty years later, I described the full moon in detail, how, once magnified, it had seemed almost too bright to look at. When a fact checker at *Harper's* magazine informed me that the moon on the night of July 20, 1969, had not been full, but had been a waxing crescent, I refused at first to believe her. When I looked it up for myself and discovered that she was right, I was faced on one hand with a memory so strong I was sure it had to be true, and on the other hand with an objective truth significantly different than what I remembered. At that moment I came to understand, if not embrace, the true nature of the phrase *creative nonfiction*.
>
> When I remember that night, the moon I see in my mind's eye is still full.[16]

In *Jim Crow Wisdom* I accept Nora's notion that memory and history are fundamentally at odds with each other. The historian in me recognizes that the past is messy and that the scholar's task is to offer a reasoned judgment about what can be known. History may do violence to memory; it may be the original cut that invites the scar, but it's likely the best we are going to do in our efforts to understand the past. At the same time, I just as eagerly accept Earley's determination to embrace a faulty memory as a kind of reality, even in the face of a confirmable and objective truth. I recognize that it is paradoxical to hold both ideas simultaneously and to value them equally—but that is precisely the point of my movement between the first- and third-person perspectives in the pages that follow.

By way of illustration, there is much in my own memory that I can track down and confirm as true or false. But in *Jim Crow Wisdom*, the literal truth is less important to me than the act of remembrance itself. This is the act that shapes a consciousness and an identity, and this is the act that I find most compelling in telling stories about the black past. In charting this course, I am embracing what Jeremy Popkin considers one of the historian's greatest fears (and the reason most historians refrain from writing about themselves): that in exploring and sharing my own experiences I will complicate or even contradict "generalizations [that I and my] colleagues have painstakingly elaborated to make sense of the past."[17] So be it.

Making this methodological decision required that I think carefully about this work's relationship to the archive. Trained as a historian to seek out archives to answer questions and to rely on archives as arbiters of truth, I now recognize that archives are repositories of a constructed truth—one that is highly mediated by government officials, estate executors, authors, and families in advance of a collection's donation. When considered in this light, one can understand Michel-Rolph Trouillot's perceptive claim that the archive is a place where facts are "assembled."[18]

I still rely on and value deeply these brick-and-mortar archives, but my research in *Jim Crow Wisdom* has taught me to value the archive of the imagination as well. Like any archive, the imagination is a place that is fundamentally about assemblage: a mixture of our best efforts to remember the past accurately, the eroding effects of time, and a desire for narrative clarity and poignancy. Relying on the imagination for its archival properties is central to this book and helps us develop a richer sense of memory *and* of history.

Imagination, of course, is not only about a reconstruction of a truth. Quite often it is the result of a fabrication of a truth, either through a determination to leave out certain details or through a commitment to a flat-out lie. In his work examining southern identity and memory, W. Fitzhugh Brundage addresses the tension between memory and forgetfulness, pointing out that elisions are deliberate acts that must be understood as such. "One conspicuous manifestation of both the interpretive character of historical memories and standards of credibility," he writes, "is the propensity of groups to suppress as well as to recall portions of the past. Within collective memories a dialectic exists between the willfully recalled and deliberately forgotten past."[19] Building on the same logic as Brundage, Jennifer Jensen Wallach adds falsehoods to the equation. Writing about the tension between what can be known (history) and what can be felt (memory), Wallach argues, "Historical reality, specifically the inside of a historical moment, can be composed of both lying and truth telling, remembering, forgetting, and perhaps reinventing."[20]

Robert Penn Warren, though, says it best. In the foreword to his book *Who Speaks for the Negro?*, Warren recounted a conversation with a black leader who questioned Warren's faith that other blacks would be honest with him during interviews: "What makes you think that Negroes will tell you the truth?" Warren simply replied, "Even a lie is a kind of truth."[21]

Lying. Forgetting. The archive. The imagination. All are part of the process of fashioning a collective memory and identity. While I pay specific attention throughout *Jim Crow Wisdom* to African Americans' memory work and its attendant nuances, the fact is that everyone participates in the construction of racial memory. It just so happens that some people are more aware than others of the silences, lies, and imaginations that construct that memory and identity and that these same individuals are equally unaware that the memory of the "other" has a direct effect on the memory of the "mainstream." In fact, as this book hopes to make clear, black collective memory is a memory of the forgotten, a memory of those whose very presence made the rest of the country white, a memory of those who lived lives struggling against a denial of their citizenship so that others would know how to claim their stake in America. The narrator in Ralph Ellison's *Invisible Man* says as much when he discovers that the secret behind Optic White, the brightest and most pure white paint produced by the Liberty Paint Factory, was ten drops of "the stuff"—a jet-black solution that enhanced Optic's brilliance.

Although the precise date eludes me, I remember perfectly well when I began to understand that black memory was in a deep conversation with and had a profound effect on the formation of the American character. As it happens, the setting for this event told much of the story: Daughters of the American Revolution (DAR) Constitution Hall in Washington, D.C. My parents, aware of my growing interest in jazz, took me to see Dizzy Gillespie, one of the masters. Even though Gillespie was headlining the event, I imagine that this was a free concert that residents of the district's metropolitan area know as one of the frequent charms of the city. A military big band was playing with Gillespie, probably the United States Air Force Airmen of Note.

The audience that afternoon or evening was as one might expect, given the state and style of integration in 1980s America. This was a black, white, and brown audience that represented the area's upper middle class. Given the setting, I imagine that this was also a "mainstream" audience, one that was fairly innocent of the broader range of jazz styles, that could cite only a handful of Gillespie's most famous tunes, and that mainly knew Gillespie for his utterly unique embouchure and trumpet. Since I was sufficiently confident of my future status as a legendary saxophonist, I remember thinking that I was somewhere above the audience that joined me at the DAR hall to listen to Gillespie. I am at a loss to explain exactly why that was, however, since I was not especially versed in anything but Gillespie's "Salt Peanuts" and "Night in Tunisia."

The opening act featured an exciting version of Chick Corea's "Spain," a technically challenging piece that my high school jazz ensemble happened to be wrestling with at the same time. Granted, there was no comparison between the two groups' mastery of the material—the Airmen of Note were quite a bit better than the Winston Churchill Bulldogs High School Jazz Band—but the very fact that I was working on the same piece that the professionals were playing only reinforced my sense of insider knowledge.

Once the Airmen had sufficiently warmed up the audience, Dizzy Gillespie strolled out to adoring applause. The real show was about to start. In my estimation, the audience was going to receive a history lesson on America's most famous native art form. What I did not and could not anticipate was that Gillespie would offer a lesson on American social and political history even before the first downbeat or syncopation.

His stunning musical talent aside, Gillespie was beloved for his sharp sense of humor and his ability to win the crowd over with the physicality of his playacting—the arched eyebrow, the mugging for the audience, the short dance steps during an interlude. On this occasion, however, Gillespie chose a different path. As he walked onstage, he paused and dramatically looked around the theater. He slowly approached the microphone, taking in every last bit of the performance space. Eschewing even a simple greeting, Gillespie instead marveled aloud, "So this is what this place looks like inside. I thought I'd never see it."

All of my accumulated sense of self evaporated as the audience laughed loudly at his mock wonderment. I am confident that some members of the audience laughed louder than others and with a deeper, more psychologically personal understanding of Gillespie's comment. The observation, however, and the humor behind it, were completely lost to me. I looked at my parents, wondering what they knew that I did not as they joined in on what had to be the largest inside joke I had ever witnessed.

Until that moment, I thought I knew that Gillespie's humor tended toward sweet and innocent clowning onstage. After the concert, when I spoke with my parents about my confusion, I discovered how Gillespie's humor could also be filled with the pathos of individual and communal pain remembered across generations. I can now say with a historian's accumulated confidence that, *of course*, with his joke, Gillespie was thumbing his nose at the venue that hosted him. Some forty-five years earlier, the DAR notoriously refused to let famed contralto Marian Anderson perform in Constitution Hall, since her appearance would violate the hall's strict race rule that prohibited blacks in the audience and on the stage.[22]

Gillespie knew that Anderson's experience with the DAR and then her eventual and triumphant Easter Sunday concert on the steps of the Lincoln Memorial served as an important marker in U.S. cultural and political history. Just a few of the basic facts surrounding the controversy underscore the concert's significance: First Lady Eleanor Roosevelt resigned her membership with the DAR over the organization's refusal; remarkably, the 75,000 people who attended that morning's concert could not find signs indicating where "colored" or "white" must sit; and finally, Secretary of the Interior Harold Ickes introduced Anderson's performance, claiming, "Genius, like justice, is blind. . . . Genius draws no color line." Gillespie's mock astonishment, then, was a sly reminder of the DAR's unintentional role in altering the nation's consciousness about the possibilities of African American citizenship.

Years after I attended Dizzy Gillespie's concert, when I was researching my dissertation, in fact, I finally understood just how important Marian Anderson's concert was. One of my interviewees, an octogenarian native Washingtonian, recalled, "After that concert, everything looked different in America as far as blacks were concerned." This gentleman was not making a literal claim about difference; rather, he spoke to a communal sense among African Americans that addressed the possibilities of the future while remaining cognizant of and always responding to a long memory of racialized subjugation and second-class status. Although there clearly isn't a causal link between the concert and what followed, it is not unimportant that almost exactly a year after Marian Anderson's performance, *Native Son* was published, and that less than a year later A. Philip Randolph began to organize the march on Washington.

Clearly, in the worlds of culture and politics, new sets of possibilities were being contested. In the efforts to articulate a new black mentality, new memories were being assembled. This is a story about these memories and how they were used to shape the contours of African American identity in the long second half of the twentieth century. This is a story about the complicated subtexts that class-based narratives presented in the face of the more obvious and unifying logics that race offered. This is a story about the traumas and evasions as they were found in the academic world of ideas, the popular world of ideas, the consumable world of ideas, the public and private worlds of ideas, and the built environment of ideas. This is a story of Jim Crow wisdom.

1

EDITING AND THE
ART OF FORGETFULNESS
IN SOCIAL SCIENCE

Any historical narrative is a particular bundle of silences.
—Michel-Rolph Trouillot, *Silencing the Past*

"But, Mr. Wright, there are so many of us who are *not* like Bigger!"
—Richard Wright, "How 'Bigger' Was Born"

Aunt Maggie was the family griot. The sister of my paternal grandmother, she was born in 1905, the youngest of eleven children. By the middle 1990s, she was the last surviving sibling of her generation. I barely knew her myself, but I know that she was a woman of accomplishment. Trained at Bennett College and holder of a master's degree in social work from Wayne State University, she served as the dean of women at Tuskegee University in the mid-1960s. Perhaps because of her own achievements she seemed to be obsessed with being the right kind of individual, hailing from the right kind of family. Anyone less than exemplary, or publicly noted for being so, was a stain on the family's past, present, and future. Unfortunately, her two sons were merely good husbands and fathers and solidly middle class to upper middle class. And even though they cared for her, she still did her best to cut them down to size.

At six feet, seven inches, my brother Brian is a rather large person, and perhaps thinking that Aunt Maggie could not reduce him, he went to visit her in late 2001. My brother is deeply invested in learning the family history. As much as possible, he wanted to get his stories from as close to the original source as possible. Guided by this passion, Brian traveled to Detroit to visit Aunt Maggie. He folded himself into a small chair next to her bedside and began talking with her about family history—hoping that he had arrived on a good day, when her memory was sharp and when she felt like talking.

Brian knew much of the recent family history, but he wanted those memories that belonged to Aunt Maggie. After some general questions about Maggie's descendants, Brian asked about Maggie's ancestors. Because Aunt Maggie hailed from Asheville, North Carolina, and was born near the turn of the century, my brother reasoned that she could likely recall members of the family who were born into slavery and perhaps lived parts of their lives as slaves.

Aunt Maggie, who had been sharing her memories with my brother willingly, in fine detail, and, remarkably, in good cheer, suddenly snapped: "We don't talk about that in this family." She added that there were stories he didn't need to know, that she did not intend to share, and that would accompany her to the grave. She then turned away, stared off into some unseen place, and with her body language and stony silence marked the end of the conversation. A few months later, Aunt Maggie died. True to her word, with her death many stories about the slaves in our family's past and their histories of social degradation, violence, and, importantly, survival disappeared forever.

With her silence, my grand-aunt was participating in a long-standing practice of editing her memory, an artful forgetting for the sake of affirming her family's social position. Hers was a logic that middle- and upper-class blacks consistently relied on in the early years of the civil rights movement to preserve their status in black and white America. By narrating a history that was only about good breeding, middle- and upper-class blacks could preserve their respectability in black America during an era of profound social, economic, and political change. They could also retain their positions as the interpreters of blackness for the white community.[1]

This sort of thinking drove Richard Wright mad, and he wrote against what he felt to be the black bourgeois desire to forget. As he makes clear in "How 'Bigger' Was Born," Wright maintained great disaffection for the black middle class's penchant to edit out certain stories of the larger black experience:

> I knew from long and painful experience that the Negro middle and professional classes were the people of my own race who were more than others ashamed of Bigger and what he meant. Having narrowly escaped the Bigger Thomas reaction pattern themselves—indeed, still retaining

traces of it within the confines of their own timid personalities—they would not relish being publicly reminded of the lowly, shameful depths of life above which they enjoyed their bourgeois lives. Never did they want people, especially *white* people, to think that their lives were so much touched by anything so dark and brutal as Bigger.

Their attitude toward life and art can be summed up in a single paragraph: "But, Mr. Wright, there are so many of us who are *not* like Bigger! Why don't you portray in your fiction the *best* traits of our race, something that will show the white people what we have done in *spite* of oppression? Don't represent anger and bitterness. Smile when a white person comes to you. Never let him feel that you are so small that what he has done to crush you has made you hate him! Oh, above all, save your *pride*!"[2]

Aunt Maggie was raising her sons in the 1940s when Richard Wright was following through with his determination to fascinate and terrify the nation's readers. A. Philip Randolph was organizing the March on Washington Movement, and millions of blacks were leaving the South for jobs in the North, Midwest, and West. Put another way, private battles to preserve and extend a class-based respectability that were linked to a narrative of racial exceptionalism were being waged at the same time that people found themselves wondering what to do with a new black cultural and political consciousness being expressed in entirely new black enclaves throughout the nation's cities.

Given the scale and significance of so much change, it is perhaps unsurprising that this was an era of dramatic growth in the social sciences as they related to the study of race in the United States. The field's literature reveals much about the strategies and rationales of blacks for self-articulation, particularly in terms of class status. Most importantly, when read in the light of a middle-class desire to forget, the social science race literature of the 1940s reveals itself to be concerned with producing a highly edited taxonomy of who was the Negro and what made a proper Negro. By the choices they made as editors, the era's social scientists indicated that telling stories of the right kind of person, the right kinds of institutions, and the right set of mores had a compelling logic, since it increased the chances that a constructive narrative about black life could be formed.

HOMEGROWN EDITING

Social scientists such as economists Abram Harris and Sterling Spero, political scientists Ralph Bunche and Emmett Dorsey, anthropologist Allison

Davis, and sociologists Charles S. Johnson and E. Franklin Frazier were prolific, producing important essays and books throughout the 1930s and 1940s about the black worker, race and economics, the changing social structures of rural life, and the effects of rapid urbanization on black families.[3] These writers were part of a generation of scholars who produced work that simultaneously introduced unknown aspects of black life to a larger reading public and applied the lived experiences of their black subjects to new methods of modern social science.[4] They also happened to serve as inspirations to Richard Wright when he was struggling to find his writer's voice. As he moved about Chicago in the late 1930s, trying to make sense of the city, he "encountered the work of men who were studying the Negro community, amassing facts about urban Negro life [that] . . . gave me my first concrete vision of the forces that molded the urban Negro's body and soul."[5] Wright's essay "How 'Bigger' Was Born" reflects the influence the social scientists had on him: It is filled with references to personality types, classifications of pathologies, participant observation, and ethnographic field reporting.[6]

The popularity of Wright's nonfiction—*12 Million Black Voices: A Folk History of the Negro in the United States*, a 1941 photo-essay about blacks in the Great Migration, was rushed to print in the wake of *Native Son*'s fantastic sales[7]—indicates a trend toward a scholarship that could be deciphered and then consumed by a larger reading public. E. Franklin Frazier, for example, published his first major work, *The Negro Family in Chicago*, in 1932. This book broke new ground in talking about the effect rural-to-urban black migration had on the black family structure. Seven years later, and in response to a strong demand for an expanded picture of his sociological examination of the black family in Chicago, Frazier published *The Negro Family in the United States*. This latter work won plaudits as one of the best books on contemporary race relations and elevated Frazier to the top of his field. Within the world of sociology only Charles S. Johnson, then the head of the Department of Social Science at Fisk University and, like Frazier, a protégé of University of Chicago sociologist Robert Park, could be seen as his peer.

In addition to chairing the Department of Social Science, Johnson established the Fisk Institute of Race Relations, and through this institute he and his research team churned out data-rich analyses of black life in the middle South that were a technician's dream. But, in line with the democratizing move seen in so many of the social sciences, Johnson also worked toward the mainstream. His 1941 book, *Growing Up in the Black Belt: Negro Youth in the Rural South*, clearly reflects this trend. Written as part of a series prepared for the American Youth Commission, *Growing Up in the Black Belt* offered its readers very little in terms of raw numbers and statistics but devoted most of its energy to vignettes of southern black youth, their social and cultural place in their local settings, and their attitudes about such phenomena as race, marriage, and relations with whites.

In the preface to Johnson's book, Robert L. Sutherland, the associate director for Studies of Negro Youth, a unit of the American Youth Commission, perhaps inadvertently captured the era's sensibility when he hailed the book primarily as a "human interest document." Sutherland continued in a similar vein: "Seldom has a scientific report brought its readers so close to the intimate lives of the people who were studied. Seldom have life history materials retained their naturalness and human flavor as they do in the personal quotations which are presented in every chapter." Although he made sure to acknowledge that *Growing Up in the Black Belt* would be valuable to social scientists for its "extensive use of carefully planned statistical and case study methods," Sutherland seemed most enthused by the fact that the general public would benefit because the "reader can draw from the real life situations of Negro youth reported in their own words."[8] Sutherland's appraisal evinces an enthusiasm for the book that borders on spectacle. Here is a book, Sutherland seems to declare, that will finally tell us what we need to know about black youth. Sutherland's preface, then, can be read as a preface to an introduction to the race.

While not using these precise words, Johnson comes very close to saying as much in his own opening to *Growing Up in the Black Belt*. He states, "The scheme of this volume is to present by way of introduction to the study of the personality development of southern rural Negro youth, brief though fairly complete pictures of ten youth in their intimate setting."[9] Taking Johnson's word, we need to think about what an introduction to the race might entail, because in his and other scholars' hands such an introduction could take on whatever construction they desired to make. The irony cannot be missed: When taking the opportunity to introduce the race, the leading social scientists of the day, the very ones who inspired Richard Wright, chose to introduce the race according to the very terms of the middle-class sensibilities Wright abhorred.

In any author's hand, a thorough introduction to the race would provide the reader with a general sense of history, population numbers, geographic density and spread, and social, economic, political, and cultural phenomena. Such an introduction would be necessarily broad sweeping, but if successfully executed, it would give the reader a sense of context and of possibility. Johnson does all of this with ease, digesting census tract information, psychological test data, and other socially scientific means of understanding a community and sharing his insights in highly readable prose. Johnson refines this introduction further by intermixing this data with observations drawn from interviews and life histories of ten youth from the Black Belt. The experiential specificities drawn from these individuals give Johnson's introduction an immediacy and reality that a "mere" introduction could not provide.

But what of Johnson's book-length introduction to the race? What does Johnson talk about? The book focuses on youth, of course, but in the process of describing these individuals, who places them into their respective social and cultural frames? One chapter, for example, is titled "Status and Security" and provides an analysis of who occupies which social classes in black America and the tensions that grow out of striving to retain or attain a certain class standing. Johnson devotes much of his attention to the black middle and upper classes, their constant struggles to hang onto their respective social standing, and their almost obsessive need to perform the Victorian rituals of proper behavior and decorum. Even though he admits that the great majority of southern rural blacks resided in the lower classes (he says 82 percent at one point), Johnson's attention is firmly set upon the other 18 percent of the population and the stresses and social pressures related to class mobility.[10] But what of lower-class youth? Where do they fit into his discussion of status and security?

Johnson affords the lower-class youth a scant three pages in this twenty-nine-page chapter and explains that while most blacks are part of this lower class, their family situations are largely "hopeless." Even though he acknowledges that many blacks are trapped in the lower classes owing to social and economic forces beyond their control, there is an overrepresentation of social misfits residing at the bottom, trapped in a cycle that defies escape. As Johnson puts it,

> The hopelessness of their status contributes to a type of free living that acknowledges little responsibility to accepted standards. Education is used by the lower classes less as a means of escape than as a means of handling some urgent practical problems like counting and reading notices. With less opportunity for recognition through education, money, or status, the youth of these families may seek their self-assurance in free sexual activity, in a reputation for physical prowess or for being a bad man, and in other forms of antisocial behavior. The "bad men" who can cut and kill and get away with it, the ones without conscience concerning various types of sexual behavior, the hopeless ones seeking to escape

their troubles and status through chronic drunkenness, are likely to be found more frequently in this category than in the others.[11]

There is an earlier sole paragraph in this same chapter that talks about "The Underworld" in black America and that describes this world as occupied by people who "fall outside the recognized and socially sanctioned class categories . . . persons who are free from the demands of society—the 'wide' people, the vagabonds, the 'worthless' and 'undeserving poor' who are satisfied with their status, the 'outcasts,' and 'bad niggers,' prostitutes, gamblers, outlaws, renegades, and 'free' people."[12] But beyond this paragraph and the three pages mentioned above, there is nothing else in this chapter and extremely little worth noting in the rest of the book that points to aspects of black life and behavior that fall outside the social norms of greater middle-class society. Only part of the race is introduced.

There is no doubt that Johnson had to make choices about what kind of story to tell and what evidence merited the most attention. Johnson's class status affected his gaze when he was writing the manuscript. Authors' choices, governed by conscious and unconscious forces, always play a role in what they choose to share with the reader. But here the willful exclusion of what the author declares to be the majority of the race in a book that is intended to introduce the race begs the question again: Who, exactly, is being introduced? There is a follow-up to this question, and its answer may be even more important: Why are certain portions—perhaps even very large portions—of the population *not* being introduced?

In analyzing Johnson's research program and its findings, members of his research team—an interracial group of professional sociologists, psychiatrists, graduate students, and social workers—had different measures of success in extracting data from the individuals they interviewed, surveyed, or tested. However, the source of this raw data, the material that helped the researchers divine the issues black youth faced in the deep South, is as important as the information itself.

In a revealing memo that ran as Appendix A in *Growing Up in the Black Belt*, white psychiatrist Harry Stack Sullivan related his struggles interviewing rural black southerners. Sullivan wrote,

The Negro of the deep South seldom escapes serious warping influences and a large proportion of them doubtless come to be measurably close to the reality underlying the prevailing white views of the Negro. I did not succeed in establishing contact with any of those who were described by my informants as "just average niggers." I learned in the first few days that I could not bridge the cultural gap with most of the plantation workers. The Negro seems to have a notably great capacity for sensing by intuition interpersonal reality. This faculty led to a good many pseudoconversations, early in my stay.[13]

In other words, the black plantation workers told the white outsider exactly what they "intuited" he wanted them to say. This was first-person editing as a practical means to survival.

If we take the tone of Sullivan's comment at face value, he seemed mystified that the folks others considered "just average niggers" were unreachable to him and that they, in his view, had some natural ability to anticipate sociocultural differences. He seemed not to appreciate that these black workers had been forced by the collaborating circumstances of racism and economic exploitation to anticipate trouble whenever it might arrive. For those who had to answer to a socioeconomic system designed to exploit them, a white northerner asking too many questions was trouble personified. The irony, of course, is that in the attempt to introduce a segment of black America to a reading public, at least some of Johnson's researchers discovered that many black informants rationally concluded that they could not let themselves be introduced.

Wright portrayed this phenomenon powerfully in *12 Million Black Voices*. Using the first-person plural to project a compelling intimacy, Wright described a typical southern scene:

When a white man asked us an innocent question, some unconscious part of us would listen closely, not only to the obvious words, but also to the intonations of voice that indicated what kind of answer he wanted; and, automatically, we would determine whether an affirmative or negative reply was expected, and we would answer, not in terms of objective truth, but in terms of what the white man wished to hear.

If a white man stopped a black on a southern road and asked: "Say, there, boy! It's one o'clock, isn't it?" the black man would answer: "Yessuh."

If the white man asked: "Say, it's not one o'clock, is it, boy?" the black man would answer: "Nawsuh."[14]

Johnson and his researchers, regardless of their social and cultural limitations, were talking about rural blacks who had a clear investment in editing out their truest thoughts and feelings. But these examples of self-policing were not limited solely to the rural folk. They appeared in other "black spaces" and, depending on the space, took on greater or deeper meaning.

This notion of self-editing for the race's sake was permeated by the kind of politics of middle- or professional-class sensibilities that Richard Wright decried. But Wright was frustrated with adults acting on their own behalf. In *Negro Youth at the Crossways*, E. Franklin Frazier illuminates how the black middle classes imbued their children with their editing choices. Acknowledging that "sometimes the efforts of upper-class parents to protect their children go to fantastic extremes," Frazier related a particular instance when "a teacher would not let anyone use the term 'Negro' or 'colored' in his house because he did not want his son to acquire the idea of racial identity and the inferior status involved in the idea." Speaking more broadly, Frazier continued:

> Whenever . . . children of upper-class families hear or read things which are derogatory to the Negro, their parents are quick to combat such influences with ideas of their own and build up a conception of Negroes more suitable to their hearts' desire. Thus, the youth in the upper-class families acquire "ideal" defenses for their egos, which become the fabric of their conventional selves. For the investigator it often proves an almost insuperable task to pierce these defenses and discover the real attitudes and feelings of upper-class youth in regard to their status as Negroes.[15]

In these ways Frazier shared common ground with Richard Wright, but there was a significant difference between Frazier and Wright in how, as authors, they conducted their own editing. Whereas Wright forced his vision of all parts of black society on his readers, Frazier was more in line with social scientists like Johnson. In a book approaching 300 pages, only in the appendix does the reader encounter a direct conversation about pathology in black communities. Dependency, delinquency, and crime are linked to a family structure that is "disorganized," a result of the traumas of migration, a matriarchal structure, and "inferior standards of excellence"—the last borne of the toxic stew of segregation.[16]

Even though Frazier is criticized for his suggestions of a dysfunctional, disorganized, matriarchal black family structure when he clearly talks about the black family's reorganizing capability after a period of readjustment, there is no avoiding the fact that his politics, and in this book his projections, were all about perpetuating a logic that kept the middle and professional classes firmly in place as the interpreters or editors of the race.

FOREIGN-BORN EDITING

As central as Johnson's and Frazier's scholarship was to the early 1940s discussions of race, there is little debating the fact that Myrdal's *An American*

Dilemma was the most important social science project of the 1940s. Its significance does not necessarily spring from the fundamental accuracy of its thesis—although the thesis, that the true heart of the Negro problem in the United States was white Americans' failure to live up to the country's ideals, is compelling. Rather, the importance of the project springs from the sheer scope of the research team, its tangential publications, and the length of time it was cited or relied on in the policy world following its publication.[17] As unusual as the project was, however, its internal logics, in particular a reliance on willful forgetfulness that grew out of middle-class sensibilities, meant that it was very much in line with the era's other leading social scientists.

The project was the brainchild of Frederick Keppel, president of the Carnegie Corporation, who sought to finance a "comprehensive study of the Negro in the United States, to be undertaken in a wholly objective and dispassionate way as a social phenomenon."[18] As news of the massive investment by the Carnegie Foundation spread, so did speculation about who would be in charge of the project.[19] There was a deepening pool of talent as far as black social scientists were concerned, and there was a sentiment that, clearly, the person best suited to offer an incisive analysis of the Negro problem was an African American social scientist.

Keppel felt otherwise and hired Gunnar Myrdal, an economist and member of the Swedish Parliament, instead. Keppel's logic was straightforward: Myrdal was an ideal choice because he had a proven record of handling large research projects in his native Sweden. More importantly, Keppel believed Myrdal could be objective—as a white European from a non-imperial country, his worldview regarding race was uncompromised. Despite protests, Myrdal led the project.

Myrdal, much to his credit, appreciated the fact that there were scores of talented black scholars who could contribute to his study, and he set about hiring as many of them as he could, essentially as contract workers. Myrdal's chief research assistant was Howard University political scientist Ralph Bunche. With Bunche's steady and guiding hand, thirty-eight scholars and several teams of research assistants went out into the field to assess the state of black America.[20]

After six years—the onset of World War II delayed the project on several occasions—Myrdal released his findings to great acclaim.[21] His book was an extended critique of the systematic denial of opportunity for blacks to attain their full citizenship rights. More than that, though, *An American Dilemma* represented an opportunity for Myrdal to allow blacks to be heard as experts on major conceptual and institutional forces involved in the making and shaping of black life. There's no mistaking the fact, however, that Myrdal's

Cartoon editorial, Gunnar Myrdal *and* An American Dilemma
(Ralph Bunche Papers [Collection 2051], Department of Special Collections,
Charles E. Young Research Library, UCLA)

was the mediating voice. He rejected many research reports—some of which would appear as stand-alone projects in the years to come—and aggressively edited and interpreted the memoranda he accepted.[22] Regardless of the voice or presence of contributors in the final text, Myrdal understood the stakes involved in the project and that this was his special chance to introduce the race to the curious public and, critically, the policy-making world.

With his teams assembled, Myrdal coordinated fieldwork around the country, particularly in the Southeast. The teams conducted interviews and surveys, wrote community histories, and analyzed cultural, economic, social, and political organizations that were foundational to the country's black communities. With Bunche's assistance, Myrdal processed the incoming data and produced extended discussions on economics, population and migration, politics, social inequality, and social stratification. The Negro church, businesses, and political machines are also detailed in full. Indeed, over the course of 1,483 pages, 45 chapters, and 332 subchapters, one develops a very clear picture of the processes of racial formation, the effects of systemic racial discrimination, and, importantly, the functional and healthy structures of black life and the failure of whites to recognize the essential decency of blacks and their desire to enjoy the full fruits of U.S. citizenship.

This is not to say, of course, that Myrdal's portrait is complete. While no honest scholar would claim to have developed a *complete* depiction of "a people," there was more than a notion that Myrdal had come as close as possible. The length of the study, the size of the research budget, and the collective expertise of the research team suggested to many that *An American Dilemma* was definitive, with Myrdal's voice ascendant.

No matter how authoritative and collaborative *An American Dilemma* appears, however, one cannot ignore that some powerful and, it would seem, corrective editing was going on that demonstrated a profound unwillingness to show the reader practically any of black Americans' dirty linen. For example, only in the penultimate chapter does one get a glimpse of conduct that did not conform to the most upstanding aspects of civilized, dignified black behavior.

In this chapter, "Non-institutional Aspects of the Negro Community," Myrdal explores black deviance. A subheading such as "Crime" appears straightforward enough at first glance, but most of the section is dedicated to explaining the statistical problems in reporting on black crime rates and the cultural hysteria that links blacks to crimes of passion.[23] In a similar vein, another subchapter, "Peculiarities of Negro Culture and Personality," suggests that poorly behaving blacks were exceptions to the rule, even though in daily life their bad behavior was what captured the mainstream press's attention. Much of this subchapter is actually devoted to middle- and upper-class blacks who were committed to proving that all blacks were not criminal or unrefined.

Myrdal explained that the behavior of striving blacks may have appeared "peculiar," owing to the intensity of their efforts to control and project their image:

Upper class Negroes, in their attempt to avoid the unfavorable traits commonly associated with Negroes, are conservative in their dress and public behavior. They avoid everything that is loud, gaudy, and cheap. But they are also driven by a desire for status and so engage in conspicuous consumption of another type. They imitate the staid, old-fashioned patterns of those upper class white people who have not become emancipated. Their clothes are most "respectable" and most expensive; their homes—though small—are furnished in "good taste"; their social gatherings are costly and ceremonial. They even go to extremes of conspicuous consumption in their desire to gain status, as many other channels of gaining status are closed to them. They try to copy the "highest" standards of white people and yet get absolutely no recognition for doing so.[24]

The irony should not be lost here: Much like the striving blacks who desired to project a certain image about their place in society, one of the most important social science documents of the 1940s was also a highly edited affair that was fundamentally constructed to provide a certain kind of portrait of black America. While one can easily and perhaps even justifiably say that *An American Dilemma* was a necessary tonic to the prevailing description of pathological black life, one ought not to ignore the project's clear objective. Although it was not written as any sort of correction to Richard Wright's *Native Son*, one can clearly see throughout *An American Dilemma* a sentiment very much in line with Wright's middle-class critics who admonished him for showing the race's "bad side."

Considering that Myrdal edited out the least flattering aspects of black America, one is reminded of the concern that a foreigner simply could not know or get access to black America. Given the challenge a foreign scholar might have getting honest responses from poor southern blacks, one might conclude that Myrdal's arguments weren't so much edited opinions but a reflection of the best he could do. But this claim ignores the fact that Myrdal had many black researchers working for him who, one would presume, would have better access to honest answers from individuals in the field. This claim would also ignore the fact that Myrdal's class position needs to be kept in mind. Even though he was not as invested in or attuned to America's racial hierarchies, he undoubtedly understood the way that social class shaped human possibility. And perhaps this is what, more than anything else, animated his editorial decisions. The thoroughness with which he confined his analysis to those blacks who clearly occupied or were committed to a politics and economics of aspirational striving underscores the desire to project a class-oriented respectability.

Throughout *An American Dilemma*, exclusive of the chapter "Noninstitutional Aspects of the Negro Community," Myrdal endeavored to write a narrative about black Americans indicating that the great majority of them already possessed or aspired to normative middle-class mainstream American values: "In his cultural traits, the Negro is akin to other Americans. . . . He believes in the American Creed and in other ideals held by most Americans, such as getting ahead in the world, individualism, the importance of education and wealth. He imitates the dominant culture as he sees it and in so far as he can adopt it under his conditions of life. For the most part he is not proud of those things in which he differs from the white American."[25]

Implicit notions of respectability are woven throughout this comment: an assertion of black proximity to white normativity and an insistence that blacks frowned upon those parts of black culture that were out of alignment with the white mainstream. Later, on the same page, Myrdal builds on the idea that black misbehavior, in addition to being shunned by the better sort of blacks, was also something beyond blacks' control. For Myrdal, black misbehavior, the pathological elements of black society, was the inevitable manifestation of institutional and social logics structured to deny opportunity:

> The instability of the Negro family, the inadequacy of educational facilities for Negroes, the emotionalism in the Negro church, the insufficiency and unwholesomeness of Negro recreational activity, the plethora of Negro sociable organizations, the narrowness of interest of the average Negro, the provincialism of his political speculation, the high Negro crime rate, the cultivation of the arts to the neglect of other fields, superstition, personality difficulties, and other characteristic traits are mainly forms of social pathology which, for the most part, are created by the caste pressures.[26]

We can see throughout *An American Dilemma* Myrdal's passionate commitment to the importance of normative values in American life and an embrace of the American Creed—systems of living that Myrdal quite plainly believed were structured and preserved by white Americans.[27] And even though Myrdal also made clear that he did not feel that "white culture is 'higher' than other cultures in an absolute sense," we are compelled to contemplate how the relentless push to embrace normative values and codes also involved a fair amount of what one can call "racial policing" that too often neatly aligned with America's caste system.[28]

FEARFUL EDITING

As I discovered one afternoon, this racial policing was part of my family history as well. I have no idea what moved my father to be reflective and raise the topic—he was usually steadfast in his insistence to remain in the present and equally determined to avoid relating his own past encounters with stories involving negative racial encounters—but once he started reminiscing, I knew enough to be quiet.

My parents met as college students at Ohio Wesleyan University. My father had just graduated and was back in town visiting friends when this lovely freshman coed caught his attention. Very soon, they would start dating and, before too long, become engaged. It was a long-distance engagement, since my father was in officer training for the U.S. Air Force. Whenever he had a chance, however, he would go back to Delaware, Ohio, to see the woman who would become his wife.

As much joy as I would like to project backward into those moments of reunion, they were not always ideal. The happy couple, for example, had to endure endless harassment from local white toughs who, typically from the safety of their passing cars, shouted obscenities at the fair-skinned woman with "good hair" who was in the company of a black man. Never mind the fact that the darker-skinned Negro was wearing an officer's uniform. He was still a nigger who didn't know his place and dared to go out in public with someone they thought was a white woman.

The troublemakers who verbally abused my parents saw past my father's uniform only to remain fixated on what they incorrectly assumed to be an interracial couple. In the 1950s such interracial relationships remained taboo. Miscegenation propelled whites—especially white men, it seems—to the greatest levels of personal anxiety.

Early on in *An American Dilemma*, Myrdal addresses this phenomenon when he discusses the "rank order of discrimination." In a ranking schema that included political disfranchisement, discrimination in the courts, and employment inequities, the nearly unanimous finding was that "highest on this order stands the bar against intermarriage and sexual intercourse involving a white woman."[29]

I do not know why my father's story of racial harassment for allegedly violating the greatest taboo from whites' perspective was something he would tell me only once. I do not know if it was the shame of being harassed while in uniform or of his lingering anger over the things the men said about his fiancée. What I do know is that my father seemed absolutely determined not to tell stories about his past that were guided by what he could not control. It was as if the ignorant whites who hurled their insults and who were thus acting as racial police officers had a lingering effect on my father's desire to share part of his history. It is not too much of a stretch to see how their profound anxiety about interracial amalgamation served as a sort of

Kay and Wendell Holloway, newly married (author's collection)

psychologically enduring editor's pencil that profoundly affected the story my father decided to share or not.

The white racists who committed themselves to drive-by opportunities of hate were the most vulgar type of editors. But the anxiety-induced fear of interracial amalgamation reflected a widely and deeply felt determination by whites to control black self-articulation. Indeed, just as Gunnar Myrdal claimed that the highest "rank" in social discrimination revolved around intermarriage and interracial physicality, the same anxiety—and a resultant determination to edit the black voice—found its way into another signature piece of 1940s social science scholarship: Rayford Logan's *What the Negro Wants*.

The genesis of *What the Negro Wants* is directly traceable to W. T. Couch and Guy Johnson, two liberal white academics affiliated with the University of North Carolina (UNC) at Chapel Hill. Both men, attuned to the uproar over Myrdal's selection as the head of the *American Dilemma* project, contacted Howard University historian Logan and invited him to produce his own piece of scholarship about the state of black America. Neither Couch, the director of UNC Press, nor Johnson, an eminent sociologist, were happy with the fact that the readers of *An American Dilemma* would be learning about the scope and shape of black America through Myrdal's mediating presence. Couch and Johnson firmly believed that the country needed a book that offered an assessment of black life directly from the perspective of blacks themselves. Logan wholeheartedly agreed, and the project was begun.

Conceptually, the project itself was simple enough: In an era of rising interest in and concern about the position of blacks in the American scene, what, exactly, did blacks want? On its surface, Couch and Johnson's plan was enlightened, since the scholars recognized that blacks were not of a single mind or approach to issues and problems facing black America. To this end, and with Logan's consent, they developed a plan: Logan would identify fourteen African American leaders who occupied the full spectrum of political orientation and strategic engagement and would ask them to write an answer to the same question: What does the Negro want?

Logan, well acquainted with a broad range of black leaders, scholars, and activists, went to work. By the end of the project, W. E. B. Du Bois, George Schuyler, Mary McLeod Bethune, Doxey Wilkerson, Frederick Patterson, and Langston Hughes, among others, had contributed essays. Couch and Johnson, one might safely conclude, were thrilled. Upon reading the manuscript, however, these liberal white southern academics had quite a different reaction. Instead of delight, they expressed dismay and outrage.

Clearly, Logan must have coached his respondents; clearly, he did not follow the conceptual directions of the project and merely ask what Negroes wanted; clearly, he had edited their thoughts too aggressively. How else, they reasoned, could fourteen leading members of the race, spanning the spectrum of political orientation, independently articulate the same desire? From communist to accommodationist, from insider to intellectual, to a person, all of the authors said that blacks wanted civil rights and the fruits of citizenship.

Angry that Logan had followed his own agenda, both men criticized the historian for failing to produce the project that all had agreed upon. Couch went a step further, arguing that since Logan did not abide by the terms of the project, Couch would not publish the book. Logan insisted he was faithful to the project's concept and made it clear he gave no direction to the contributors beyond the request that they provide an essay that offered their opinion as to what the Negro wants. Never one to shrink from a fight, Logan then threatened to sue the press for breach of contract. Logan's response surprised the UNC liberals. The book was, of course, eventually published, but not before some very revealing arguments and commentary about the contributors' responses emerged.[30]

Both Couch and Johnson believed that blacks deserved rights but that the pace of the change the book's authors advocated was too fast. Couch and Johnson also expressed concern about the scope of the change that the leaders claimed blacks wanted.

In correspondence with Logan, Johnson worried that readers would see blacks' push for civil rights as nothing less than an expression of black male desire for white women. Couch took this private concern and morphed it into a public complaint. Still unhappy with Logan and the book's contributors, and still angered by the fact that he had little choice but to publish the book, Couch wrote a "publisher's introduction" that would fall between Logan's introduction and the body of the book.

Over the course of fifteen pages (near in length to several of the book's essays) Couch presented a scathing indictment of the presumptive logic of equality that he felt was the biased engine driving *An American Dilemma*; he dismissed anthropologists' cultural relativism as a methodological absurdity; and he offered a series of questions that progressively reveal what was truly animating his anxiety:

> Is the southern white man to blame for everything that happens? Do fate and the Negro have no part? . . . Can Negroes and whites learn to work together, to develop and use all their talents, to live in peace and mutual respect — can they discover the meaning of human rights, can they learn to practice what they discover? Can they remain racially separate and distinct and at the same time avoid inflicting disabilities on each other? Does the white man have no right to attempt to separate cultural from biological integration, and help the Negro achieve the first and deny him the second? Can biological integration be regarded as a right? What happens to the case for the Negro if it is tied up with things to which he not only has no right, but which, if granted, would destroy all rights?[31]

In the following paragraph Couch again moved to the disingenuous inquisitive: "What problem would be solved if the white South dropped all barriers and accepted amalgamation. Would anything be gained if overnight the whole population could be made one color?"[32]

Whether or not Couch and UNC Press deserve any credit for publishing a book in which the head of the press declares in his introduction that he "disagrees with the editor and most of the contributions on basic problems" is, in the end, beside the point. What is valuable here is to observe the intensity of Couch's public racial policing. The irony may be plain to the modern reader and maybe even to readers in the 1940s, but it seemed utterly lost on Couch. He commissioned a project out of frustration with Myrdal's approach to studying black life in America. His new project would address Myrdal's presumptive authority to speak about blacks by relying on the insights of blacks into their own condition. In the end, Couch tried to kill the project because the findings did not align with his worldview and, even worse, advocated, in his feverish interpolation, the most egregious excess: racial amalgamation. Couch's public disavowal of the project was a fundamentally ideological editing job; it was more than just an artful social science forgetfulness. Couch's editing was the most willful expression, perhaps even a desperate attempt to maintain control of a narrative that was invested in a commitment to impossibility.

Couch could not imagine that blacks would be so irresponsible as to fail to realize that immediate integration would harm them (although he never actually says why or how this would be the case). Nor could he comprehend that black men might not, after all, desire white women after achieving full citizenship rights. But most incredulous to Couch was the idea that Rayford Logan could have played the role of professional editor but instead chose not to.

Recognizing the way that "impossibility" drives Couch's conception of the ideas expressed by the project's contributors helps us think anew about the role of the editor in the era's social science literature. Myrdal was clearly operating in a mode very similar to what one could find in Charles Johnson's *Growing Up in the Black Belt* and E. Franklin Frazier's *Negro Youth at the Crossways*. Black misbehavior and pathology could not be part of a larger corrective conversation about black America. Couch, on the other hand, could not conceive of a black community whose animating narrative revolved around a commitment to social change. His was not a case of artful forgetting so that a new narrative could appear that suggested black functionality instead of pathology. Instead, Couch's role as editor was to *deny* the formation of an alternate narrative in the first place.

If Couch had had his way, *What the Negro Wants* would never have been published, and he would have successfully silenced—or edited away—the project and the authors' views. This is the kind of aggressive narrative-making to which philosopher Ernest Renan referred when he observed that "forgetting . . . is an essential factor in the creation of a nation."[33] Editing was constantly happening in the hands of social science authors, in the voices of the people they interviewed, and in the manuscripts of those from whom they solicited ideas. The social scientists' pen, however, was mightiest: The experts had the most control over the narrative, and they vested in themselves the ability to write a story that had the potential to influence the opportunities of those who toiled below.

With the explosion of social science literature in the 1940s, expertise crossed the race line. The idea of this crossing did not necessarily bother white scholars like Couch or Johnson, but the implications of the change were bedeviling. While neither St. Claire Drake nor Horace Cayton were included in *What the Negro Wants*, these two major Chicago-based social scientists were undoubtedly in accord with the general desires expressed by the contributing authors. As Logan was fighting to get his book published, Drake and Cayton were putting the finishing touches on *Black Metropolis: A Study of Negro Life in a Northern City*, a book that would become the most important nonfiction examination of black urban life for the next two decades.

FICTIONAL EDITING

Richard Wright effused about *Black Metropolis* in his 1945 introduction to the work. Calling *Black Metropolis* a "landmark of research and scientific achievement," Wright lauded the extensive sociological and anthropological logics deployed by the authors and pointed out that his own literary ambitions as a social realist would have been directionless without their data.[34] Drake and Cayton spent years creating research models and surveys and conducting participant observations of Chicago's black enclaves.[35] Wright praised the book as a text essential for understanding the breadth, depth, and apparent intractability of the Negro problem. It was a book every American should read. Wright noted that although the expertise that informed the book was grounded in the social sciences, it also grew out of deeply felt personal experiences that would be instantly recognizable to blacks who struggled through the social, economic, cultural, and political challenges of migration and urbanization. Like Wright, Drake and Cayton migrated to Chicago and spent their formative years there, and "in that great iron city, that impersonal, mechanical city, amid the steam, the smoke, the snowy winds, the blistering suns; there in that self-conscious city, that city so deadly dramatic and stimulating, we caught whispers of the meanings that life could have, and we were pushed and pounded by facts much too big for us. Many migrants like us were driven and pursued, in the manner of characters in Greek play, down the paths of defeat; but luck must have been with us, for we somehow survived."[36]

These were graceful yet brutal words for a social science text. Such was Wright's style, of course. But the drama of these opening thoughts serve one of Wright's fundamental claims about the book and also serve the book's curious hybrid style—one that had to have been instantly recognizable to Wright himself.

Wright declared that this book needed to be read because it confirmed much of the social science literature that preceded it; he even cited *Black Metropolis*'s confirmation of *An American Dilemma*'s claim that "the Negro's position in the United States results from the oppression of Negroes by white people, that the Negro's conduct, his personality, his culture, his entire life flow naturally and inevitably out of the conditions imposed upon him by white America."[37] But, more importantly, *Black Metropolis* needed to be read because it removed the veil separating black and white life. Wright warned the reader that "this is no easy book. In order to understand it, you may have to wrench your mind rather violently out of your accustomed ways of thinking." He continued that Drake and Cayton made no effort to "understate, to gloss over, to doll up, or make harsh facts pleasant for the tender-minded. The facts of urban life presented here are in their starkest form, their crudest manifestation; not because the authors want to shock you, but because the environment out of which those facts spring has so wrought them."[38]

For Wright, then, the book was important because it was an expression of cutting-edge method and it simultaneously confirmed and broke with social science literature before it. Wright claimed that Drake and Cayton presented a narrative of black life structured by social and economic circumstances that no one dared tell before. Further, Drake and Cayton succeeded in *Black Metropolis* because they did not shy away from black and white Americans' "deep seated resistance against the Negro problem being presented even verbally, in all of its hideous fullness, in all of the totality of its meaning." Drake and Cayton did not follow, according to Wright, the temptation of so many organizations committed to interracialism to "dilute or blur" their scholarship by injecting "foggy moral or sentimental notions."[39]

Like any good social science scholars, Drake and Cayton committed a lot of energy in *Black Metropolis* to context. In telling the story of how

"Midwest Metropolis" (their frequent stand-in for Chicago) became an ideal setting to study black life in urban America, Drake and Cayton spend just over 100 pages describing a long history of settlement predating the Civil War and the ways in which Chicago became a beacon of hope to black southerners who sought better-paying jobs, political possibilities, and a measure of recognition of their fundamental humanity.

The second part of the book provides a sociological analysis of black life in Chicago and the structural and cultural obstacles that defined that landscape. Here readers first become acquainted with Chicago residents, their thoughts and experiences sprinkled liberally throughout. At triple the length of Part 1, this second part is the analytical foundation of *Black Metropolis*. It is mostly clinical in tone, allowing the community to come alive principally in the voices of black Chicagoans whose excerpted observations are used to bolster the authors' analyses.

By the time readers arrive at the third part of the book, they are equipped with a solid history of Chicago, its demographic changes over time, and a deeply sociological analysis of the black Midwest Metropolis. Drake and Cayton have consistently proven their mettle as careful and ostensibly objective observers of social phenomena. The text is replete with maps, charts, and interview excerpts, but one suspects that it is in this section that Drake and Cayton connect with Wright. Here, in the midst of chapters that have long sections filled with participant observations, Drake and Cayton offer detailed portraits of black life that affirm its diverse and largely wholesome nature while also talking about the unsavory aspects of life in the black ghetto.

With the opening lines of Part 3, Cayton and Drake move away from detached observation when they describe a typical street scene in "Bronzeville." In doing so they convey a warmth and liveliness absent from much of the book: "Stand in the center of the Black Belt—at Chicago's 47th St. and South Parkway. Around you swirls a continuous eddy of faces—black, brown, olive, yellow, and white. Soon you will realize that this is not 'just another neighborhood' of Midwest Metropolis." Multiple editions of black newspapers are stacked at the corner newsstand. "In the offices around you, colored doctors, dentists, and lawyers go about their duties. And a brown-skinned policeman saunters along swinging his club and glaring sternly at the urchins who dodge in and out among the shoppers."[40]

Drake and Cayton go on to draw a detailed picture of life in Bronzeville, rich with the complexities of a diverse black community. Churches of various sizes and faiths and businesses predominate in these pages, as do discussions about different types of race leaders one could find at the pulpit, in the lawyer's office, or in the backroom. This is a portrait of a functional and highly ordered black community—one that other social scientists of the era labored to present in their scholarship and one that ran counter to familiar, mainstream news accounting of black criminality.

When Drake and Cayton turn their attention to the city's lower class, their narrative is more akin to what readers would find in Wright's harrowing pages. Bronzeville's cleanliness and social order fade away immediately. Drake and Cayton show that after the veil was lifted on Bronzeville's poor, one could find

> a variety of living patterns. The twenty households, sharing four bathrooms, two common sinks in the hallway, and some dozen stoves and hot-plates between them, were forced into relationships of neighborliness and reciprocity. A girl might "do the hair" of a neighbor in return or permission to use her pots and pans. Another woman might trade some bread for a glass of milk. There was seldom any money to lend or borrow, but the bartering of services and utensils was general. Brawls were frequent, often resulting in intense violence. A supper interrupted by the screams of a man with an ice-pick driven into his back might be unusual—but a fight involving the destruction of the meager furniture in these households was not uncommon.[41]

The reference to a brawl involving an ice pick is important beyond the spectacular terms of the violence itself. It points to the only moment in the nearly 800-page book where the researchers give themselves over to a fictionalized accounting of their study of black life. In this particular instance, Drake or Cayton—the authors decline to say who—offers his eyewitness account of a Christmas Eve fight between two lovers that he saw when conducting participant observations among the city's poor. The story begins with "Dr. Maguire" returning home after a long day at work. He was preparing a nightcap and then headed to bed when he "stepped back and admired the electric star at the top of the Christmas tree and the gifts neatly stacked beneath it. . . . [Maguire] smiled, drained his glass, and headed for the bathroom. He caught himself musing in the shower. Not so bad, not so bad. Three years out of med school, in the middle of a depression. A pretty wife with smooth olive skin and straight black hair. A sweet little girl, image of her mother. And buying a home."[42]

His reverie, which included a detailing of his evening volunteer work distributing holiday baskets, writing checks to the NAACP, and an emergency meeting of the YMCA board—all wholesome behaviors that were clear markers of his middle- to upper-class status—was interrupted by a phone call. A stabbing victim needed his care. Although the victim wasn't one of his regular patients, and although it was safe to presume the patient would not be able to pay the doctor's $5 fee, Dr. Maguire piled into his car and drove to the crime scene.

When he arrived and assessed the poverty and social mayhem around him, the doctor momentarily disappeared into another, but quite different reverie:

> "Are these my people?" he thought. "What in the hell do I have to do with them? This is 'The Race' we're always spouting about being proud of." He had a little trick for getting back on an even keel when such doubts assailed him: he just let his mind run back over the "Uncle Tomming" he had to do when he was a Pullman porter; the turndown he got when he wanted to interne at the University of Chicago hospital; the letter from the American Medical Association rejecting his application for membership; the paper he wrote for a white doctor to read at a Mississippi medical conference which no Negroes could attend. Such thoughts always restored his sense of solidarity with "The Race." "Yeah, I'm just a nigger, too," he mumbled bitterly.[43]

In an asterisked aside at the bottom of the page, Drake and Cayton make it clear that the doctor's thoughts and the subsequent drunken, angry, and weeping exchanges between the two fighting lovers were fictionalized.[44] Even though the authors quickly point out that the chapter's content remained grounded in the solid social science methods used throughout the book, they do not explain precisely why it was important to include these fictional elements. This silence invites questions: Beyond protecting the identity of the people involved—something that did not require such thorough fictionalizing—what inspired this fabrication? What were Drake and Cayton hoping to gain?

Perhaps the authors decided to take this approach because they admired the kinds of art that Wright had been producing in his literary sociologies of black life. More likely, however, is the possibility that despite their extended participant observation work and interviews with everyone involved, the fictionalized account allowed them greater access to a "truth" that served their purposes. And while their purpose was to create a complete portrait of black urban life, Drake and Cayton understood that they were fighting against a deeply ingrained impulse within the black community to tell a certain kind of story—perhaps one that was fictionalized in the same way as their recounting of the ice pick stabbing. Drake and Cayton recognized that many blacks felt the need for circumspection. "Emphasis upon 'race pride' and 'race solidarity,'" they write, "is sometimes coupled with an expression of contempt and scorn for people who tell all their business to white folks. Bronzeville feels that, as a minority existing within a Black Ghetto, 'protective secrecy' is necessary if their solidarity is not to be broken." In a separate note at the bottom of the same page, the authors acknowledge that Richard Wright's praise aside, "Works like *Black Metropolis* are likely to draw the fire of very race-conscious Negroes who feel that the authors are betraying secrets that should stay within The Race."[45]

While Drake and Cayton revealed much more about the scope of black life than so many of their peer social scientists, they were not truly able to break free of the kinds of editing choices that their class sensibilities demanded of them. They showed an underbelly, but the net result was to affirm the moral clarity of the race experts and the middle or upper classes.

The assertion of the primary authority of the expert—even when he or she is doing participant observation among the lower sort—is part of the same dynamic that prevented Aunt Maggie from talking about the family past; that kept Charles S. Johnson, E. Franklin Frazier, Gunnar Myrdal, and their ilk from airing dirty laundry; and that compelled my father not to share stories about those times when he had been policed by those who disapproved of his life choices.

Willful forgetting, editing, and social policing are all types of communal forgetfulness. But a final point is the most salient and ties everything together: *No one was forgetting anything.* Indeed, it was the persistence of memory and the persistence of threats to a social order that animated all the silence in the first place.

FAMILIAL EDITING

Of course.

My father was busy hustling everyone out to the car for the road trip, but not before hectoring all of us into going to the bathroom. I was a teenager. It was the same routine every time. Hustle, hustle, hustle. Go to the bathroom first. This made perfect sense when I was, say, six or seven. But the same routine, nearly a decade later? Was he serious?

Pushed beyond frustration one day, I decided to raise the issue with my mother. We were in the car waiting for my father (he was always the last one to make it out . . . one last stop to the john, of course), and in the deep exasperation expressed in my rolling eyes I asked her why he always had to get on our case about going to the bathroom. My mother, ever wise, simply said, "Why don't you ask him?"

Now, with everyone in the car—"yes, I'm buckled up"—I decided to ask my father.

"I'm in control of my bladder. I didn't have to go at all. I went an hour ago. Why do you always insist that we try?"

"So we don't have to stop on the road."

"But there are rest stops all over the place."

Silence from the front seat. Then my mom: "Wendell, just tell him."

More silence.

"Old habits die hard," he said—or something like that. "We always had to be sure to go before we went anywhere because we didn't know when we'd get the chance again."

"But weren't there rest stops or restaurants where you could stop?"

"Rarely. And besides, if they were there, you couldn't ever be sure that people like us could use them."

Now, silence from the backseat.

Had I been younger I would have asked more questions, seeking some measure of clarity. But I was old enough now and knew enough that my father didn't have to say anymore. I have no certain memory of when this happened, but the chronological specificity doesn't really matter. I know it happened, and I also know that I never again rolled my eyes at my father's entreaties about going to the bathroom. Admittedly, part of me still found it a bit ridiculous. Things had changed, after all. Another part of me, however, also understood and knew that even despite my adolescent tendency to resist my parents or to sulk or to huff about, I wouldn't grumble about this out loud anymore.

Now that I am older, I know two things: (1) The hairs on the back of my neck still rise when I stop along the highway in those parts of the country that I consider suspect, and (2) my father didn't want to tell us why it was important that we go to the bathroom before we left the house. Although he never forgot the reasons himself, he thought it wiser to edit the reality of his past to protect his present and, embodied in his children, his future. And now, as a father of two young children who makes sure that they go to the bathroom before the family gets in the car, even though I know we will have ample opportunities to stop along the way, I find myself wondering when or even if I will introduce my children to this story.

The editing, it appears, continues.

2

MEMORY AND RACIAL HUMILIATION
IN POPULAR LITERATURE

Southern prejudice is much like a treacherous serpent, it lies in wait and
springs often without warning just when you least expect it while you are going
quietly about your business enjoying life and at peace with the world.
—Ralph Matthews, "My Most Humiliating Jim Crow Experience"

Did you ever ride on a Jim Crow train? Did you ever go to see
your mother on a Jim Crow train? Did you ever go to college on a Jim Crow train—
Fisk, Tuskegee, Talladega? Did you ever start your furlough on a Jim Crow train?
Soldier boy, training to fight for freedom, on a Jim Crow train. Did you ever take your
vacation on a Jim Crow train? War-worker from Detroit going home for a visit on a
Jim Crow train. Did you ever feel it in your soul, that Jim Crow train? . . .
Where is freedom going on a Jim Crow train?
—Langston Hughes, "Here to Yonder"

I had just climbed the staircase to the second floor of the store, the name
of which has long since faded, but I do recall it was where urban fashion
met college prep met affordability. I was ostensibly looking at designer blue
jeans. To be completely honest, however, I was just killing time. The store
was around the corner from where my morning seminar had been held, I
had just finished lunch, smartphones didn't exist (meaning I mindlessly
browsed clothes instead of the internet), and, most importantly, it was New-
England-winter cold outside. My purpose for being in that store, then, had
nothing to do with the blue jeans but was all about staying warm for another
twenty minutes before my next class started. I think my determination to

look like a real shopper and not a mere heat seeker left me slow to realize that I was being followed.

When I became aware of his presence, I first thought the salesperson was being solicitous, and I was about to answer "Oh, no thank you, I'm just browsing" to some version of the obvious forthcoming question: "May I help you find something?" or "Are you looking for something in particular?" The only problem was that the salesperson never asked me anything. I must have looked a bit baffled when I stared at him, anticipating a pleasantry when none was offered, wondering what he wanted.

When I moved further into the second floor, somewhere between the jeans that now seemed unreasonably expensive and the definitely over-priced backpacks, it was painfully obvious that this salesperson was going to shadow me throughout the store. Upset at his presumption that I was going to shoplift, or that I looked like someone who would shoplift, I left the store quickly and empty-handed, determined never to return. I felt I had secured some sort of unspoken victory over the salesperson's suspicion, since my satchel only had books, paper, and pens inside. It took me a while to understand that the salesperson probably felt a similar sense of victory: namely, I left his store with only my own possessions and none of his.

Admittedly, the inconvenience of the salesperson's suspicion was just that: an inconvenience. Since he never accused me of attempting to steal anything and since he never actually said that I was unwelcome in the store, all I had to go on was an instinct that said my presence caused him alarm. This was New Haven in the early 1990s, when property damage and violent crime were rampant. Further, the media did not hesitate to tell any of us that black men steal things. Black men with large and capacious trench coats—I was certainly wearing the calf-length duster that somehow carried me through Connecticut winters—had to present a heightened risk to store owners trying to protect their inventory.

Later that day I was still indignant when I related these events to one of my friends. Now, I find the memory of my indignation embarrassing mainly because I know that a good measure of my anger was rooted in the fact that the salesperson suspected me of being a criminal. (Technically I had shoplifted before. I was six years old, and the three or four small patches I found in the bins near the fabric store cash register looked so cool I had to have them. By the time I got home, I was crying about my theft, consumed with guilt. After telling my mother why I was so upset, we drove back to the store, and I returned the patches after admitting my crime to the sales-clerks. From that point forward, going to the fabric store with my mother made my stomach hurt.) Yes, the black men featured in the hyperventilating nightly news were threats; yes, people had to watch their inventory; but, really, how could anyone suspect *me* of being a criminal? I received my undergraduate degree from Stanford University. I was a graduate student at Yale University. I had a fellowship!

This was the first time I can recall being followed in a store by a suspecting clerk. The second instance occurred a few months later when I was babysitting my young cousins in upscale Stamford, Connecticut, while my aunt and uncle were in Italy for the week. Even though I pulled up to the front of the package store in my uncle's luxury car, and even though I was only buying milk and yogurt, the clerk could not have been more devoted to following my movement from aisle to aisle until I got to the dairy section. Aware that he was watching me, I made quite a display of picking up the items I needed and keeping them at arm's length until I got to the front of the store. See? Nothing up my sleeves or in my coat pockets. He never said a word to me while following me through the store but dared a smile when I paid him. I did not smile back. I would like to believe that if I hadn't actually needed the milk and yogurt, I would have marched out of that store as well, convinced I was winning another anonymous victory in the march toward racial justice.

I consider myself very lucky that these two minor events are the only instances I can recall where I was racially marked and followed in a store. Similar transactions occur daily in black America and often transpire in such a way that the affected party is unable to escape with his or her dignity intact. My private, nonverbal exchanges that revolved around negative constructions of blackness pale in comparison with what others have endured. Too frequently, transactions that speak to blacks' second-class status or simply blackness as a threat are stories about public moments of racial shame and humiliation that force the victims to question that day's fashion choice, their hard work, their annual income, or their place in the republic.

This is the first time that I have committed these experiences to paper. Other black writers, however, have registered their anger and pain when reflecting on instances when they felt trapped in a moment of racial shame and humiliation. Like mine, their encounters were individual in nature. However, in their retelling they were typically repackaged as representative of the daily challenges that all blacks faced when navigating their United States. In retelling their stories, they suggested a collective memory of trauma that resonated loudly with the metaphoric unified black community.[1] While these moments of suggestive, collective shame can be found across time and space, a mid-1940s magazine series titled "My Most Humiliating Jim Crow Experience" captured this phenomenon in striking clarity.

"My Most Humiliating Jim Crow Experience" was one of the first major series to appear in *Negro Digest*, the brainchild of Chicago insurance publicist John Johnson. First published in 1942, *Negro Digest* served as the foundation for what would become the Johnson Publishing empire, the eventual home to *Ebony* and *Jet* magazines, and the cosmetics company Ebony Fashion Fair.[2] Johnson believed that *Negro Digest* met the needs of a black middle class that was desperate for news about itself that existed beyond what was printed in the weekly police blotter or crime column. In the hands of its editors, *Negro Digest* became an arbiter of middle-class values as well as a vehicle for furthering interracial understanding. It is, in short, an effective barometer for assessing the strategic work of black remembering in the 1940s.[3]

At first glance, the very public acts of remembering moments of shame and humiliation that one finds in "My Most Humiliating Jim Crow Experience" seem to run counter to the efforts of 1940s social scientists to engage in a practice of "forgetting" when they edited out sordid elements and aspects of the black experience. However, as this chapter shows, the public reconstruction of humiliation by privileged blacks actually served the same agenda: the preservation of social status and authority.

The idea that blacks had been systematically humiliated through Jim Crow encounters was not new when the *Negro Digest* series first appeared. In fact, "humiliation" had long been one of the defining characteristics for the victim of any Jim Crow exchange. Humiliation involved more than just a personal feeling of shame or embarrassment because it so often evoked new and terrible understandings of reality. It destabilized an imagined sense of a world that welcomed you, and it reaffirmed the existence of a world that did not want you in it, at least not in any way that suggested you were a first-class citizen or a peer. For anyone of prominence—as all of the authors of the *Negro Digest* essays happened to be—humiliation was always to be avoided. Because the social position of prominent blacks so often hinged expressly on the approval of whites, humiliation driven by racism had graver implications.[4]

SOCIAL POSITION AND HUMILIATION

"My Most Humiliating Jim Crow Experience" appeared twenty-six times between March 1944 and June 1946. The only break in the series occurred during the two months between the penultimate and final essays. The contributors were well-known figures in black America. The first essayist, for example, was George Schuyler, gadfly journalist and writer known for his satires such as *Black No More* and syndicated columns in black newspapers.[5] A handful of the other contributors, such as Zora Neale Hurston, Langston Hughes, and Arthur P. Davis, were also important literary figures. On the whole, the essayists represented a fairly broad range of professional backgrounds. Among the contributors were Walter White, executive director of the NAACP; G. James Fleming, the regional director of the President's Committee on Fair Employment Practices; Muriel Rahn and Canada Lee, famous Broadway actors; and Adam Clayton Powell Jr., then the pastor of New York's Abyssinian Baptist Church and candidate for the U.S. Congress.

One can break down the contributors' narratives in a variety of ways. Some were written as triumphant stories in which the antagonist's ignorance was put on public display. Others were more somber, acknowledging the distance that remained before blacks had full equality in American society. Yet, whether they were clearly uplifting or critically cautious, none of the narratives were naive about the political intentions that informed the series. That much had to be obvious to the contributors. Beyond the authors' universally expressed desire for a just America, there are particular subthemes in the essays that yield fruitful considerations of the subtleties and nuances that accompany the social performance of Jim Crow and its attendant humiliations. By understanding how certain essays were informed by the politics of social position and others were driven by the politics of racial solidarity, we can begin asking important questions about the rhetoric of humiliation and its strategic value.

The first "My Most Humiliating Jim Crow Experience" essay reveals some of the class dynamics that came to define much of the *Negro Digest* series. In March 1944, George Schuyler recalled his experiences in Paris, Texas, where he was completing a tour of the South during which he reported on black life below the Mason-Dixon line. Schuyler was scheduled to catch a train out of town that evening, but before then, he was to receive a money order at the local Western Union office. The order arrived as expected, but the small office did not have enough money on hand to cash the check. The Western Union clerk, expressing no ill will toward Schuyler, directed him to the local hotel for assistance.

> I made for the hotel desk, the Western Union check in my hand. When I was half way to the desk, the clerk looked up with a scowl on his young, hard face.
>
> "Take off yo' hat . . . Boy!" he shouted at the top of his voice. He emphasized the word "boy."

I stopped in my tracks as if shot. All eyes turned toward me, curiously, challengingly, warningly. The lobby was quiet with the silence of a cemetery. It was shocking to be catapulted suddenly into dubious battle when one was intent only on getting away from the battlefield.

What was there to do? To retrace my steps—if I could—meant trying to find another place in town to cash the $75 check, with the chance of missing the last train for Texarkana. On this, my first tour of the South, I had been engaged for some two months—long enough to know that if I started back toward the door without obeying the clerk, I might never reach it. Undoubtedly, the clerk had a gun, as did over half the other men in the lobby. This was Paris, Texas, not New York City, and . . . well, when in Rome. . . .

After these lightening reflections I swallowed my pride and reluctantly pulled off my hat. My jauntiness was gone and [with] humiliation and rage tormenting my insides, I proceeded to the desk, followed by scores of glances.

Schuyler then pulled out his check and got it cashed. But almost immediately after receiving the money, the clerk's curiosity got the best of him: "What are you, president of some nigguh school?"

"No," I replied witheringly and with foolhardy Manhattan flippancy, "Where did you ever hear of a *boy* being president of a school?"

I was across the lobby in no time, acutely aware of my anger. As I opened the door and looked back, the clerk's face was red as a beet from his collar to his hair.

I strolled out of view without undue haste, but once at my rooming house, I grabbed my suitcase and typewriter, hailed a colored jitney and five minutes later was at the station. How I suffered awaiting that train, with one eye on the track and the other on the street! How delightful it was a few minutes later to sit in the Jim Crow coach and watch Paris disappear forever in the dusk![6]

In the pantheon of stories involving small towns, strangers, race, and respectably large sums of money, there is little new in this story. But if we consider how the participants' class position infused the episode, we get a clearer sense of how a certain social standing could afford at least some blacks a taste of freedom at the same time that it might amplify the prospect for some sort of humiliating encounter. The most critical element in Schuyler's story is not that he was a stranger but that he had freedom of mobility: He could leave when he wanted and go where he wanted. It is this very aspect of his narrative that most underscores the often unconscious class character and privilege that accompanied these *Negro Digest* pieces. The possibility of mobility, of leaving an oppressive situation, immediately spoke to his privileged position. Granted, Schuyler wrote his essay during the midst of the second great black migration, when movement was in the air, but "mobility" is different by a matter of degrees. It implies a fluid ease and independence of movement that was alien to most blacks. His very mobility set Schuyler apart from other blacks, and his haughty, if rash, behavior separated him in whites' minds from the lowly masses. The white clerk, unhappy as he was to serve a black patron, still cashed the check. Quite likely, the clerk had little choice but to conclude that this unknown black customer with a large check who dared to wear his hat in the presence of whites and who had the temerity to expect service *had* to be a leader of his race, perhaps even a college president. Just as the clerk could not imagine what it meant to be a college president, he could not imagine how even a black college president might share Schuyler's relief at safe passage in the Jim Crow train car out of town.

Schuyler's relief, of course, was the ironic twist to his tale of humiliation. Countless black travelers felt anger and bitterness when confronted and confounded by Jim Crow policies. Black newspapers frequently related stories of Jim-Crowed travelers. Mundane acts of race discrimination that happened on a daily basis went largely unreported in the black press, but when a notable Jim Crow event occurred—notable for the fact that it involved either a black soldier or a black leader—it was sure to be reported, and it was also sure to sound dissonant alarms throughout black America.[7]

Indeed, just a few weeks after the first issue of *Negro Digest* appeared, the *Pittsburgh Courier* ran two stories in its front section about Jim Crow and travel. The first, "Evict Negro Soldier Even from Jim-Crow Seat in Bus," detailed Staff Sergeant Clark Coleman's removal from the blacks-only section of a Greyhound bus because it was overbooked with white passengers. In the same issue of the paper, a full-page article recounted U.S. Representative Arthur Mitchell's legal challenge to Jim Crow travel that culminated in a Supreme Court victory the previous year. Soon after these stories appeared, the *Washington Afro-American* reported how police forced Hugh Mulzac, the captain of the USS *Booker T. Washington*, from a Richmond, Virginia, bus station because he refused to move to the "colored room." Although Mulzac was almost as well known as an icon of integration as Jackie Robinson would be a few years later, Mulzac's fame did not grant him special privileges. Apparently it did not matter that Mulzac was the first black to skipper a ship for the Merchant Marine or that he was a veteran of both world wars. Taken together, these three articles demonstrate that patriotic loyalty and service to the federal government even during a time of war did not release anyone from the cruel illogic of racial discrimination.[8] The lead editorial in the *Washington Afro-American* that referred to Mulzac's run-in with the police said as much:

> It has long been apparent that the army and navy uniforms mean nothing to the South. Had Captain Mulzac wrapped himself in the American flag and seated himself in the Greyhound bus station of the one-time Confederate capital, the police would have torn away the flag first and ousted the captain second.
>
> We know now that patriotic service and heroism have no meaning for Dixie either. Jim crow [*sic*] is as much for the colored man who commands a ship in sub-infested waters and delivers the goods to the troops overseas as for the humblest colored American who washes cuspidors.[9]

These episodes are merely representative of others that one finds by browsing the pages of the black press. They are also typical in that the black press reported that each Jim Crow victim acted in an assertive and self-assured manner. Staff Sergeant Coleman felt that he had been done "a great injustice," Representative Mitchell pursued his case to the Supreme Court, and Mulzac spoke with great scorn to a white police officer.[10] In this way, the responses one finds to Jim Crow experiences in the pages of *Negro Digest* are entirely different. Certainly, the authors of "My Most Humiliating Jim Crow Experience" also bristled with anger and, in different ways, condemned America's failure to abide by its own moral code of conduct. But one cannot dismiss the fact that they verbalized their pain and anger via humiliation. The desire to have its authors talk about their encounters as moments of such profound shame emphasizes the path that a magazine like *Negro Digest* traveled in order to speak to an interracial audience. Humiliation was an effective tool to create links with a black middle-class readership that certainly experienced the same emotions as the authors, and it resonated effectively with a liberal white readership that wanted black leaders who were strong and yet also in control of their emotions. Humiliation was less abrasive than a piercing, white-hot anger. Humiliation would also work with a sympathetic white public because it relied on these whites to change the nature of the political and social structure so that no one would have similar experiences in the future. In this way, those elite blacks who "confessed" to their humiliation let whites preserve power to absolve themselves, but only if whites, in turn, forced social change.

Given the frequency of racially charged episodes involving travel, it is not surprising that one-fourth of the *Negro Digest* narratives revolve around travel.[11] Historian Rayford Logan's contribution to the series lamented the fact that his first-class cabin was denied him and his wife as they attempted to cruise to Haiti on a research trip. Performer Muriel Rahn's essay recounted the airport concessionaire who refused to serve her while she was traveling with a group of public figures assisting the U.S. Treasury Department's sixth war-loan drive.[12] G. James Fleming, a mid-ranking administrator in the federal government, met Jim Crow on a Southern Railroad train. His experience, however, is notable for what it says about how humiliation played a distinctive role in articulating an elite black space, one, furthermore, that would not be challenged by white friends of the race.

As his train pulled out of Atlanta and he prepared to occupy the lower berth in the sleeper car, he was confronted by a white "solid-looking citizen" who declared, "You can't sleep in here. . . . This is below the Mason and Dixon line and no niggers ride in sleepers down here." Both parties refused to give ground and instead sought out a Pullman porter and then a conductor to resolve the dispute. When Fleming began to tell his side of the story, he was promptly interrupted by his antagonist, "Stop talking so damn proper; talk like a nigger should."[13]

Unlike the other humiliation episodes in the series that explicitly revolved around class status, Fleming's claim to social position was subtler. The fact that he was in a Pullman sleeper was a clear marker of rank, but Fleming's status is more profoundly marked by the white passenger's frustrated demand that he "talk like a nigger should." The antagonist wanted to return Fleming to the position that he thought every black should occupy; Fleming's diction marked him as different from the average black, and for that he should suffer. The white passenger's brusque and crude behavior clearly also marked him as someone quite different from—beneath, if you will—the kind of white reader *Negro Digest* sought to cultivate.

Although class-based confrontations were not always the driving impetus behind Jim Crow, the efforts of certain whites to reduce the social standing of blacks were a central feature of every Jim Crow encounter. Most often, these encounters were limited to a barrage of words that concealed, albeit barely, the threat of physical harm. On occasion, however, the commitment to attack blacks' social standing was accompanied by a more literal and immediate possibility of assault. In Frank Marshall Davis's case, this threat came from a young doctor.

Davis, the executive editor of the Associated Negro Press, wrote about his days in the early 1930s when he was the managing editor of the *Atlanta*

Daily World. In February 1931, he relocated from Chicago to Atlanta with "considerable misgivings" to assume the editorship. He had never been south before but clearly felt that the possibility of mortal danger accompanied the move. It occurred to Davis that "when you get that far in Dixie and something happens, it's not a simple matter to get back to a place of comparative safety. Even after you leave Georgia, you've still got to dash across two more Jim Crow states, Tennessee and Kentucky, before you can reach even southern Ohio, and that's still a long way from the 'Windy City.'"[14] If Davis really did have these thoughts when he moved to Atlanta thirteen years before he published his essay in *Negro Digest*—and there is no reason to believe he did not—they quickly proved prophetic.

Three months after his arrival, he was rushed by two of his reporters to tax-supported Grady Hospital, where many blacks went for free care. Davis's assistants rightly concluded that he needed prompt medical attention. He sustained a gash in his forehead after he hit a makeshift doorframe in the newsroom. Although Davis could have afforded a private physician, his assistants took him to Grady Hospital because it was only four blocks from the newsroom office.

A young, white intern arrived to care for Davis's laceration. After inquiring if his patient had been hit over the head with a brick, the intern began to close the head wound with stitches. Halfway through the procedure the unnamed doctor paused and asked Davis a question:

"Well, boy, do you think you'll survive this?"

"Yes," I said.

The young doctor stopped. I looked up. Very deliberately he directed his gaze toward my reporters and then back to me before he said: "What's the matter, darky, don't you know how to say 'sir'? Don't forget I've got you where I can do anything I want to. Remember, I'm a doctor. Now, what did you mean to say?"

Dumbfounded, I looked around. My companions dropped their eyes. The interne stood above me, suturing needle upraised in one hand as if it were a stiletto, cold color-hate shining in his eyes. My lips were dry. As I moistened them, I thought of all I had heard of Dixie. I wanted to rebel, to get out of there. But my head throbbed from the pain of the wound and I did not know what this angry, young, white doctor might do. And whatever it was, I knew that he could get by with it.

"Yes sɪʀ," I said somehow.

The interne relaxed, nodded his head approvingly, and finished the task. Nobody uttered a word.[15]

With his words and suture kit, this young doctor silenced and humiliated three blacks. He also reduced these professionals to the position of the "common Negro" whose life experiences were reduced to "boyhood" and, with their eyes dropped, were forced to defer with unearned respect to even a younger white as "sir."

Age, professional position, and education mattered not at all in the Jim Crow exchange. The amount of currency in one's pocket or bank account was immaterial where the only currency with real value was white skin. All blacks could thus be lumped together in the same group, without any distinguishing features to set them apart from one another. Many people did just that. But the authors of these stories understood themselves differently. They were aware of their blackness and thus had to suffer the daily threats of violence to their physical and psychological well-being. But they were also the most talented blacks, a class removed from those with whom they were often grouped by outsiders. Davis was "dumbfounded" that a person trained to heal would threaten him with physical harm, but might he also have been amazed that his assistants offered no support? It was only after he looked at them that his companions assumed the position of the "common black" with averted eyes. Davis's reporters were, indeed, suffering a double humiliation—one from the doctor and one from Davis. This double humiliation shows how status played an important role in delineating how shame was communicated and experienced. The higher the status a black person held, the greater the risk he or she ran of being humiliated by whites and the greater the possibility that he or she could, in turn, humiliate "lower" blacks.

Although Davis remained in the South for several more years, it is evident that he never recovered from the threat to his well-being or the assault on his social position. The only resolution one finds in his narrative is his refusal to return to Grady Hospital and his decision to retain private physicians for the remainder of his years in Atlanta. Ultimately, his high social standing and the material resources that served to intensify his humiliation at the hands of the intern also provided him the means to escape, like Schuyler did from Paris, Texas.

Not all of the Jim Crow encounters ended on notes of irresolution or lost dignity. Alternatives to the class narratives filled with painful reminders of racial difference and privilege are stories that took the humiliations of Jim Crow and turned them into an explicit condemnation of American society. On one level, these stories are laments for the American soul. But the people doing the lamenting also assert their superiority over the individuals and circumstances that violated the promise of America.

Just as humiliation cuts deeper than mere embarrassment, the act of lamentation signifies a particular status vis-à-vis the rest of society. *Negro Digest* authors who angrily and actively decried violence against American ideals also embraced their status as race leaders. Their essays, in effect, "solidarity narratives," mourn the nation's loss of its own possibility as the authors simultaneously articulate their own place as interpreters of what the American soul ought to be and do. In this way, these narratives came closest to the kind of editorializing and reporting one regularly found in the broader black press. The fact remains, however, that these encounters were presented in the context of a kind of shame that cut across racial boundaries and spoke to different reading constituencies. Narrating a humiliating experience that was clothed in the language of lament preserved the narrator's leadership position with blacks who were similarly disappointed in America's racial practices and also with whites who felt ashamed of such practices.

Arthur P. Davis's most humiliating experience came early in life, but it remained a useful memory for casting shame on American mores that denied full citizenship status to even the most innocent and for even the most innocuous transgressions.[16] He recounted a childhood experience in Hampton, Virginia, when he stayed on a streetcar one extra block so he could walk by the white section of a beach and look at the whites-only amusement rides. After his black companions disembarked and Davis did not, the white conductor grabbed him by the collar and yelled at him:

> "You little yaller son-of-a-bitch . . . You must think you're white! Why in the hell didn't you get off with them other niggers?" And then, his face distorted with anger, he called me a half-white bastard in a dozen insulting ways.
>
> I can still see the hatred in his watery-blue eyes; I can still feel the shock, the abysmal hurt which I received. I don't remember what I said or did. It couldn't have been much, because the attack was too sudden, too unreasonable, too unprovoked for me to react adequately. Its violence and viciousness simply overwhelmed me. But I shall never forget the agony of that experience. And the incident will always remain with me, not only as my most humiliating experience with Jim Crow, but also as the symbol of all the gratuitous and sadistic cruelty inherent in American race hatred.[17]

Though Davis's retelling of this childhood experience is filtered through decades of lived experience, he understood the political possibilities such retelling involved. Davis believed that his position as a recognized interpreter of the black experience also allowed him to be an arbiter of America's morality. Indeed, being able to critique without fear of retribution was the mark of someone who had already embraced his full citizenship rights.

Zora Neale Hurston was no different in this regard. By recounting her particular moment of racial pain, Hurston revealed the extent to which she pitied America and the Anglo-Saxon civilization it glorified. Hurston's most humiliating experience occurred in New York after she returned from a research trip in the Bahamas. Hurston's patron, Charlotte Osgood Mason, noticed that Hurston had fallen ill and arranged for her to see a medical specialist. Mason's friend, "the wealthy and prominent Paul Chapin," spoke with the doctor and received a promise of the best possible care. When Hurston arrived at the doctor's office, however, it became evident that the office did not anticipate that Mason and Chapin had referred a black patient to them.[18]

The receptionist was "obviously embarrassed" when Hurston arrived and then disappeared into the doctor's private office for several minutes. The doctor came out of the office, "looking very important, and also very unhappy from behind his rotund stomach," and directed his nurse to show Hurston to a private room. For a moment, it seemed that despite the doctor's apparent displeasure, Chapin's and Mason's status was going to ensure that Hurston received the promised proper care.

The extent of her patrons' protection, however, proved limited. When Hurston entered the room, she discovered that "the room was private all right, but I would not rate it highly as an examination room. Under any other circumstances, I would have sworn it was a closet where the soiled towels and uniforms were tossed until called for by the laundry. But I will say this for it, there was a chair in there wedged in between the wall and the piles of soiled linen." The doctor came into the used linen closet/examination room immediately, hoping to get Huston out of the office just as quickly. After a "desultory" examination, an extraction of bile from Hurston's gall bladder, and a prescription, the doctor asked for a fee of $20. Hurston, who was prepared to pay the doctor before she entered his office, refused. Instead, "I got up, set my hat at a reckless angle and walked out, telling him I would send him a check, which I never did. I went away feeling the pathos of the Anglo-Saxon civilization."[19]

Like Arthur P. Davis, Hurston saw in her moment of humiliation the depth of racial irrationality that resided in the soul of America. Also like Davis, Hurston used this revelation as the vehicle and justification for her pity. The experience was painful, but it imbued her with an undeniable authority to judge America's commitment to equality and, in her opinion, even Anglo-Saxon civilization. Admittedly, Hurston's position of authority is complicated by the fact that her humiliating Jim Crow experience depended on the helpful assistance of wealthy whites. But this fact did not stop her from emphasizing the sincerity and intensity of her pity. She closed her contribution to the *Negro Digest* by reiterating her sense that Anglo-Saxon civilization was doomed: "And I still mean pathos, for I know that anything with such a false foundation cannot last. Whom the gods would destroy, they first make mad."[20]

Forceful as Davis's and Hurston's closing thoughts were, they paled in comparison with those issued by Adam Clayton Powell Jr. His contribution to the series is by far the most dramatic example of a humiliating Jim Crow experience being used as a marker of whites' moral failings and as a vehicle for self-determined leadership within black America. Powell's *Negro Digest* narrative opened in November 1942 with his arrival in Washington, D.C. He came to the capital to support those senators fighting for the abolition of the poll tax. The police met Powell at the train, but he refused their escort. When Powell approached the Senate gallery to witness the floor debate, it became clear that there was an armed guard specifically posted to observe him. (At first, Powell's light skin apparently frustrated security looking for "'that damn n——r Powell.'")[21] While this personalized attention may or may not have perturbed Powell, he lost his patience when one of the guards, in the middle of searching Powell at the Senate gallery door, asked him, "Got any likker [*sic*] or a razor on you?" According to Powell, his "sudden display of contempt, disgust, and no little anger" shamed the guard.

Powell's mood only worsened when the attempt to kill the poll tax failed.

When the infamous deed was done, when the poll taxers won for the moment and democracy lay raped before the world, I moved toward the door leading from the gallery. The officer moved with me. I walked down the steps, and he remained at my side. When I came to the main corridor I paused to talk with my friends—to plan our next move. We were not defeated, merely set back. We knew we would eventually win—right always does. As I stood there talking the officer approached me and snarled, "Move on you—keep goin'. . . ."

The guard said no more, but instead made a convulsive lunge at me, yanked his holster around, unlatched its flap, jerked his pistol half out of it and barked. "I said git out of here—now git!"

I looked at the guard with the pistol. He was wizened and ill fed. He looked hungry and brittle. I knew his gun alone gave him what little security he could muster up in the face of my six feet four inches and over

190 pounds of weight. I wasn't afraid. It was a crisis, but those of us who want to live to fight on at times have to let reason supersede wrath.

The simple act of walking away with dignity was a victory:

I walked firmly from the building. My footsteps were hard and noisy—noisy like the exultant clamour of the oppressed on their day of victory. My face was flushed. My eyes glowed with the light of a man seeing visions, visions of a day when I would return to fight, change or unseat these, the mighty—when I would be sent by believing people to challenge those who prostitute our government. In this hour when I had come to the headwaters of my nation to help stem the tide of garrulous self-defilement, I had been driven from her halls of law. In this hour when it seemed that my humiliation was unmatched—I was unashamed because as I walked away, I turned to look back on the gold domed symbol of a nation a black man, Crispus Attucks, had died to make possible—to scan a city a black man, Benjamin Banneker, had helped to lay out—and thought on the national security and integrity black men even then were dying to preserve.

I looked back and pitied my country because as I looked I saw America hang her head in shame.[22]

Powell's overwrought prose drew on his charismatic preaching style. His words were also rooted in his long experience as a political agitator. In fact, he had recently won a seat on the New York city council and had just declared his candidacy for Harlem's new congressional seat.[23] Since politicians seeking to preserve the status quo already considered Powell a troublemaker for his calls to improve housing, schools, and job opportunities, it is little surprise that he was a target for zealous police attention.

It is difficult to ignore Powell's use of images that connect sex, violence, and masculinity. Democracy was "raped" by those senators who engaged in the "infamous deed" and defiled themselves when they preserved the poll tax; white manhood was only protected by a half-jerked pistol; and it was up to virile yet resolute black men to save "national security and integrity." Powell turned whites' widely held fear of black freedom and equality on its ear: True freedom, Powell implied, had nothing to do with black men gaining free access to white women.[24] Instead, those black soldiers who fought to protect Lady Liberty, the purest woman, embodied true freedom. Black soldiers died to protect America, their motherland, in the hopes that she would not have to "hang her head in shame" as a rape victim of the southern racists/johns and their northern collaborators who saved the poll tax. Powell's sense of all that was right and good, then, revolved around black men. Powell's answer to the country's seemingly implacable problems would be found in forging solidarity with the figure of the black male.

Despite his strong language, few contributors to the "My Most Humiliating Jim Crow Experience" series would have criticized Powell, especially since men wrote twenty-two of the twenty-six essays. This is not to suggest that men and women thought in absolute and separate terms on the issue of gender roles, but this gross gender imbalance does reflect the choices made by *Negro Digest* editors. The editors sought famous and influential contributors for their series, and they turned to men like themselves. Surely more than four women could have spoken of their Jim Crow experiences, and some might have spoken openly about the negative repercussions of linking racial liberation to manhood. Just as manliness was employed as a symbol of protection, democracy, and freedom, it was also used to confer authority and knowledge, implicitly excluding women.[25]

More stories like Zora Neale Hurston's could have revealed the multiple layers of race and gender oppression that so often defined black women's experiences. After all, despite Hurston's hasty departure from the doctor's office, she was only there because Mason, who liked Hurston to call her "godmother," arranged to have a white man make the appointment on Hurston's behalf. While the very people trying to help Hurston infantilized her, one can easily imagine how other black women suffered even more acutely when they did not have influential white backers, be they female or male. More women's stories of Jim Crow humiliation, for example, may also have raised the ugly specter of interracial sexual humiliation. Having Adam Clayton Powell Jr. speak in coded terms that linked authority to sex and cast southern senators as rapists was one thing. Having black women talk about the same matters in frank terms may have been too much for the bourgeois and interracial sensibilities of *Negro Digest*.

According to *Negro Digest*, masculinity bestowed authority and knowledge, but it was not bestowed equally across racial lines. In fact, it would be a mistake to assume that black men always enjoyed universal opportunities to share their insights, even just to black audiences. J. Saunders Redding, an influential essayist on black life and culture, demonstrated this fact in his contribution to the series: a recollection of the events related to a last-minute invitation to speak at a school's commencement ceremony.[26] As it happened, the previously invited speaker, an unnamed "famous" white figure, canceled his appearance at the eleventh hour. Redding still agreed to speak even though he knew he was, at best, second choice. On the day of the event, with the crowd assembled, Redding took his seat on the dais.

Moments before he was to begin to offer his words to the graduates, the rear doors of the auditorium opened, and the original speaker strolled down the aisle with his entourage. No one spoke to Redding as he was gently, but physically, moved from the stage to make room for the originally scheduled speaker and his handlers. Redding was never offered an apology; apparently, no one felt the need to offer one.[27] The presumption of white knowledge and the premium placed on whites' insights were enough to foul Redding's memory for years. *Negro Digest* readers never learn what Redding was planning to say. But his experience makes clear that a black-authored narrative of racial pride and progress—the kind of rhetoric one expects at a graduation ceremony (and what one could generally expect elsewhere in *Negro Digest*)—could quickly become lost in the shadow cast by white presence.

In many ways, a "white presence" was found in every issue of *Negro Digest*. The editors frequently cited or claimed *Negro Digest*'s appeal among black and white troops fighting in Europe. They appealed to readers, black and white, to do their part to improve race relations by getting whites to subscribe to the magazine. They conducted fundraising drives to pay for *Negro Digest* gift subscriptions to southern white schools, and they ran articles with titles such as "Some of Our Best Friends Are White" and "A Negro Magazine for Whites Also."[28] On the back cover of the June 1945 issue, the editors removed all doubt about the role they perceived their magazine was playing in America:

> We hope in the future to publish more and more original material on Negro life that would not ordinarily find its way into the pages of white magazines. An example is our current series on interracial marriage, which is an untouchable subject in most magazines.
>
> NEGRO DIGEST feels that it is pioneering in this field since virtually no Negro magazine in the past has attempted to reach a broad interracial audience with articles which ordinarily are taboo in white magazines. Today a good percentage of readers on our subscription lists are white.
>
> . . . We believe that open and above-board debate of these issues contributes to better racial understanding and helps to douse many of the wild, hysterical rumors which sometimes lead to unfortunate tension and violence.[29]

At the same time that the editors viewed their strategy as a way to "contribute to better racial understanding," they also saw their commitment to open dialogue as fundamentally American: "Free discussion is the American way and we hope to make NEGRO DIGEST a champion of the American way of life."[30] The surest way, of course, to make your commitment to American-ism plain at this time was to declare your solidarity with the troops fighting in foreign lands during World War II. *Negro Digest* did this through ar-ticles that pointed to the commitment and heroism of black soldiers despite race discrimination. The editors were not above using sly self-promotion to "prove" their dedication to the war effort. On the back page of the very first edition, for example, the editors suggested that *Negro Digest* was critical to preserving and promoting morale. The editors reasoned that by subscrib-ing to *Negro Digest* and thereby participating in the propagation of stories of black excellence, U.S. soldiers would be reminded of the ardent support coming from the home front.[31] At first, such editorial comments implicitly referenced black troops. By the end of the *Digest*'s second year, however, its editors connected its morale-boosting strategies with its commitment to an interracial ideal.

To this end, in September 1944, the editors proudly highlighted a let-ter from the crew of the USS *Booker T. Washington*—less than a year after its captain, Hugh Mulzac, ran afoul of Jim Crow in a Richmond, Virginia, bus station—that requested a two-year subscription to *Negro Digest* and "begged" for back issues to distribute among the troops. Commander John O. Garrett, the letter's author, added, "We are proud of your magazine and democratic spirit." *Negro Digest* editors pointed to this letter and "the hundreds of similar letters that we get each month from Negro and white servicemen overseas" with great satisfaction, arguing that these letters col-lectively demonstrated the *Digest* was "buoying morale on the distant bat-tlefronts of the world."[32] Whether or not these claims were materially true, the editors clearly valued the connection between morale, Americanism, and interracial understanding.

This desire to spread interracial understanding fit well with *Negro Di-gest*'s plans to be unique among its competitors. Its determination to de-velop a white reading audience was a means to that end. It was not enough, however, to express such determination. The trick was securing it. If, as Gunnar Myrdal argued, white Americans were "entirely unaware of the bit-ter and relentless criticism of themselves" by the black press, John Johnson and the editors at *Negro Digest* had to find a way to attract white readers.[33]

The answer to this predicament came in the form of another series that was exclusive to *Negro Digest*: "If I Were a Negro."

"If I Were a Negro" became one of the landmark series in *Negro Digest*'s early years. In fact, when the magazine published First Lady Eleanor Roo-sevelt's "If I Were a Negro" essay, it became the best-selling issue in the *Digest*'s short history. For years it remained publisher Johnson's favorite essay from the *Digest*, if mainly, perhaps, for the way it boosted sales and put *Negro Digest* on the national scene. The popularity of Roosevelt's contribution, specifically, and "If I Were a Negro," more generally, speaks to the high level of fascination that each race held for the other and confirms the marketing savvy of John Johnson and his editors.[34] Seen in a different light, other aspects of this commitment to interracialism complicate how one reads "My Most Humiliating Jim Crow Experience." Assessing "If I Were a Negro" better illuminates the kinds of social pressures under which black leaders such as the authors of the Jim Crow experiences operated. This series reveals the mindset, even among so-called friends of the race, that created humiliating Jim Crow experiences in the first place.

RACIAL SYMPATHY AND HUMILIATION

"If I Were a Negro" began its run in December 1942—thus predating "My Most Humiliating Jim Crow Experience" by more than a year—and appeared forty-two times through October 1946. Like "My Most Humiliating Jim Crow Experience," the "If I Were a Negro" series highlighted the thoughts of prominent figures. In "If I Were a Negro," however, the writers were white, and instead of sharing memories, they proffered their opinion of what their life would be like if they were black. The results were a mix of the predictable, the occasionally insightful, and the shocking.

The most predictable sentiments were those that claimed to be aware of how frustrating and embittering it would be to be black. To fight this bitterness, several "If I Were a Negro" authors said that, as blacks, they would join unions to secure economic justice and demand civil rights.[35] However, just as quickly, many of these same authorities cautioned that change takes time and that, as blacks, they would be patient with white America. Hand in hand with the call for patience was the authors' insistence that they would refrain from placing all whites together in one group. Whites deserved to be appreciated as and treated like individuals. A few contributors felt the same should be said for blacks, but more frequently these authors made blanket statements about a general and universal blackness.

The contribution of best-selling novelist Louis Zara exemplifies this. Midway through his essay he declared, "I would judge every man who did me an injustice as an individual, and not as a member of a race or creed—for that is the way I would want to be judged myself." Later, on the same page, he acknowledged the "tremendous creative energy of the Negro people."[36] Guy Johnson, the executive director of the Southern Regional Council, a group dedicated to promoting racial justice and democracy—and the same person who recruited Rayford Logan to edit *What the Negro Wants*—offered a slight variation on this same theme. Like Zara, Johnson insisted that he would "try to remember that white people are individuals and [would] never let [himself] get into the habit of lumping them together in a stereotyped way or of imagining that *all* whites are prejudiced against *all* Negroes."[37] Johnson added, however, that he would "avoid attributing all of the problems of *my group* to discrimination and segregation. The removal of these barriers will make life fairer and pleasanter, but will not work miracles in the hearts of men or eliminate conflicts between the races."[38] Here, Johnson placed part of the onus of garnering social and civil rights reform on blacks' shoulders and simultaneously insisted blacks had to act properly in order to change whites' hearts.

The contributors to the "My Most Humiliating Jim Crow Experience" series, however, proved the lie in Johnson's claim. In each of their stories, they acted respectably and yet remained victims of at times vicious Jim Crow exchanges. Admittedly, as is the case in any memoir, these personal stories were self-serving. The authors certainly would not have portrayed themselves in a negative light. But given the psychological investment most prominent blacks made in the idea of respectability, there is little chance that they would allow themselves to act inappropriately in public, particularly in racially mixed company. For the authors of the humiliation series, then, the pain of the Jim Crow exchange was intensified because racial conflict came precisely when they were acting just as the white authors of the "If I Were a Negro" series hoped blacks would act. An observation from Ralph Matthews's Jim Crow memoir speaks directly to this point: "Southern prejudice is much like a treacherous serpent, it lies in wait and springs often without warning just when you least expect it while you are going quietly about your business enjoying life and at peace with the world."[39]

Guy Johnson's directive to blacks shows the privilege that accompanied whiteness. Even progressive whites could insist, without a trace of irony, on the principle of white individualism at the same time that they talked about generic black characteristics. The only blacks who were recognized as individuals were the race's leaders. This recognition, moreover, came with the articulated expectation that these individual, exceptional blacks had an obligation to their group.[40]

A few of the most insightful contributions to the "If I Were a Negro" series recognized the inequity in this equation. Oswald Garrison Villard, the former editor of *The Nation*, pushed Johnson's view to a more balanced position. He, like his less progressive white contributors, agreed that "more than ever there is an obligation upon Negroes, both men and women, to put their best foot forward, to be patient and enduring, and above all to be well-mannered." But Villard added an important caveat to his call for respectable behavior. In a variation, perhaps, of W. E. B. Du Bois's double-consciousness framework, Villard made it clear that he understood that individual blacks unfairly bore a "double obligation." Villard recognized that this double obligation grew out of the fact that the black individual "represents not only himself but his race, and upon his behavior depends . . . how the battle for complete legal equality will come out."[41] Noted author and conservationist Wallace Stegner echoed Villard. If he were black, Stegner wrote, he would know "that any career I undertook was in a sense a career of my whole people; that everything I did would be put down to the credit or discredit of my whole people. I would know that in the face of enormous difficulties I was obligated to do better, be better, think better than most Americans. I would know that my purposes could not be selfishly my own, that I had common cause with thirteen million other colored Americans."[42]

Villard's and Stegner's recognition of the inherent inequity in the way whites and blacks should view each other and their respective obligations, if any, to their group were rare moments in this *Negro Digest* series. Dominating most of the series were pieces that would seem more at home in *Reader's Digest* for their rosy optimism about blacks' future place in society.[43] As might be expected, however, there were a few shocking departures from this general tone. Channing Pollock's and Fannie Hurst's essays made plain how even those who considered themselves friends of the race embraced ideologies that only perpetuated Jim Crow dynamics in the first place.

Playwright and lyricist Pollock urged blacks to take the most cautious approach to full citizenship. "As a Negro," Pollock declared, "I should find happiness in my own world, among my own people, striving for the time when my race should have *demonstrated* equality, rather than demand it."[44] Pollock, who was born in Washington, D.C., in 1880, made sure to highlight his credentials on the topic to his reading public. He first presented his warm friendship with Booker T. Washington and then with Robert Russa Moton, Washington's successor at Tuskegee, as evidence of his finely honed sense of race relations. In further testimony to his close sympathies with black America, Pollock pointed to long-standing friendships with two other blacks: his "helper" of twenty years and his butler. Even if these last two relationships were entirely reciprocal, it is evident that Pollock lacked an appreciation for the fact that they were forged in, at best, a hierarchy in which he, as benevolent white, dictated the terms of the relationship.

Novelist Fannie Hurst's contribution was little better than Pollock's for the way it saluted black accomplishment while unconsciously damning blacks to a subordinate position in American life. Hurst, who at one point was a member of the board of directors of the New York Urban League, recognized the difficulties blacks faced on a daily basis but also wanted to congratulate them for their perseverance. Hurst offered, "If I Were a Negro I would want to be capable of a sense of high pride in those singing qualities of heart and spirit; those rhythms of mind and body, which have helped the race survive. I would want to experience gratitude for the godliness, the friendliness, the joyous adolescence of the Negro. Qualities which have enabled him to laugh off, sing off, pray off some of his gargantuan social burdens. That would give me courage and self-confidence."[45]

(It is worth noting that Hurst's impressionistic 1946 opinions seem less than one day removed from sociologist Robert Park's 1924 observation that the Negro "is primarily an artist, loving life for its own sake. His *metier* is expression rather than action. He is, so to speak, the lady among races.")[46]

Closer to Hurst's time, Edwin Embree, president of the Rosenwald Fund, provided a list of "basic steps" whites and blacks should pursue in order to secure democracy. Among other things, he told whites to cease racial discrimination in the military and "equalize schools and other public facilities." He told blacks that in addition to joining labor unions and patronizing their own stores, they needed to "take pride in [their] own distinctiveness." Therefore, blacks should "keep on laughing, singing, dancing, making jokes. Make fun of the ofays if you want to, but anyway keep making fun. Keep on eating good food and wearing gay clothes, and enjoying life. Keep swinging."[47] What is particularly troubling about all of these comments is the fact that Park, Embree, and Hurst were sincerely interested in improving the quality of black life. One wonders, therefore, what effect the articulation and propagation of these ideas had on those blacks who were expected to lead the race and those whites who wanted to preserve the idea that blacks were simple and childlike and thus needed to be figurative wards of the state.[48]

Blacks, of course, had no interest in being the objects of an infantilizing discourse. Infants' memories and identities had no bearing on the world. Infants could not be the agents in making their own, independent future. Prominent blacks, particularly those who fashioned themselves to be race leaders—and every contributor to the "My Most Humiliating Jim Crow Experience" was, whether he or she liked it or not, viewed by white America as a race leader—fought hard to have their own ability to act be recognized and respected.

The ability of blacks to withdraw from the social difficulties associated with blackness largely depended on the willingness of whites to allow blacks to live their lives in peace. Whites consistently deployed Jim Crow ideologies and practices that reduced individuals to groups regardless of a black person's wealth, education, profession, age, or gender. "My Most Humiliating Jim Crow Experience" centered on this phenomenon: individual black respectable behavior negated by white intolerance.

The twenty-six essays in the Jim Crow series were of uneven quality, and the humiliations ranged across time, space, and circumstance; but it is evident that the essays were united in purpose. The Jim Crow experiences show us that despite the elite standing of the authors in black America, their social position was always potentially under threat from young, white medical interns or hotel clerks or passengers in Pullman cars or trolley car conductors or officers of the peace—in short, from any white person. These horrible incidents, however, also presented moments of opportunity. The public airing of these humiliations actually served to protect the authors' own elite standing in the black community. Just as whites could humiliate elite blacks so that they could remember their alleged proper social station, there was little stopping prominent blacks from airing their own Jim Crow grievances and thereby establishing links, forged from common experience, to the larger black community.

MAKING MEMORIES BEYOND HUMILIATION

Negro Digest's publisher John Johnson made clear in his autobiography that he envisioned the magazine as a vehicle to help blacks earn respect.[49] Johnson was determined to sell an upbeat message to the country as well as an upbeat image of black America. Granted, "My Most Humiliating Jim Crow Experience" was not the vehicle to do either of these things, but it was an important way for prominent blacks, relying on their memories, to stake a claim to their fundamental citizenship rights and to act as racial interpreters to white America.

I was born too late to have read the earliest versions of *Negro Digest*. Faced with fiscal realities and a changing national consciousness, Johnson decided to suspend publication of *Negro Digest* in 1951. The magazine would reappear in 1961, but its postwar, middle-class, take-it-slow sensibilities were out of place in the new era of major civil rights activism and then the emergence of black power militancy. Aware of the changing social scene, the editors broadened the magazine's appeal, seeking also to broaden its reader and subscription base. In 1970, *Negro Digest* editors made a significant alteration to the magazine's format and renamed it *Black World*, reflecting a much more overtly political and transnational editorial agenda.

By this point in its publication run (which would end in 1976), a typical issue of *Negro Digest/Black World* would have essays such as "On Racism and Racist Systems," "The Black Aesthetic," and "The Cultural Arm of Revolutionary Black Nationalism."[50]

While I can't be absolutely certain that a magazine with this kind of focus entered my house, I find it unimaginable that my parents would have subscribed to it. They did, however, have long-standing subscriptions to Johnson's other magazines, *Ebony* and *Jet*. Almost from the moment of its first publication in 1945, *Ebony* was without peer in the world of black periodicals. In fact, its success led directly to *Negro Digest*'s first demise. Whether it was running imaginative essays such as "If I Were a Negro," politically challenging essays like "My Most Humiliating Jim Crow Experience," or even crowd-pleasing occasional columns like "Movie Star Quiz," *Negro Digest* just could not compete with *Ebony*'s popularity.

Envisioned as a black version of *Life* magazine, *Ebony* sought to use photo-essays to showcase a high-functioning, middle- and upper-class black world.[51] Its editors made no secret of their ambitions: "We like to look at the zesty side of life. Sure, you can get all hot and bothered about the race question (and don't think we don't) but not enough is said about all the swell things we Negroes can do and will accomplish. EBONY will try to mirror the happier side of Negro life—the positive everyday achievements from Harlem to Hollywood. But when we talk about race as the No. 1 problem of America, we'll talk turkey."[52]

Even though the first letters to the editor *Ebony* published were full of congratulations for "helping America understand a very important part of our total population" and for "rendering unique service not only to the Negro public, but to America at large," some readers were displeased with the editors' affection for "zest."[53] Complaints came in about the "pin-up" girls featuring low-cut dresses and the frequently off-color humor in the magazine's cartoons. If the editors were going to be true to their claim to show the best parts of black life, they needed to rethink their penchant to dabble in flesh and base humor.

Reflecting the same kinds of anxieties and motivations that centered on black memory work (how and what blacks remembered and forgot), *Ebony*'s editors and readers alike were deeply concerned about how the race was presented in the magazine's pages. Although they shared a concern about what stories needed to be told, there were instances when the editors and at least some readers parted company. For example, in a particularly pointed letter to the editor, reader Kathleen Daveson expressed her dismay about an article concerning black poverty: "Your magazine is nice but for

God's sake, lay off this mess about Negroes living in a ghetto and the horrible conditions that the Negro lives under. We know you mean well, but you might as well get it through your head that if the kind of Negro who lives in a rat-infested kitchenette didn't like to live like a pig in a sty, he would not."[54] The trenchant tone of the letter was unlike anything that readers would see in the body of the monthly. Further, *Ebony* readers rarely came across pictorials that had anything to do with poverty or racial degradation of any type. More typical would be a photo-essay on the stylish living on Sugar Hill, an enclave for Harlem's political and social elite, in which the reader would see photographs of spacious Manhattan interiors or two leaders of the race sharing a casual conversation across the net at a local tennis club.[55]

(Unsurprisingly, just as Daveson disagreed with *Ebony*'s editors, readers disagreed with her. Two months after Daveson's letter appeared, six different readers responded to her critique—all of them attacking her for being shortsighted. The most pungent letter observed, "Kathleen Daveson has committed a great injustice to her race [or does she still own us] by publicly expressing her selfish thoughts. By publishing her letter you brought to light a far greater menace to the race than the rat-infested kitchenette can offer. Why not send Kathleen's letter to 'The Man' [Bilbo]. He has found a true black companion.")[56]

Growing up as a casual reader of *Ebony*, I can't say that I ever read letters to the editor. In fact, by the time I picked up my first copy of *Ebony*, the editorial agenda was strikingly consistent: share local black success stories; visit movie stars or athletes or musicians at their homes; emphasize glamour and entrepreneurship; and above all, make sure everyone is smiling and has beautiful skin, hair, and teeth. In truth, I assume the agenda was a bit more complicated than that, but this is what stuck. *Ebony* was about black accomplishment. I also remember that I was the only one in the house who ever picked up the magazine. I read it not because I was determined to consume narratives of black triumph or because I needed to find out about the latest interior design of Ruby Dee and Ossie Davis's living room. Rather, I was bored, my homework was done, and, if it was the weekend, I hadn't yet learned to enjoy watching sports on television. I don't truly know what the variables were, but I always knew that if I were searching for something to do, I could find the latest issues of *Ebony* prominently displayed on the coffee table in the living room. In this regard, *Ebony* was a performance piece in my household. It said that we were simultaneously middle to upper class and very comfortable in our blackness.

Jet magazine, however, was quite different. Debuting in 1951, *Jet* effectively replaced *Negro Digest* as a resource for black news in short form. It

At the net, Lester Granger and William Trent Jr. (right), *my maternal grandfather* (Ebony, *November 1946, Yale Collection of American Literature, Beinecke Rare Book and Manuscript Library)*

was published weekly and, to judge a book by its cover, was less socially reserved than *Negro Digest*. In its early years, *Jet* consistently featured an attractive woman on the cover and lured its readers inside with taglines like "10 Ways to Get a Mink Coat," "Where People Make Love," and "How Negro Beauties Charm Europe's Men."[57] A few years into its publishing run, *Jet* added to its commitment to "zest" when it began running a center photograph of a "Beauty of the Week"—a suggestive, but not luring, photograph of a black woman in a bathing suit. We had *Jet* in our house as well, and I definitely remember reading it solely to see that week's black beauty. Actually, to be honest, if I read a page of *Jet*, I would be astonished. Notably, *Jet* was not next to *Ebony* on the coffee table. You had to go a bit further into the house to find my father's copy of the magazine (and it was clearly my father's). Of course, I don't recall anyone else in the family reading *Jet* either. Maybe my father's friends picked it up when they came over.

It would be unfair to limit my description of *Jet* to its willingness to be a bit more provocative than its predecessors. Importantly, *Jet* also made a name for itself for its civil rights reportage. Given its format—weekly issues with very brief stories, some not much longer than newspaper headlines—*Jet* could call its readers' attention to civil rights battles across the country in what would pass for real time in 1950s print culture.

The magazine's most famous moment occurred when it published a civil rights story, the 1955 essay titled "Nation Horrified by Murder of Kidnapped Chicago Youth." This was the story of Emmett Till, the fourteen-year-old who, while visiting family in Mississippi, was kidnapped, assaulted, and murdered for whistling at the wife of a local store owner. After Pullman porters spirited Till's body back to Chicago, his mother insisted that the mortician leave his severely mutilated face untouched so that "all the world" could bear witness to the atrocity. During a four-day memorial, thousands passed by the open coffin. *Jet* ran several images of Till, barely recognizable as a human being. The nation was shocked.[58]

I was not yet born when Till was murdered and *Jet* ran the infamous photographs that served as a call to action for thousands. And while I would never equate the humiliation of being kicked off a trolley car or being followed in a store with Till's kidnapping, violation, and murder, I know that blacks of my parents' generation saw in Till's death the gruesome extension of their daily battles with racial shame and humiliation. I came to this realization around 2000 when I joined a colleague for Easter Sunday dinner at her house. Her parents were visiting from Los Angeles—or, more precisely, the very wealthy enclave Palos Verdes Estates. Her father was a self-made success who, I learned that afternoon, was also a displaced southerner.

He was, he told me, born about the same time as Emmett Till. And although he was not from Mississippi, rural Louisiana was close enough in literal and figurative ways to matter deeply. I could not help but notice that this normally stately and debonair man who was maybe just a few years younger than my own father was still rattled by the memory of Till's murder: "Once I heard what they did to him, I was determined to leave the South as soon as I was old enough. It was clear: there simply wasn't any future for black boys like me. And I kept my word. It wasn't until this past summer's family reunion that I stepped foot again in Louisiana. That was almost fifty years ago."[59] His voice wasn't quavering when he told us this story; too much time had passed for that. It was plain to see, however, that after so many years the bitterness was still present. The memories of lost time, broken families, and humiliations that ran the spectrum from racial epithets to lynching were as alive as the day of their first discovery.

3

THE BLACK BODY
AS ARCHIVE OF MEMORY

If any one aphorism can characterize the experience of black people
in this country, it might be that the white-authored national narrative
deliberately contradicts the histories our bodies know.
—Elizabeth Alexander, "'Can you be BLACK and Look at This?'"

I want my whiteness back!
—Jeff Gerber, *Watermelon Man*

THE FINGER

I don't recall the year, but I remember the moment perfectly. My brother
sat me down with the promise to show me something that was earth shat-
tering, something that was so racy and daring that I couldn't even tell Mom
and Dad about it.

Obviously, he had my complete attention.

Brian turned on the television, and I sat there a bit confused as we
watched a tall black man in a long leather coat emerge from the subway
in New York City's Times Square. This was back in the days when Times
Square was little more than a red-light district, so the scene was already
filled with a tension that, while visible and palpable, was beyond my sensibilities to process beyond the most basic reflections.

It was the opening scene from *Shaft*, the 1971 film that is heralded as one
of the crowning moments in the short-lived history of early 1970s "blaxploitation" cinema. As John Shaft, or rather Detective John Shaft, rolled
past the illuminated promises of adult entertainment, Isaac Hayes's funk
offered something viscerally exciting. I was too young to understand the

67

simultaneous thrill and threat of Hayes's lyrics when the singer observed that "Shaft is a bad mother" only to be interrupted by his righteous backup singers who tell him to "shut your mouth!" I didn't get it, but I knew something older than me was going on that I was not allowed to know. It turned out, however, that watching Shaft move through these city streets or listening to the backup singers interrupt Hayes is not what Brian wanted me to see. Instead, he wanted me to see a gesture.

Less than one minute into the opening, the camera pans out as Shaft, the master of his surroundings, purposefully strides past one broken promise after another and starts to jaywalk through an intersection. He weaves around a couple of taxis with ease until a car begins to speed past traffic and toward the intersection. The driver slams on the brakes to avoid hitting Shaft. That's when it happens. Before the driver has an opportunity to curse the jaywalking black man, Detective John Shaft gives the finger to the driver and provides the movie's first lines: "Up yours!"[1]

My childhood was innocent enough that I immediately knew that this had to be the moment. Giving the finger was a violation of some sort of social contract—even though I didn't have the words then to put it that way. What I wasn't prepared for was my brother's observation that Shaft's gesture was important because the public hadn't ever seen a black man act like that before, especially a black man with a badge. I had to take my brother's word for it, as he was much more experienced about the racial ways of our world.

When I watched the opening sequence in *Shaft* (my brother didn't allow me to watch any more than that, concerned, I think, that I might tell our parents that he had introduced me to such fare), I'm not sure if Brian was even aware that the movie was part of a dawning phase in the history of American cinema in which blacks and an ostensibly black world—one that was hypermasculine, violent, laced with drugs, and defined by ill-gotten gains, corrupt (white) police, and large-breasted women in skimpy outfits—became highly marketable commodities. A few months before *Shaft* appeared, filmmaker Melvin Van Peebles inaugurated this blaxploitation moment when he released his independent art film, *Sweet Sweetback's Baadasssss Song*. Much less concerned than *Shaft* would be with offending white sensibilities, Van Peebles's film was, from beginning to end, one extended middle finger to white America. (Some of the film's promotional material affirmed as much, stating that it was "The film THE MAN doesn't want you to see!" The movie itself closed with an on-screen warning to white America: "A Baad Assss Nigger Is Coming Back To Collect Some Dues.")

But out of the many differences between the two films, one distinction is salient: Whereas Van Peebles's main character, Sweetback, lived outside the mainstream, John Shaft embodied an entirely new concept of what the establishment might actually look like. This fact alone made the movie a hit in black America. Also, since Shaft exuded a cool aesthetic that affirmed law and order even while suggesting black power, he could be an object of desire to white America as well. In my brother's opinion, that the object told the desirous to screw itself was the source of the shock.

A couple of decades passed before I finally saw more than the opening credits of *Shaft* or any part of *Sweet Sweetback's Baadasssss Song*, but my brother's story never left me. I have no evidence that his observation about Shaft's gesture was correct, even though it certainly seems right the more I learn about the early 1970s and the era's battles about who could belong to the social and political establishment. Right or wrong, my brother's mid-1970s claim is a useful starting point for a careful consideration of the fascination and fear of what blackness meant for the country in the decades immediately preceding John Shaft's gesture. To stretch the metaphor further than I probably should, we can see that Shaft's finger points backward to a history of racial desire and anxiety that were incorporated into the physical manifestation of blackness: the finger, the arm, the mind, the flesh, and so on.

But what, precisely, was this blackness? Was it the result of a set of experiences that only blacks could know? If so, was this a communal memory that could be shared if there were a way to embody those experiences? One thing is evident: In the 1950s and '60s, while blacks and whites were wrestling with the experiential, spatial, and representative meanings invested in the black body, it became clear that the terms of the negotiation were being informed by different sets of knowledge and experience. That is, blacks' understanding of their collective, representative body was constructed by a set of literal and figurative memories that were unknown to whites.[2] This much had always been the case, of course, but as this was an age of increasingly (but always fraught) conversations about the place of blacks in the larger society, the stakes of cross-racial understanding were never higher. Looking across the marketplace of culture—popular literature, modern dance, and documentary and feature film—we find numerous examples where the black body becomes a means, or at least appears to become a means, to access an understanding of blackness that was informed by trauma, framed by assertions of the authentic, and always troubled by the complexities wrought by class.

If you were white, crossing the color line was the only way to grasp the authentic black experience and, famously, journalist John Howard Griffin did just this. Griffin, long disturbed by the challenges facing black Americans and the deepening refusal of white southerners to accept the era's social and legal changes, decided to go undercover. If Griffin knew about the *Negro Digest* series "If I were a Negro," he didn't mention it. Also, even if he did know about the series, he likely wouldn't have been satisfied with the safe musings of white people. Griffin wanted to know the black experience as his own, and the only way to do that was by taking medicine that darkened his skin. A southerner himself, Griffin crossed the color line and rediscovered his native land over the course of six weeks in 1960. Although he and his family received threats of various types and even had to relocate for their own safety when the book was published in 1961, Griffin's *Black Like Me* became a best seller and an international sensation. Still in print fifty years after its original release, *Black Like Me* was even required reading in high schools in the 1960s. Finally, it seemed, here was an honest treatment of black life even if the truth was only the result of a performance.

Not meant to be a guide, *Black Like Me* certainly functioned as one, with its list of dos and don'ts when it came to black life in the Deep South. In fact, from the very moment that he emerged—literally, since Griffin entered a house as a white man and left at midnight as a (temporarily) black man—Griffin was accosted by anxious uncertainty: "How did one start? The night lay out there waiting. A thousand questions presented themselves. The strangeness of my situation struck me anew—I was a man born old at midnight into a new life. How does such a man act? Where does he go to find food, water, a bed?"[3] In short, Griffin needed to know how to perform essential blackness.

Griffin wrote *Black Like Me* with no apparent awareness of the literal guides that had been published for years that had been helping blacks find a place to rest or eat as they traveled to new places. These documents—*The Negro Motorist Green Book*, or merely the *Green Book*, and *Travelguide (Vacation and Recreation without Humiliation)*, first published in 1936 and 1947, respectively—addressed many of the problems that Griffin would write about in his first hours as a black man. Whereas Griffin, realizing that he did not know where or how to begin in his life, was lost in a sea of a "thousand questions," neither the *Green Book* nor *Travelguide* concerned themselves with the reasons for their existence. They did not speak about the broken promises of America's founding documents or the structural inequalities of the intervening centuries. Instead, they simply told black travelers where they were welcome to sleep, eat, and have fun without, as the *Green Book* editors put it, the risk of embarrassment.[4]

There was no need to think too deeply about the reality that justified their value. The racial ugliness that permeated society, especially that which accompanied African Americans traveling as strangers to or through a town, was a story whose beginning, middle, and end were all well known. So instead of stories of denial and second-class citizenship, these guides projected possibility, though tinged with caution.

Travelguide "worshipped leisure and the open road." Its covers, for example, were telling: light-skinned and trim African American models with good hair stood next to never-ending convertibles in which an ever-present bag of golf clubs signaled security, access, and acceptance. The *Green Book* typically featured highways on its cover, with cars heading toward a horizon that was really an unseeable future. It mixed middle-class aspirational consumerism with a note of caution. At the bottom of every cover, one could find what was essentially the *Green Book*'s tagline: "Carry your Green Book with you. You May Need It."[5] Not to put too fine a point on it, but the *Green Book* and *Travelguide* were trying to keep African Americans alive.

It is clear that in those first moments of Griffin's newly donned blackness and in the subsequent days as he tried to establish a routine in New Orleans, he would have profited from these real guides. Griffin was perpetually unsure of where to go and how to act until he established a relationship with Sterling Williams, a local shoeshine and someone in whom Griffin confided his whiteness.

When Griffin set out for Mississippi and thereby left Williams's guiding hand, the same problems relating to safe space reemerged. As he was about to exit a Greyhound bus that took him across the state line, a fellow passenger, believing Griffin to be black but knowing that he was new to the area, asked Griffin if he had a place to stay. Griffin recalled, "I told him no. He said the best thing would be for me to contact a certain important person who would put me in touch with someone reliable who would find me a decent and safe place."[6] Griffin may not have enjoyed the luxury of the *Green Book*, but through good fortune he kept meeting blacks who already knew the logic that created the market for guides of some sort and who were willing to share their knowledge of the local landscape.

Although *Back Like Me* was and remains the most famous book of its type from the era, Griffin was not the only white person who hatched a plan to pass as black in order to gain firsthand knowledge of what it meant to be black in America. Indeed, ten years after Griffin's famous experiment, Grace Halsell, a journalist who specialized in deeply immersed experiences across the globe in order to better understand her subject matter, set out to reproduce Griffin's work. Surely, she reasoned, much had changed since Griffin crossed the color line. At the same time, it was clear to her that "most white people still think of Negroes as somehow different and apart. They see their skin and nothing else. The depths of sensitivity, attitudes, abilities, emotions escape the superficial, subliminal view."[7]

Before contacting numerous doctors and even Griffin himself, she spoke with Roscoe Dixon, the "cleanup man" at her apartment building in Washington, D.C., where she worked as a staff writer in Lyndon Johnson's White House. Halsell talked about Griffin's experiment and shared her interest in conducting a similar trial. She asked Dixon if he thought that she could pull it off. Dixon immediately responded in the negative, saying that Griffin's success was so much dumb luck. No white person, male or female, could endure all the shame that accompanied blackness. When Halsell suggested that "millions of black men and women did it every day," Dixon merely replied, "That's different—when you're *born* black, you get prepared for the shame."[8] Here, Dixon was referencing the kinds of storytelling that black parents shared with their children as they prepared them for a difficult world and the years of racial slights that would accrue to an increasingly thick skin. Essentially, Dixon was describing a process in which social degradation became embodied in blackness and in black memory.

Halsell, however, was undeterred. She had traveled extensively by herself in places where white people, much less white women, were not guaranteed safe passage. She was not about to let one person's snap judgment get in her way. Her resolve was only deepened when she met Griffin himself and presented her plan to him. According to Halsell, Griffin had dissuaded numerous other people from trying to replicate his experiment and was especially discouraging to white women. Until, that is, Halsell told him about her desire to pass for black and seek work in Harlem and then again in the Deep South.[9]

Predictably, Halsell encountered the same challenges and affronts that defined Griffin's time across the color line. To be sure, there were differences, most often determined by gender, but both authors wrote at length about their shock over whites' irrational ugliness and blacks' almost heroic humanity. Understandably, both authors were deeply anxious as they took their first steps into the black world. But whereas Griffin was contemplative in his anxiety Halsell was dramatic:

The bus wheels turn and I talk to myself in a monologue of reassurance that fear doesn't accompany me. I summon the memories of my going to live in a junk with the Chinese, of floating down the Amazon, 2,000 miles on a tug, the only woman, not afraid. Nothing physical ever frightened me—so why the big deal?

Why had I not wanted to get on this bus?

Why do I fear entering this black enclave as I have never feared any other place?

Because there are signs you don't see, big, lurid signs all over this country. They shout out: you are white, you are a white woman and have no business going into that ghetto—it belongs to *them*. And the rest, *all* the rest, belongs to you.

These thoughts tumbled from Halsell's typewriter as she recounted her first day in Harlem. Losing her white privilege seemed even more terrifying than the physical risks accompanying her new blackness. By the time Halsell moved her experiment to Mississippi, she had a deeper appreciation for the limited opportunities that defined the black world. While she remained mystified and horrified at the poor treatment she consistently encountered when interacting with whites, her prose became observational. Her attempt to secure a job by visiting the state employment office reflected her new awareness: "The white woman calls me forward, without ever looking at me. I know it is beyond her wildest imagination to think of me as anything but a person beneath her." Projecting a flat affect, Halsell continued, "Pretending to be destitute, I ask about getting welfare assistance and am directed to the floor below, where a woman in spike heels places me out in the general hallway with the spittoons and passerby. I sit for half an hour, time enough to wonder about the lives around me, the clerks returning from their coffee break, idly gossiping. No white person looks at me, sees me. I'm behind a glass, as it were, that enables me to see out while they can't see in."[10]

As tempting as it is to engage a DuBoisian interpretation about the racial veil, it is more appropriate here to consider that Halsell's imagery invokes a museum setting where the blacks were objects on display for the white passerby to notice or to ignore. Living "behind a glass" meant that blacks were closer to the Aboriginal figurines posed in their native landscape as they hunted local game in the Hall of Natural History. They embodied a still life that was arranged just so, in a perpetual state of static performance.

In these instances, Halsell's thoughts—dramatic in the former instance, cool-headed in the latter—effectively reaffirm her privilege. It might have been easier to float down the Nile precisely because she and everyone else knew that she was different. When she passed for black, however, the privilege afforded by racial difference no longer existed. Yes, she could still be an effective and maybe even powerful performer. But she was now behind the glass with the rest of the exhibit, and that fact was more than disorienting; it was profoundly destabilizing.

Halsell followed Griffin by ten years, and by sheer coincidence Griffin followed *Pittsburgh Post-Gazette* writer Ray Sprigle, also by ten years. Sprigle's *In the Land of Jim Crow* sprang from the same curiosity that inspired Griffin and Halsell to pass for black. At the time of Sprigle's writing, however, science had not advanced far enough to allow him to darken his skin chemically. Instead, Sprigle had to rely on extended suntanning sessions and, from the very beginning, a black compatriot—a black authenticator—to accompany him throughout his journey, as "it took no great acumen to realize that no Northern white man, even though fairly well disguised as a Negro, could make his way through the black South alone, and completely on his own."[11] Sprigle's black companion—an anonymous figure throughout the book except for the fact that Walter White, executive secretary of the NAACP, recommended him—authorized Sprigle to other blacks. Very soon, the companion was the director for Sprigle's staged performance. He taught Sprigle how to act (right) and how to hit his marks. In this way, Sprigle's project was different from Griffin's and Halsell's, whose directions came from a number of authorities. This difference, however, did not mean that Sprigle was immune to the multiple realizations of inconvenience that accompanied life on the wrong side of the color line.

For example, early in his adventure, Sprigle discovered the logistical challenges that black sojourners faced. He encountered the absurdities of segregated train travel and the importance of paying attention to every sign—even those not posted—as local custom often informed blacks where their place was. He learned about the informal social networks that provided safe lodging and meals for blacks, since establishments that rented rooms to blacks, much less provided a meal, were rare beyond the larger southern cities. More than anything else, however, he learned that blacks lived in a perpetual state of anxiety. Sprigle wrote, "Fear walks beside the black man in the Southland from his earliest boyhood to the bed in which he dies. And fear was the lesson that I learned first and the lesson that I learned best in my four-week lifetime as Negro in the South."[12] He continued:

> Why, the mere recital of the briefing I underwent before I switched races betrays the fear in the heart of the Southern black. These men who gave

me my short course in how to survive as a black man were men of position and substance in the black world of the South. If any Negro in the South could feel himself secure and beyond reach of white malice, these men could. Yet here are the things they stressed in their instructions to me—repeated over and over again.

"Don't ever fail to say 'sir' when you speak to a white man, whether he opens the conversation or you do."

"Don't ever strike back if a white man hits you—whether he's drunk or sober. You don't have to like it but you do have to take it."

"Don't ever speak disrespectfully or familiarly to a white woman. If you should be unfortunate enough to bump into one, or offend her by stepping in front of her and she becomes insulting, don't reply, don't try to defend yourself. Just take off your hat and keep backing away."

"Don't ever argue with a white train or bus or streetcar conductor, or with any white man. Do as he tells you and keep quiet."

I could fill a couple of pages with it—but what's the use? The fact remains that the black man in the South lives in fear.[13]

The fact that "men of position and substance" were able to give Sprigle such an exhaustive list—and he tells the story in a way that suggests that the men were in accord and actually built upon one another's observations and suggestions about how to be black in America—speaks to a larger phenomenon: the fact that black life in the South was essentially a set piece. Local practices might change from town to town, but the logic of racial control was overwhelmingly consistent. Put another way, the southern scene was a static diorama in which blacks posed as the silhouetted figurines in an unchanging landscape.

Although there were some differences in structure and certainly in the authors' tone and style, *In the Land of Jim Crow*, *Black Like Me*, and *Soul Sister* can be read as a two-decade-long performance in journalistic blackface—an action driven by a desire to understand blackness and rife with experiences that captured a fundamental anxiety, either of a white person hoping to know blackness or of a passing black person afraid for his or her life or of having his or her performance revealed for what it was. Sprigle, Griffin, and Halsell all stated clearly that their views were not meant to represent blacks' views, and they were all horrified at various times about the racial cruelties they either witnessed or experienced personally. Taken together, we have the thoughts and experiences of three white liberals, at least on the question of race and rights in the American landscape. But the landscape in which Sprigle conducted his experiment in 1949 was significantly different from the one in which Halsell conducted hers. Laws had changed (though not enforcement), but so had the degree of general white interest in "the black condition." Whether that interest was motivated out of sincere curiosity, morbid fascination, fear, or hatred, it's certain that the demand for information, the more personal or intimate the better, about black life was increasing exponentially.

THE ARM

In the world of high culture, the demand for an intimate knowledge of authentic blackness was met onstage in the form of modern dance. At first a site of rupture with classical dance traditions that overwhelmingly took their clues from Europe, modern dance moved from the margins to the center of America's cultural landscape in the 1950s and '60s, often relying on Afro-Caribbean and Brazilian gestures and movement.

The Kennedy Center for the Performing Arts in Washington, D.C., did not exist when modern dance was taking the national stage by storm. The Kennedy Center was built in 1971 to bring a high-culture arts scene to what some had considered the barren landscape at the nation's capital. Since we weren't much of a theatergoing family, I remember with clarity each time I went to the Kennedy Center: There was the matinee of *Pippin* with Ben Vereen (I was mostly irritated that my mother took me out of a soccer tournament so that she and I could go; once the play began, though, I recall being mesmerized); an evening performance of *The Wiz* (in rehearsal, when the tickets were less expensive); a weekend performance of a national company of Chinese acrobats (my father was working for a congresswoman at the time, and we were part of a large group of congressional staffer families who received complimentary tickets); Alvin Ailey American Dance Theater (AAADT) (with my family, balcony, stage right); AAADT (with my brother and sister, orchestra seats, my parents sent us); and, again, AAADT (best seats yet, except for the woman with an impossibly tall beehive hairdo sitting directly in front of us). If I'm forgetting anything from my childhood experiences at the Kennedy Center, it would only be another performance of the AAADT.

Seeing the AAADT perform was clearly special to my parents. To this day, I don't know if my mother forced the issue on the family, if my father got the tickets of his own volition, if these came to us in another round of complimentary tickets, or if there were some sort of parental agreement that the children had to see Ailey. I do know, however, that attending the Kennedy Center to see the AAADT perform was high on the Metropolitan

D.C. black middle class's annual list of things to be done. I also know that with each performance of *Revelations* (in my childhood and beyond), I felt reaffirmed in my blackness. I strongly suspect that these two "certainties" were intertwined for many people in those audiences because Alvin Ailey knew how to tell stories in his ballets, particularly *Revelations*, which allowed the black audience members to share in communal memories that spoke to triumph over struggle, the resiliency of faith, and a fundamental black authenticity.

Alvin Ailey was born in 1931 in rural, Depression-era Texas. He and his mother moved frequently as she searched for work. Eventually, they settled in Los Angeles as Ailey was on the cusp of adolescence, and he soon started exploring the city's broadening cultural opportunities. Ailey was first introduced to concert dance on a high school field trip. At age eighteen he began to pursue a career in dance when he joined modern dance artist Lester Horton's studio. Ailey quit almost as soon as he started, however, once he recognized the limited professional possibilities available to black dancers. It took another four years before Ailey fully committed to a career in dance.[14]

Not quite a decade later, Ailey created his own dance troupe, which he named after himself. He could not have known in 1958 that he had created a company that would become the most prominent cultural export in the world of dance in the United States and that, in fact, the Alvin Ailey Dance Theater would become the most popular modern dance troupe in history. The foregoing is not meant to suggest that Ailey was fundamentally unaware of his troupe's potential but, rather, that no one could have anticipated that Ailey's success as an American cultural ambassador rested primarily on a ballet that was grounded in a commitment to an authentic African American past that, in Ailey's words, was part of his "blood memory."

This was not an incidental description. Ailey biographer and dance studies scholar Thomas DeFrantz points out that Ailey would return to the notion of "blood memory" when asked about his inspiration for *Revelations*. Quoting an interview from 1961, DeFrantz captures Ailey's near-mystical recollection of his childhood: "These are dances and songs I feel very personally about—they are intimately connected with my memories of the Baptist Church when I was a child in Texas—baptismals by tree-shrouded lakes, in a lake where an ancient alligator was supposed to have lived—the holy-rollers' tambourines shrieking in the Texas night."[15] More than twenty-five years later, Ailey still used this phrase to explain his inspirations for *Revelations* and another ballet, *Blues Suite*.

Interviewed in 1986 for a Danish television production titled *An Evening with Alvin Ailey American Dance Theater*, Ailey spoke at length about his upbringing. The viewer does not hear the questions, but Ailey's responses offer a clear sense of what made for an authentic black experience:

> Well, the first ballets were ballets about my black roots. I lived in Texas, in the South of the United States until I was twelve. Came to Los Angeles when I was twelve. So I had lots of what I call blood memories.
>
> Blood memories about Texas, oh, blues and spirituals, about gospel music, and ragtime music . . . all of the things—folk songs, all those work songs, all that kind of thing that was going on in Texas, in the early thirties, the Depression years. And I had very intense feelings about all those things. The first ballets I made when I came to New York as a choreographer were based on the feelings: *Blues Suite* and *Revelations*. . . . The first idea was to make a company, a large black company, which would concentrate on southern material. A ballet which would be . . . I mean ballets which would be all about those folk songs, those blues, those gospel songs, you know, evenings of ballets that celebrated the black experience. So, those ballets were the first that I made when I came to New York. Those I have very intense feelings about.[16]

Ailey's invocation of blood memory is an acknowledgment that his inspiration for the ballets came from a deep wellspring of personal experience. Ailey's blood memories, predating his move to Los Angeles when he was twelve, suggested that the authentic black experience was a southern, rural one that drew upon the spirit and a culture of creativity in the face of unspeakable challenges. In this way, the blood memories for Ailey are connected to his childhood but, more fundamentally, to Texas and the music and performance that were inscribed in the traditions of the southern Baptist Church and the secular songs heard at work and the pleasure songs of Saturday night.

Ailey referred to both *Blues Suite* and *Revelations* as blood memories. *Blues Suite* is still an active part of the company's repertoire, but the nature of its narrative about black cultural survival is less palatable to a broad audience. The ballet is set in the "backwoods music hall/whorehouse for working-class African Americans," and its protagonists are prostitutes and johns engaged in social and economic violence from which their only escape was the communal grief and catharsis of the blues.[17] Although *Revelations* tapped into the same kinds of group memories of pain forged through systems of white supremacy, its story was ultimately uplifting. In *Revelations*, the arc of the African American past tilted toward a salvation that was secured in the redemptive power of the southern church. It became Ailey's signature piece.

Revelations is a ballet in three suites: "Pilgrim of Sorrow," "Take Me to the Water," and "Move, Members, Move." The ballet tells the story of the African American past through dance that is choreographed to noted spirituals and gospels "I Been 'Buked," "Didn't My Lord Deliver Daniel," "Fix Me, Jesus," "Wade in the Water," "I Want to be Ready," "Sinner Man," "Honor, Honor," "The Day Is Past and Gone," "You May Run On," and "Rocka My Soul in the Bosom of Abraham." Although the great majority of people who saw *Revelations* did not share Ailey's blood memories from his Texas childhood, his decision to connect the physical performances with this music gave his audience two means to access the black past.

The first access point was the music. Ailey's integrated audiences might not have known the lyrics to "I Been 'Buked," for example, but they certainly understood the connections between a black past and Negro spirituals. Indeed, the audience, most of whom likely had a very impoverished knowledge of the music's histories, probably fashioned an overdetermined connection (that bordered on stereotype) between the music and the history.[18] Everyone, though, could understand the lyrics that offered a plainspoken acknowledgment of having faced unimaginable challenges and yet resounded with an insistence that nothing would diminish the singer's faith:

I been 'buked and I been scorned.
Yes, I been 'buked and I been scorned, children.
I been 'buked and I been scorned.
I been talked about, sho's you born.

'Dere is trouble all over this world.
Yes, 'dere is trouble all over this world, children.
'Dere is trouble all over this world.
'Dere is trouble all over this world.

Ain't gonna lay my 'ligion down, no.
Ain't gonna lay my 'ligion down, children.
Ain't gonna lay my 'ligion down.
Ain't gonna lay my 'ligion down.

The second means Ailey offered the audience to access the black past is apparent in the opening moments of *Revelations*. The curtain rises on an austere stage upon which nine dancers in shades of brown and tan stand in a tight triangle, partially illuminated by an overhead spotlight. They rarely leave the light throughout the performance, as if the sorrow of the lyrics requires that they stay close to one another, securing strength in their proximity. As they perform a series of deliberate horizontal and vertical moves

"I Been 'Buked" (Alvin Ailey American Dance Theater in Alvin Ailey's signature masterpiece Revelations. *Photo by Nan Melville. Courtesy of Alvin Ailey Dance Foundation, Inc.)*

with their arched arms, one might be inclined to imagine that they are about to take flight. However, the context of the music, the earth tones of their costumes, and the shaded lighting all suggest the opposite: that their arms are not wings preparing to soar but are themselves 'buked, burdened with the weight of so much sadness throughout history. The dancers are the children of Jesus who share with him a painful familiarity with the cross. Their gestures toward heaven, though uncertain, retain an insistent hopefulness.[19]

In the rest of this first suite, Ailey's performers tell the story of a community's faith in the possibility of salvation ("Didn't My Lord Deliver Daniel") and a woman's faith in a minister to save her soul ("Fix Me, Jesus"). In the second suite, "Take Me to the Water," the dancers invoke the connections in the African American past between water and freedom: both the rivers that were used by self-emancipating people to throw off tracking hound dogs and the lakes where communities bore witness as individuals sought a certain freedom in baptism. The concluding piece in this suite, "I Want to Be Ready," is an aching solo in which a man who seems to be trapped in a tight overhead spotlight prays that he will be ready for his freedom and salvation, meanwhile never really knowing which will welcome him first.

In the final suite, "Move, Members, Move," the energy and physicality of the ballet changes dramatically. From the pyrotechnic leaps of a trio of sinnermen who seek protection from an angry Lord who told them they should have been a-praying, to the closing number when the entire company performs together in a Sunday afternoon country church ("Rocka My Soul in the Bosom of Abraham"), the audience is figuratively summoned to the stage to bear witness to desperation and then to celebrate salvation.

Using the music and movement as shared idioms to express the black past allowed Ailey's African American audiences to connect to the dancers and choreography. By employing familiar cultural signs and symbols, Ailey's black audiences could understand him as a "black poet of dance" who fashioned, with their enthusiastic and consuming approval, a modern mythology of a singular blackness that affirmed a shared set of memories underscoring their collective resiliency.[20] For a consuming white public, the cultural markers that seemed so familiar yet were so often at a remove were brought close by Ailey's dancers, who offered an invitation to intimacy that proved irresistible. Because *Revelations* proffered "cultural memory as body wisdom" through the performers' movements, the Ailey dancers could affirm (their black audience) and they could teach (their white audience).[21]

Whether affirming or teaching, *Revelations* contained an undeniable element of spectacle. Ailey was open about this and saw in spectacle the opportunity to build an audience and to entertain. For Ailey, spectacle was also about connecting a social statement to a political statement—both of which he saw as fundamental to his entire company. (In his 1986 interview for *An Evening with Alvin Ailey American Dance Theater*, Ailey made his feelings plain on this accord, stating, "I'm concerned about making social statements because I'm a black person who has grown up in a country that is intensely racist.") Indeed, the very idea of the company, Ailey argued, was a social statement. It was a statement not just because most of the dancers in the company were black, but also because the company's existence was Ailey's way of saying "something that in addition to fine choreography is about the beauty of black people, about the elegance . . . about their ability to entertain, about their intelligence, about their . . . love of self, about their . . . wanting to transmit through discipline their feelings to the audience that watch them dance."[22]

By creating a company that commented on the American scene as well as speaking about blacks' "elegance, intelligence, and love of self," Ailey believed he was continuing a tradition of storytelling and memory work in the world of performance. In addition to speaking to an unacknowledged tradition of black choreographers as storytellers, Ailey also felt his company had a unique ability and opportunity to connect with collective black memories, the blood memories that he would invoke from the moment of *Revelations*'s creation until his death in 1989. Ailey clearly understood that his personal memories extended outward to black America. As he said in a 1986 interview, "I always wanted to have the kind of company that my family could relate to, that my people in Texas could relate to, that my aunts and uncles, you know, on the farms or wherever they're from, or from the ghettos in the States could understand. The dance, in particular, is for everybody. That the dance, I believe the dance came from the people and that it should always be delivered back to the people."

Earlier in the same interview, when talking about the final suite in *Revelations*, Ailey referenced his family, "my uncles, my family, my mother," and its long tradition of worship in the southern, country church vernacular. Later, when talking about his aspirations for his company, Ailey again referenced his family, "my people in Texas," but opened up further, invoking a symbolic black family "from the ghettos" that could see in dance a shared heritage that was, in the end, redemptive.

When I went to the Kennedy Center to see the AAADT as a preteen, there was little, if anything, in the setting that connected Ailey's work to his "family" in the ghettos, and it was questionable if his company was delivering dance "back to the people." The formality of the Kennedy Center, with its grand opera halls, its proximity to some of the district's most expensive real estate, and the quasi-formal attire of the audience (racially mixed and surely middle to upper class) would seem to have changed the dynamic that Ailey sought to construct and convey.[23]

Ailey had choreographed many dances for his troupe by the time I first saw the AAADT in the mid-1970s. The company also had works by many other choreographers in its repertoire. The audience, however, came to see *Revelations*. As this was my first time seeing Alvin Ailey, I did not know this, of course, but even in staid Washington the audience seemed particularly alert when the curtain rose for "I Been 'Buked." I have to confess that any further specific recollection of that first experience with the AAADT is ill defined in my memory. Beyond where I sat in the performance hall and the electricity that shot through the audience during *Revelations*, virtually all other distinctive details of the actual performance have merged with the two other times that I saw the company perform in the Kennedy Center.

The only other detail that I recall perfectly from my first time with Ailey is the white dancer.

I believe that we were watching *Blues Suite*, Ailey's other signature blood memory ballet, when I became completely distracted by the white dancer's longish hair. His ability to interpret what even I could tell at that young age was a black experience further left me confused. There is no other way to put it other than to say that I was deeply suspicious. He could not know what I knew.

This final assertion was ludicrous, since this "imposter" surely knew far more about the history of black cultural expression than I. Also, I would later realize that my racial chauvinism was further misplaced; Ailey had made it a point to integrate his company almost from the moment of its founding. With the benefit of hindsight, I can understand that the white dancer's presence caught me off guard because even at that young age, I could *feel* the Ailey company authenticating and affirming my blackness, especially when it performed *Revelations*. Over the years, and as I learned more about the black past, seeing the AAADT perform has elicited in me ever-stronger reactions about my authentic blackness.

Part of this reaction was simply a manifestation of familiarity. While most of any particular evening's ballets were unknown to me, I knew the music and choreography of *Revelations*. I had mastered the two clear ways that Ailey invited his audiences into his memories. I also knew to anticipate the audience reaction once the first notes of "I Been 'Buked" filled the hall. I knew that "Rocka My Soul in the Bosom of Abraham," the ballet's closing number, had evolved into a full-throated, full-throttled revival that inevitably included some members of the audience standing in aisles, bearing witness to African Americans' indefatigable faith. Finally, I knew that when I left the theater, I would be exhilarated and uplifted as if I had been to a revival meeting and had testified before the Lord. This was part of the authentic black Sunday church experience, after all. This was in my bones, part of my cultural-racial genetic code.

Even though I know these feelings are real, they are also completely false. My family rarely went to church when I was growing up. At some point, my parents left behind their own upbringing in this way. In fact, I was so removed from any knowledge about my family's relationship with religion that I was floored to discover in my late twenties that my father had been a licensed minister before he left for college. (How was this not part of the family lore?) I also recall being eleven and mystified when I accompanied my mother to a wedding and everyone in the church—including my mother—started reciting something in unison without looking in a book or reading the wedding program. (It was the Lord's Prayer.) Indeed, my connection to the family's religious tradition was so feeble that I was beyond college before I knew that I came from a Methodist and African Methodist Episcopal Zion background. Sure, I had gone to family church services when we visited the grandparents; I just never paid attention to any of the names outside the building or on the programs.

Considering this personal background and the twin facts that I had never been to a church revival or to a southern rural Baptist service, I might as well be the symbolic perfection of the distracting white dancer onstage. It would seem that I was someone who could perform a culturally articulated authentic blackness but who did not know it in lived-in-the-skin fashion. This was the genius of Ailey and of *Revelations*, and it speaks to the evocative power of dance as a means to access memory. Seeing the AAADT as an African American was an act of racial affirmation and authentication, a psycho-cultural authorization that blacks, too, had a collective memory worth celebrating, even if it wasn't a lived memory. Put another way, Ailey's performative choices made his blood memories mine; they provided the fictive connections to an authentic past that felt completely real to me.

Of course, I was not the only person who felt comfortable claiming a deep familiarity with Ailey's memories. Indeed, I was part of a phenomenon that seemed integral to the Ailey "experience." In 1956, two years before Ailey formed his company, famed jazz trumpeter Dizzy Gillespie and his band went on a federally funded tour of the Middle East. Supported with funds from the White House as well as the International Cultural Exchange Service, Gillespie was the first headliner in what would become a roughly fifteen-year project of the U.S. State Department to share American cultural excellence with the world. Signing up Dizzy Gillespie and, soon after, other luminaries such as Louis Armstrong was remarkable in itself, since jazz, though an American idiom, had yet to be considered a "highbrow" musical tradition. The State Department's embrace of jazz legitimated an art form that, for many Americans, remained part of the vernacular of poverty, blackness, and excess (alcohol, sex, and crime).[24] By 1962, the State Department's cultural exchange mission had matured and broadened. And it was in this year that the AAADT went on its first state-sponsored international tour.

Although jazz seemed an unlikely choice, the State Department's use of this "black idiom" to highlight American cultural excellence was actually predictable in the context of the Cold War. Gillespie and others served as cultural ambassadors, allowing the State Department, and thus the United States, to congratulate itself for demonstrating to the world that the promise of American democracy was real. Much of this was simply pretense, and even though ambassadors like Gillespie and Armstrong often gave the State Department fits when they went "off message," the jazz tours still stood as symbols of possibility in the present and the future.[25]

When the AAADT joined the State Department tours, however, it introduced a different dynamic into the conversation about cultural promise. On one level, relying on *Revelations* as the anchor for its performances, the AAADT offered a narrative of uplift and salvation that fit neatly into the State Department's ideas of American exceptionalism and a color-blind universalism in which everyone was free within their respective cultural frames. At the same time, because *Revelations* was the embodiment of Ailey's blood memories, the ballet offered a powerful counternarrative to American universalism that spoke to the brutality of the country's pre-emancipatory and white-supremacist past. Were the audiences watching an "authentic" black past being danced onstage able to separate Ailey's memories from the country that sponsored his tour?

During the 1960s, as the State Department tours and their narratives of American exceptionalism became fixtures on the international arts and culture scene and as the civil rights movement intensified and garnered increasing attention in the national media, a curious and anxious public wanted to know more about black Americans, their past, and their present. Experiencing an Ailey performance might alleviate some of this anxious curiosity. But the public desire far exceeded the AAADT's ability to narrate an answer. Increasingly, major institutions like the Ford Foundation and special investigatory groups such as the National Advisory Commission on Civic Disorders (more often known as the Kerner Commission) called on scholars and creative intellectuals of all types to develop a more informed recounting of the black experience.[26]

This institutional determination to know more about black America resulted in a boom in black documentary films and television shows. These productions most often focused on current events and so, at first glance, seem not to have any explicit connection to the black past. But a closer look reveals that, like the blackface journalists and Alvin Ailey before them, the black documentarians of the 1960s turned to the black body as a means to narrate African American life in the moment. Further, while establishing the embodied visual language to tell that particular story, the black documentarians were also creating a black past that was as much the product of collective memories and the fictions built into them as they were about well-sourced and historically grounded considerations of that same past.

As a result, 1960s television and film documentaries such as *Take This Hammer, The First World Festival of Negro Arts, Black Journal,* and *Still a Brother: Inside the Black Middle Class* demonstrate that many forces were in play: the documentarians' understanding of the black past, the tension between the institutions sourcing the documentarians' work, and how expectations of telling the story of the black present and past began to change during an age of cultural, political, and social revolution.

REVOLUTIONIZED MINDS

There is no definitive beginning of the black documentary tradition. Film scholars point to the 1910 silent film *A Day at Tuskegee* as the first in the genre, or they reference the short-subject and newsreel films in the mid-1940s. Regarding "modern" documentary, though, the clear consensus is that filmmaker William Greaves is the "dean" of black documentarians.[27]

Greaves began his career as a stage and screen actor but became fed up with the dearth of complex roles for black actors. When he discovered that the director who cast him as a Pullman porter for a Broadway show with Gloria Swanson wanted the character to be a servile, shuffle-along minstrel, Greaves quit. Realizing that he wanted to be in control of stories and performances, Greaves began to take courses in filmmaking. Greaves reflected on this moment: "It became obvious to me that either I would stay in America and allow myself to be made a fool of, or become a very neurotic person, or be destroyed. Or leave."[28] Greaves opted for sanity and moved to Canada in 1952 to pursue his ambitions. There he joined the National Film Board and eventually worked on more than eighty films before returning to the United States in 1963.[29]

Once back in the States, Greaves found his footing and began to direct films for the United States Information Agency (USIA). That Greaves found work with the USIA is equally ironic and understandable: The federal government of a country where he could not find work a decade earlier now sought him out. For its part, the USIA was motivated to secure a black filmmaker so that it could congratulate itself for appearing open-minded. Race relations became more complicated in the 1960s, and as the country moved from sit-ins to protest marches to assassinations to race riots, the USIA appreciated being able to turn to someone like Greaves because it felt he would be able to get to the truth of "black stories."[30] In an interview in which he discussed *Black Journal*, the pioneering black public affairs television series that he led in the late 1960s, Greaves pointed out that the series owed its existence to the Carnegie Endowment, the Ford Foundation, and the Corporation for Public Broadcasting. These organizations saw in *Black Journal* an opportunity to defuse the racial tensions of the late 1960s because the series would address the fact that the "black community had no access to the media, and there was no outlet for it to express its needs and interests in the media"—concerns expressed by the Kerner Commission.

In the same interview, Greaves clearly took to heart the concerns about the black community and the fact that its stories were not being told, that black people were simply lost in the larger narrative of the United States except when they were protesting or rioting. For Greaves, then, the black documentarian had an obligation to make films that made a difference. Black documentary films, he said, are "usually activist, advocacy-oriented productions, weapons in the struggle for freedom, dignity, equality, liberation, self-expression and human rights."[31]

Greaves's activist orientation was not unique among black documentarians. Film studies scholar Janet Cutler writes about the "urgency" driving the work of black documentarians. Arguing that African Americans have been cut off from their "ancient history and heritage" and that their cultural contributions have been "marginalized," Cutler asserts that it was up to black documentarians to "assume the role of cultural historians, filling gaps and creating significant, sometimes imaginative connections to the past and to collective experience, countering misrepresentations perpetuated by the dominant culture, and constructing more telling narratives of the black experience."[32]

Here, Cutler connects Greaves's insistence that black documentary films had to have a purpose with the need for a useable past. The "factness" of the matter was outweighed by the simple need for a set of facts that the black community could use for a greater good. This was, essentially, a call for the creation of a collective memory that could support the efforts of blacks to share a story about their community on its own terms.[33] For Greaves and other documentarians, their work was about a "revolution of the mind"—a phrase that Greaves would use to great effect in his late 1960s documentary *Still a Brother: Inside the Black Middle Class* to signal the need both to look at things from a different perspective and to recognize that black consciousness and self-conception themselves were in a state of flux.

This need for a past, a call for recognition, and a demonstration of a new consciousness resonated in documentary work even earlier in the decade. In 1964, for example, San Francisco public television station KQED aired *Take This Hammer*, a documentary that collectively addressed these issues. Shot in the spring of 1963, *Take This Hammer* featured famed writer James Baldwin, who had just returned from his self-imposed exile in France to support the civil rights movement. His visit to San Francisco was part of his own conscious, nationwide effort to speak to and for black youth. He felt this was a population that needed to be heard, as it represented the race's future. It was also a population that needed to know its past. This was Baldwin's first visit to San Francisco, but over the course of a few days traveling across the city with a KQED film crew and Orville Luster, the executive director of the local social service agency Youth for Service, Baldwin developed strong and, some would come to feel, alienating opinions about the famed progressive city.[34]

The film opens with an unnamed, twenty-year-old black male responding to an interviewer who wants to know more about San Francisco: "The South is not half as bad as San Francisco. You want me to tell you about San Francisco? I'll tell you about San Francisco. The white man, he's not, he's not taking advantage of you out in public like they doing down in Birmingham. But he's killing you with that pencil and paper, brother." Complaining about being laid off and then unable to find work because the white man controlled everything, the interviewee set the tone for a documentary that said the entire country was in crisis, not just the U.S. South.

The first time Baldwin speaks in the film, he alludes to the popularly held notion that San Francisco is a liberal bastion, untroubled by the civil rights and racial problems elsewhere, and he also preemptively defends the factual bases of his observations. Immediately following the angry twenty-year-old in the opening sequence, the camera cuts to Baldwin, who, the editing suggests, has just heard the opening statement of the film: "This is the San Francisco Americans pretend does not exist. They think I'm making it up."[35]

Baldwin is determined to convince the viewers that he is not, in fact, "making it up," and he speaks with passion and urgency about the state of affairs in black America. Like the unnamed man whose interview began the film, Baldwin invokes recent events in Birmingham to pull the viewer in: "And Birmingham is an instant, you know, which may become a shrine. What is really crucial is whether or not the country, the people in the country, the citizenry, are able to recognize that there is no moral distance, no moral distance . . . which is to say, no distance, between the facts of life in San Francisco and the facts of life in Birmingham. We've got a cause, you know, one's got to tell it like it is. And that's where it's at."

Of course, the "where it's at" in the film was literally San Francisco but figuratively everywhere in the United States. By likening daily life in San Francisco to events in Birmingham—a theme that surfaced throughout the film—the documentary made several important rhetorical moves: It forged a connection for the viewer to the "authentic" black experience that people had seen played out on newsreel footage throughout the spring of fire hoses and police dogs directed at civil rights marchers; it invoked a collective memory of vicious state-sponsored assaults on the black body; and it provided the space for someone like Baldwin, who had proven on other occasions to be unafraid to speak the truth to power, the opportunity to step up to the bully pulpit and offer his narrative of the black experience.

Toward the end of the film, Baldwin and Luster stand on a street corner, discussing the privilege of white liberals—the people who, in Baldwin's estimation, alleviated their anxiety about the country's state of affairs by helping out the Negro, albeit on their terms. The problem, Baldwin observed, was that as soon as white liberals discovered that their narrative of blackness did not align with blacks', liberals became hurt, disillusioned, or scared.

The camera floats over Baldwin's shoulder—in a figurative sense trying to see the world from his perspective—as he turns to Luster to offer as an example his experience with a white liberal who told him how hurt she was when a room of twenty black college students told her that she was of no use to them because she did not understand their world. Baldwin became infuriated when she said defensively that she was sure she had "done more for Negroes than they've ever done." When Baldwin pressed her, trying to gauge the extent to which she was willing to make further sacrifices, she declined, explaining that she could not afford to risk damaging her children. Her reluctance to pay the same dues to society that black parents were expected or forced to pay every day pushed Baldwin over the edge. The speed with which his words tumbled out of his mouth prevented an articulate delivery:

> You know, it's kind of an insult. I've, I, here I am, you know, as they say, I've no visible scars. I'm not a, I'm not isolated. I've got a family. You know. And a history. And I've got nieces and nephews. I can't protect them. You know. They're, they're in tremendous danger, all, every hour that they live, just because they are black, not because they're wicked, you know. And I mean this is, uh, from the, from the baby niece to the, to the oldest nephew who is only sixteen. Now if this is the way that, if this is the way that they are, you know, and I know that every time I leave my nephew I don't know what'll, what'll happen to him by the time I see him again, I mean not only inside, but physically. How can you expect me to take seriously somebody who says "I'm willing to fight for you, but I, but I can't afford to let my children, I can't afford to let my children be damaged"? And furthermore, how can I take seriously somebody who doesn't realize that children *are* being damaged by this, by the continuation of this, of this, of the system?[36]

In this moment, very near the end of the film, the documentary clearly invokes embodied black memory. Baldwin begins his monologue by referencing the fact that his body is unblemished—it has no scars—but that the damage is much deeper, in the soul, perhaps. Baldwin also invokes his family and black history to suggest, by extension, collective memories of shame, and damage that all blacks understand. Although Baldwin is not behind the camera or directing the scene, he certainly has the same impulse as the black documentarians who strove to create films with a purpose and to fashion a black past that had been denied for so long.

While I have no evidence that William Greaves ever saw *Take This Hammer*, it is clear that he and Baldwin shared the sentiment that blacks needed their past to be a useable past. That is, Greaves and Baldwin understood that mainstream social, political, and cultural expectations regularly denied blacks individual pasts and typically only saw their collective past as a problem to be solved. In Greaves's hand, documentary film could address the limitations of this worldview by showcasing black cultural excellence and by affirming a collective black cultural memory. In his 1966 documentary, *The First World Festival of Negro Arts*, Greaves did just this. That the film was simultaneously a powerful meditation on black identity and memory and a commissioned piece for the USIA is remarkable enough. That the film garnered critical acclaim for its nuanced interpretation of black memory despite the fact that it was not released in the United States for decades after its completion is testimony to the power of its narrative and insight.

In the wake of the Civil Rights Act and Voting Rights Act triumphs, the USIA commissioned Greaves to produce a five-minute newsreel on an arts festival in Dakar, Senegal. The political motivation for the film was clear: call attention to the U.S. support of the celebration of African arts and culture, thereby offering a counternarrative to critics of the country's Cold War politics and its suspected involvement in the recent coups in Zaire and Ghana (the latter coup occurred just months before the festival began). Greaves accepted the job but was so overwhelmed by the spirit of the gathering that he turned in a film quite different from the one he was commissioned to make. The resulting forty-minute tone poem became the most comprehensive visual record of the First World Festival of Negro Arts as well as the most popular USIA film in Africa for the next decade.[37]

Although unseen in the United States due to the USIA's mandate, *The First World Festival of Negro Arts* featured many of the country's leading artists. They were filmed in performance, of course, but also while observing the work of other artists from throughout the African diaspora. Greaves built the documentary around this exchange, often speaking in free verse about the mystery of origins, asking in various ways throughout the film, "Who am I?"

Shot entirely in sepia, the documentary begins with Langston Hughes on a beach, watching fishermen's boats come in. In the background, Greaves asks, "Who am I? Perhaps I am a poem by Langston Hughes." Answering by illustration, Greaves reads Hughes's anthem "The Negro Speaks of Rivers," the poet's declaration that black memory stretched across the millennia to the dawn of civilizations around the world. Beginning with Hughes's poem, and using rivers and seas as a motif throughout the film, Greaves offers a narrative that pulls together clips from the festival's performances, attempting to showcase performers from as many different countries as possible, while constantly trying to answer the question, "Who am I?"

During a long section dedicated to dance, we see folk dancers from several African countries while Greaves as the disembodied narrator muses, "The dance is an old friend of mine. It is a river in which the spirit swims and plays. It is a river in which the spirit weeps." After an extended clip featuring dancers from Chad, the narrator returns, and the question "Who am I" still resonates: "I am the American Negro spiritual. See how these Americans, these dancers of Alvin Ailey, search for me in their movements." We then see the opening two minutes of *Revelations* ("I Been 'Buked") as Greaves returns to Hughes's poem with which he began the film: "I've known rivers, ancient dusky rivers. My soul has grown deep, like the rivers."[38]

Greaves makes no effort to hide his intention: African arts and cultural practices may be widely varied and may now be dispersed because of political and economic forces, but they are, in the end, a unifying, universal power that unites black people. The creative power of the arts was also a healing power. It healed by bringing people together, and it healed by allowing them to share in one another's stories. In this way, histories became memories and memories were woven back into history.

In the film's closing moments, Greaves's narrator changes his approach. The "I" we have heard throughout the film is now a "we." It is the people and cultures of Africa. It is the multivocal motherland. It is, more than anything else, the place that we must remember if we are to know who we are: "You who have journeyed to this place in 1966, we hope you have found much to delight and inspire you. We are glad to see you leave in such high spirits. When you return home tell everyone what you have learned here at our festival. Let us meet often. We will continue this conversation we have already begun."

The scene shifts to American artists in the Dakar airport, heading toward a waiting plane. The closing narration is now speaking to the Americans directly. The last person we see, the final person to board the plane, is Alvin Ailey himself. As he turns to wave, the narration concludes, "Goodbye. Remember what has happened here. Remember. Remember."[39]

Throughout *The First World Festival of Negro Arts* Greaves was calling for a remembrance, certainly, but also a fundamental shift in how African

Americans should recognize their own past and their position in the world. With this extended visual poem he called for a revolutionized consciousness that could appreciate the roots of black memory throughout the diaspora. Clearly, Greaves was inspired by his experiences in Senegal. When he returned to the United States, however, the realities of a nation in profound turmoil pressed down on him.

By the late 1960s it was clear that the legislative victories of the Civil Rights Act and the Voting Rights Act were unable to stop the bloodshed in the nation's streets. The war in Vietnam was escalating and relying on a disproportionate number of black bodies on the front lines. And the nation's black leaders were being murdered. As the decade of civil rights triumphs turned into the decade of discord and race riots, new opportunities appeared for black documentarians to tell the story of black America. What did black America want? What would bring peace to the streets? Whose stories needed to be told?

A direct attempt to answer those questions came with *Black Journal*, an hour-long public affairs program that declared itself to be produced by, for, and about the black community. Hosted by Greaves and Lou House (who would later change his name to Walli Sadiq), *Black Journal* first appeared in June 1968. Airing just a few months after the assassination of Martin Luther King Jr., the first episode of *Black Journal* featured a story of Coretta Scott King's commencement address at Harvard University, the Black Panthers, and famed comic and actor Godfrey Cambridge.[40] (In fact, Cambridge was the first individual on screen in *Black Journal*. He appeared as a painter who silently painted the viewer's television screen black. When he was done, the graphic of the show's title appeared.)

Ostensibly, the show directly addressed the need for a black perspective in the nation's media.[41] However, since Alvin Perlmutter, the show's executive producer, was white, the majority of the black staff on *Black Journal* thought they were participating in a lie. When their requests for new senior leadership were not met, eleven of the twelve black staff members walked out in protest. By September, Perlmutter was gone and Greaves was serving as the show's executive producer and cohost. Although the episodes produced under Greaves's aegis were not substantially different from those that appeared before, the young black filmmakers on staff felt that they had a new liberty to "express themselves artistically" and to speak with confidence to the needs of black America.[42]

While they could not have necessarily known that Greaves would grant them the artistic independence they sought, the filmmakers knew that he was the most accomplished documentarian of the day. Working with him would be, at minimum, a first-rate apprenticeship, a "once in a lifetime opportunity."[43] St. Clair Bourne, one of the filmmakers on staff who became a leading documentarian himself, explained why Greaves was so important to the world of black documentary film:

> If you look at black filmmaking as an inverted pyramid, he's the base which everything else comes out of, because it was he who set up the three-point dictum that we were supposed to work by: one, to define the reality, the black reality, which in those days, as now, was usually problem/struggle; two, to define why the struggle/problem/situation evolved; but most important, he said—and if you didn't do this, then you were really derelict in your duty, and three, to suggest a way out. It did not have to be *the* way out, but you had to show people trying to attempt to resolve the difference.[44]

Perhaps because Greaves was so adept at "defining the black reality"—what Klotman and Cutler refer to as "creating a more authentic narrative of the black experience"—his reputation preceded him throughout the larger filmmaking world by the time of the *Black Journal* walkout.[45] He was particularly well known by executives at NET who had just aired his striking documentary *Still a Brother: Inside the Black Middle Class*.

On the surface, *Still a Brother* seemed to be simply concerned with offering a new perspective on what constituted the black community. White Americans needed to know that all blacks were not endlessly rioting, nor were they all destitute and angry. Further, blacks who were poor needed to know about the black middle class so that they could find in them effective role models.[46] At least, this was the thinking going into the project.

The documentary that Greaves completed reflected his own projection of the importance of the black middle class. In effect, he constructed a different reality—a black reality—and created a film that clearly had a purpose. It exceeded the expectations of the NET executives. Greaves was fully aware that he was submitting something other than what NET executives anticipated. Greaves recalled,

> We had difficulties once *Still a Brother* was finished because NET had not expected that kind of film. They had expected an *Ebony* magazine kind of film, but we brought them this documentary that talked about mental revolution and showed increasing militancy in the black experience. . . . So when NET executives saw the film they sort of blinked because they didn't know whether or not they really wanted to put it into the system. They weren't clear whether or not it would be acceptable.

There was a great deal of anxiety because these executives were looking at their mortgages and didn't know whether they would be tossed out of their jobs.[47]

To their credit, the NET executives honored their commitment to Greaves's vision and let the program run. Over the course of its ninety minutes, *Still a Brother* offered a multilayered interpretation of race and class in the American scene.

Structurally, *Still a Brother* seemed conventional: It acknowledged a problem, identified a little-known phenomenon, and said that it would tell the story of that phenomenon, suggesting that within its truth there lay a solution. It was 1968, and everyone knew that America was caught in the throes of social change; people began to pay special attention to the challenges of black urban life and the apparent unspooling of civil rights gains. In his role as narrator, actor Ossie Davis told the viewer that despite the troubles, there were other African Americans who had been working hard to make their presence known and who could be a stabilizing force for the country. These people were the black middle class.

One of the first talking heads to appear in the film is sociologist St. Clair Drake. He offers an illustration of the kind of person one finds in the black middle class.[48] Drake tells the story of two black men who worked in the local stockyards (the film does nothing to challenge gendered mores; black men are at the center of the documentary from beginning to end). They both leave work, get home late, and find themselves locked out. They both yell upstairs to their wives, who eventually let them inside. There are differences in their narratives, however. The first stockyard worker stops by the bar before going home and has too much to drink. Meanwhile, his wife is drinking at home. When the husband gets home, he and his wife get into a shouting match, most of which happens in public. The argument becomes physical, again in public. They finally go inside after much of the neighborhood has seen them—once again, since it seems to be a routine—and go to bed.

The other stockyard worker passes the same bar as his coworker, but he turns his head and ignores it. He and his wife get into an argument when he gets home, but the argument—which also involves raised voices and the possibility of a physical confrontation—only happens after the husband has been let in, the front door closed, and the shades drawn. Their fight remains private. Further, when the fight is over, they sit down in the kitchen and decide "how much money to set aside for the kids' education fund and how much to give to the church on Sunday." To Drake, the latter worker is middle class, while the former one is lower class.[49]

Drake begins his illustration pointing out that both men make the same amount of money each month. So, for Drake, middle-class status was an expression of how one viewed the world and how one wanted to be viewed. It involved having faith in the future (saving for a college education) and hewing to a moral code of respectability (avoiding temptations to excess and keeping one's private affairs private). Greaves relies on Drake numerous times in the film, but this is the most important moment, since it frames so much of the narrative that follows: Being middle class, according to Drake and, by implication, Greaves, is not primarily about material claims but about a state of mind.

This state of mind is central to Greaves's film. As he tells stories about material possessions or life chances exclusive to people with high incomes, Greaves organizes them around the liminal space these blacks occupy: vacations in black enclaves like Oak Bluffs in Martha's Vineyard or Sag Harbor in Long Island; expensive soirées where wealthy blacks and whites mingle freely. They are often seen trying to explain their own struggles about not quite fitting into the black or white worlds. Interspersed throughout the film are small gatherings of middle-class blacks who are viewed engaging in fierce debates about the state of the country and the place of blacks within it. These well-off African Americans wrestle openly—in the privacy of their salons, that is—with their role in the freedom struggle and their obligations to the community.

One man speaks at length about his dawning awareness of how he saw himself in the world and how he struggled with the changing contours of the country's political landscape:

> For some reason or another I never associated myself with the welfare recipient, the unemployed person, and now I realize that these are, uh, my people; and that I should be able to do something for them or with them. But yet I haven't so that I think is where the guilt comes in.
>
> I have empathy for my people, but yet in my middle-class value I still kind of think of them as "those people." And I'm aware of it and I think a lot of people in my particular class, if you will, are aware of it, but we are reluctant, we are just imbued with this white middle-class value where we think "white." So I take the position that these people have been denied—and I continue to say "these people," notice that, I continue to say "these people"—and, uh, like I'm not one of them when, in fact, I am one of them.[50]

Although this man's frankness is both gripping and unnerving, Greaves intersperses his subject's slow and contemplative narration with other visuals to keep the viewer interested. The first cutaway happens when the subject says that he has never associated with the welfare recipient and the unemployed person. At this moment, viewers see an extended shot of blacks in an urban setting. They are in the street; they seem to be poor and unfocused. They appear lost—lost to one another and lost to society. The second cutaway is longer, almost thirty seconds, and begins when the subject points to his own realization that he is talking about "those people" as if he were not part of them.

An important visual statement reinforces Drake's assertion that in the black world, at least, poverty has a public face: All of the scenes of "those people" are filmed outside. "Those people" are also rendered silent. The poor truly are subjects on display—and, disturbingly, too often on display in prone positions, with the right to remain silent. These visual choices develop as the film proceeds. Later, another middle-class black man narrates the mental challenges of his own discovery of how class and race mix, while unsettling visual projections of "those people" play on the screen. In this instance, Horace Morris, the associate director of the Washington, D.C., Urban League, recalls a harrowing story of his experiences in Newark during that city's race riots in 1967.

Morris decided to visit his family in Newark after attending an Urban League conference in New York. He picked up his stepfather and then, together, they went to see his brother with a plan to borrow a car to visit other nearby family. As Morris and his stepfather got into the car, three Newark police cruisers turned the corner. The officers got out of their vehicles and, without provocation, opened fire on Morris, his stepfather, and another forty or fifty residents who were gathered on the stoop of the brother's apartment building. With a deceptively flat delivery, Morris remembers the massacre: "My stepfather was mortally wounded and I had another brother who was wounded twice who required an operation and extensive hospital care. We were under fire, I would say, for approximately ten minutes by the Newark police. They said they were looking for a sniper on the roof or the upper floors of the apartment building, but they were still firing at ground-level range." Morris continues:

And once we had, once I had the opportunity to collect my senses, really evaluate and think this thing through, it came through to me in stark reality: regardless of how far up the economic ladder any Negro goes, that there still is this oppressive thing of prejudice that he's subjected to on the part of the white man and I realized that I was extremely fortunate not to be killed myself. And that even though I had two degrees, even though I had played football for Syracuse, even though I was an elementary school principal and had educated white children, even though I work with white people in the Washington Urban League, even though there are white people that I consider close friends, that in . . . as the boys say, when it gets down to the nitty gritty, right down to where it really matters, you are still a Negro, and you are still identified with every other Negro in America, be he in a ghetto or in a suburban neighborhood. You are still a brother. I think we just have to recognize this.[51]

Morris's interview marks a turning point in the film. The tone of curious musing about the state of mind of the black middle class morphs into more determined and angry declarations of how justice might be secured. Viewers hear this shift in Morris's words but also see the shift in how poor black bodies are displayed. As Morris offers his closing comments that he was "still a brother" despite his unusual life chances, Greaves runs footage from the Newark riots. Police roughly pull black men out of cars. Many of the officers interlace their directions with "boy." We see police assault blacks who, while getting beaten, continuously declare their innocence. Then we start to see death—a series of stills of black men lying in pools of their own blood, one sprawled across the backseat of a car.

Greaves's editing implies that black men will be victimized by a system that will not hesitate to kill in order to preserve the status quo. This interpretation is only heightened when bongos start to play a violent rhythm in the background and the film cuts to a funeral scene, and then to several sequential shots of a city in flames. As the martial bongo continues in the background, another layer of music builds and rests on top. It is "America, America." This disharmony slowly begins to fade as we enter another middle-class salon where we hear a black man essentially giving a lecture to his peers about John Brown and revolutionary zeal. It turns out that Richard B. Moore, identified in the film simply as a "Harlem Bookstore Owner" (no mention is made of his prominent community role as a longtime civil rights activist, communist, and black nationalist), is the source of the opinions.

Morris's recognition that he is "still a brother" offers a reading different from what we've seen earlier in the film. Before, even though the speakers did not literally use the phrase, they evinced a social anxiety that was a collective declaration to lower-class blacks that they, the middle class, remained black. Even if some were only just realizing this connection, they were sensitive to the ways in which they suffered some of the same challenges that defined racial life in the United States. But experiencing Morris's narrative, however, we see the recognition that regardless of their class standing, middle-class blacks were still (only) a brother in the eyes of whites.

Greaves interprets the middle-class response to an increasing racial militancy as a reflection of a revolution of the mind—a moment of rising consciousness that linked still (only) being a brother with still being a brother. The middle class was on the verge of reconnecting to the larger black community, catalyzed by a new sense of self-esteem and an appreciation for a collective memory filled with accomplishment. Sitting in front of a sign that reads "Black is beautiful and it's so beautiful to be black," Atlanta psychiatrist Dr. J. Denis Jackson speaks to this issue directly, referencing the cruel dualities in society that inevitably had a negative effect on African Americans.

Jackson says that this duality—a philosophy of good versus evil—"makes us ashamed of just being black." He continues:

> There is a bone-deep shame about being black which pervades the entire black community and it has no respect for class. The black bourgeoisie is just as ashamed of being black as are the masses of Negroes. This was done due to a concerted effort over many years and generations by the white propagandist. We intend to counter-propagandize. We intend to tell black people that they are valuable; that they are important; that they have made contributions to the world and will continue to make contributions to the world. But first they must look upon themselves in a better light. Hence, black is not ugly. Black is not evil. Black is beautiful.[52]

Just as in those previous moments in the film where Greaves cut away from the interviewee to make visual statements about the black body—the black body as a site of anonymous poverty and the black body as a receptacle of violent intention by the state—Jackson's interview was followed immediately by a reading of another black body: Bayard Rustin.

As one of the nation's most prominent civil rights activists and perhaps the most important political adviser in the black community, Bayard Rustin was widely celebrated as an arbiter of positive change. In the film, Rustin acknowledges a new mentality among blacks and salutes it: "Black people now," he says, "are proud of being black. They are proud of their hair. When I was a child I was taught that if a Negro was light complexioned and had straight hair he was somebody. And I was taught that because I had nappy hair and was black I was nobody. Young Negroes today are proud of their black skin; they're proud of their nappy hair and . . . . That's what they are. Now that is new and, to me, that is good."[53] As Rustin completes his thoughts, the camera pans up and closes in on his full head of naturally "nappy" hair, an Afro, with a slight fade on the sides. There is no doubting the fact that even though the revolutionized mind meant that the meanings of the phrase had changed, he is still a brother.

Riven throughout with social anxieties operating at different registers, the film's depictions of the black body and black space (core elements of Greaves's "black reality") force a reconsideration of the film's title. What does it mean to still be a brother? While wrestling with that question, the film reasserts an authentic Negroness that the blackface journalists sought, affirms the history of struggle that performers in the AAADT projected with their bodies, and abides by the documentarians' commitment to create a useable narrative of the past for the sake of the present and future.

MEMORY, SKIN DEEP

I do not remember if my brother called me into the family room to watch another seminal moment in the era's cinematic cultural race battles, but I recall being there all the same. Previously, at my brother's invitation, I had seen John Shaft give the white man the finger and, in doing so, create entirely new ways to read the black body. My only memory of this second moment—of the entire film, in fact—is an image of a black man sitting in a bathtub filled with gallons upon gallons of milk.

That man is Godfrey Cambridge, the same person who opened the first installment of *Black Journal* two years earlier and who was an early guest on the show. He was immortalized in my mind for this particular frame (not even the scene, just the frame) from *Watermelon Man*, the 1970 project of filmmaker Melvin Van Peebles that marked his return from Europe. Like Greaves before him, Van Peebles could not find compelling work in the United States and left to develop his skills and pursue his craft. While in France, Van Peebles directed *The Story of a Three-Day Pass*, his first feature-length film. The film caught the eye of Hollywood producers, and soon he was signed to direct *Watermelon Man*, a social commentary clothed in a comedy built on a fantastical premise.[54] The movie tells the story of Jeff Gerber, an unbearably loud and obnoxious bigot who doesn't know what to make of the black activists he sees on the nightly television news and with whom his liberal wife sympathizes. Although having little obvious in common except for their two children and the privilege that accompanies their white skin, the couple has a comfortable suburban life and appear faithful to each other, even if Gerber endlessly lobs unwanted advances toward the office sexpot.

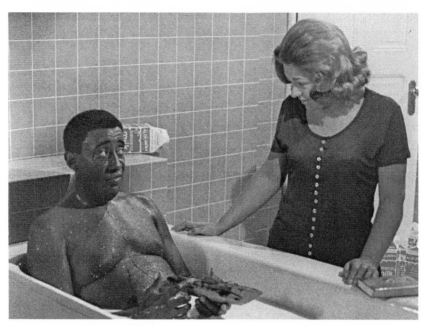

Trying to bathe the black away, Watermelon Man (*WATERMELON MAN* © *1970,
renewed 1998 Columbia Pictures Industries, Inc. All Rights Reserved.
Courtesy of Columbia Pictures.*)

Everything seems to be in order in Gerber's life until he wakes up one
morning to discover that he is no longer white (Cambridge plays Gerber in
whiteface for the first twenty minutes of the film). At first he believes his
dark skin to be an overreaction to the tanning bed he uses religiously, but
as the days wear on, he becomes increasingly desperate and experimental,
trying everything to force his skin back to its normal pigmentation. After
every skin lightener on the market fails, he bathes in gallons of white milk.
Before we see him steeping in a tub of milk, however, we hear him repeat-
edly chanting "ooga booga dooga do." When the camera enters the bathroom we understand: While bathing in the milk, he is also reading *Voodoo
without Killing Chickens,* apparently "number one in Haiti." He is willing
to try anything to remove this curse.

This is the moment that I remember: a forlorn and dark-skinned black
man, sitting in a bathtub filled with white milk (presumably whole milk, as I
think of it), veering dangerously close to losing his mind. I did not recall the
"jungle chanting" his wife hears before she finds him in the bathtub reading
his book of voodoo, nor did I remember their exchange. The image, though,
was indelible, much like Gerber's skin color.

After a few days of calling in sick, Gerber decides he has no choice but to go public in his new skin. Predictably, mayhem ensues. From causing a near street riot when he is "caught" by the police as he is running to catch the bus, to being asked to move out of his home by his neighbors because his presence was bringing down property values, Gerber suffers an endless slew of humiliations that were familiar (if exaggerated for the sake of filmed entertainment) to so many real African Americans. The shock of these negative experiences is mitigated—but always only temporarily—when he takes advantage of his neighbors' racism, forcing them to double what they originally offered him to move out of the neighborhood. Additionally, the office mate who had been repulsed by his "white" masculinity and endless come-ons aggressively pursues him as a hypermasculine sexual object. (After they consummate their relationship, Gerber becomes disgusted with her for her obvious racist presumptions of black male sexual prowess. He leaves her apartment in haste, and, confirming his sudden and shocking critique, she slings racial epithets at him and then yells "rape" from her apartment window as he makes his way in the street below.)

As Gerber continues to navigate life in this skin, the viewers see other changes happening. The children had already been sent away, but his wife soon follows, failing to realign her liberal race politics with the color of his skin and the reality of their new life together. Understandably, he seems to lose his mind, though not long before Van Peebles makes it clear in the film's closing scene that Gerber has gained a hyperclarity.

In the film's final minutes, Gerber talks on his phone with his wife. She is clearly still in love with him but is also unable to reconcile her emotions with her husband's reality. Despite being embittered by her unwillingness to embrace her stated politics, Gerber is polite enough and reassures her that he is doing well. As they are hanging up, however, the film cuts to an overlapping scene in which we see Gerber going through rudimentary military training for the literal revolution with other radical blacks, all of whom are using the tools of subjugation—mops and brooms—instead of rifles. Gerber, the film implies, is not only no longer in blackface; he is now fully and truly black. With each spearlike thrust of his headless mop, Gerber embodies the revolutionized mind of the late 1960s. He is prepared to do more than give the finger to the system, and his arms have already begun to strengthen as they prepare to carry the burdens of blood memory. We know that the newly black Gerber who flung himself across his bed earlier in the movie while wailing, "I want my whiteness back!" is gone. The desire to forget black memory is released, and black embodied memory is embraced.[55]

4

BLACK SCHOLARS
AND MEMORY IN THE AGE OF
BLACK STUDIES

A black student cannot merge "into the university scene"
without consciously striving to forget his past.
—William Sales, "Response to a 'Negro Negative,'"
Columbia Daily Spectator

If our history has taught us anything, it is that action for change
directed only against the external conditions of our oppressions is not enough.
In order to be whole, we must recognize the despair oppression plants
within each of us—that thin persistent voice that says our efforts are useless,
it will never change, so why bother, accept it.
—Audre Lorde, *Sister Outsider*

My first tenure-track job was at the University of California, San Diego (UCSD). I was in one of the most beautiful places in the country and in a first-rate department, but all wasn't perfect. I was only an acting assistant professor, since I had yet to complete my dissertation. Although I was able to remove the "acting" from my title at the end of that first year, I began my professional academic career acutely aware of how tenuous things could be and that I needed to be mindful of doing all the right things (publish a lot, teach effectively, be a good citizen) if I were to earn tenure down the line.

In my third year on the faculty, I was leading a lecture course on black politics in the twentieth century. Things were going well enough. My lecture notes, a mad improvisation the year before, were coming together nicely, and I even had a teaching assistant. In truth, I didn't actually have an assistant, just an undergraduate who seemed to think that she was helping me out by actively supporting my comments. (It was still a small lecture class, and she could turn her chair around when she wanted, face the rest of the class, and underscore my points with her own. She also doled out unsolicited advice to her classmates.) Since I was still a new teacher and learning how to manage a lecture course, I was trying to find a way to offer my unofficial assistant some gentle, corrective advice about her contributions. Coincidentally, just when I was about to engage her in that uncomfortable conversation, she started accompanying me after class as I walked to my department, where I was about to hold office hours. We would talk the entire fifteen minutes it took to cover this ground, going over topics from the course, and beyond. I had to admit that she knew the material extremely well.

These exchanges continued another week or so until we had what turned out to be our final conversation. We had arrived at the department, and I thought we were about to part company—she never actually came to my office hours, instead claiming my free time between the class and my office—when she said that she had an observation that she wanted to share with me. I had no idea where this was going but thought it would at least prove interesting, so I told her to go ahead. It turns out that her observation wasn't about my lectures, the books I selected for the course, or the mixture of exams and papers I assigned. Rather, it was about my appearance and mannerisms. Apparently, my style of dress (in my opinion, pretty unremarkable: khakis and a button-down, long-sleeved shirt) and my way of talking (proper English?) made it seem like I was "trying too hard to appear legitimate."

I like to think I'm fairly good at masking my emotions, but I was completely unprepared for her comment. I was so taken aback that instead of biting my tongue—an instinct I had carefully cultivated in my adolescence—I responded acidly, "I actually like these clothes. This is how I speak. And, to be honest, I already thought I was legitimate." For the first time since she started taking my course, I saw a flicker of uncertainty cross her face. She stammered a bit while saying, "But, Professor Holloway, you know what I mean, right?" Before turning to head upstairs to my office, I offered a fully loaded, quick reply: "Yes, I believe I do."

I lost my assistant that afternoon. She continued with the course and I'm sure she earned an A, but for lack of a better phrase, she kept to her place from that moment on. Given her "post-legitimacy behavior," I can only conclude she understood the fraught terrain she entered during our exchange.

I also believe she understood that my acknowledgment of her intent was more complicated than it immediately seemed.

I had heard stories like this from my handful of grad school friends who were also in their first jobs. It didn't take long for me to realize that the only people who seemed to have these stories were my friends who were underrepresented minorities, women, or, of course, both. Even though I knew that I wasn't alone in this experience, my "teaching assistant" did, in fact, rattle me. While I put no special thought into what I wore or into how I spoke, I admit that I was burdened with a lingering anxiety over my job. Although I'm not sure if I ever wondered if I were "legitimate" or not, I certainly wondered if I would be an effective teacher. Also, like every other assistant professor, I worried about publishing enough. Finally, even though I loved my job, I was curious to learn if it would matter to my career as a historian that I did not have a "straight" history job but was in the Department of Ethnic Studies instead.

I had no doubt about the political and intellectual importance of ethnic studies and knew that it lined up well with my own personal, political, and intellectual interpretation of the narrative about the history of the United States. Thinking about this country's popular memory and the way that it had been fashioned around an erasure of the contributions made by people of color (not to mention all women, poor people, political radicals, and non-European immigrants) made the work of ethnic studies that much more critical. I shared a conviction with my departmental colleagues that presenting a different narrative of the nation's past actually made the country a stronger, more vital, and certainly more honest place.

Of course, my own declarations about the merits of ethnic studies traveled only as far as willing ears would listen. For those who weren't terribly concerned about the triumphalism in the American narrative, I expected a certain level of hesitance or confusion. The questions ranged from the relatively benign, "What does ethnic studies mean?" to the disappointing, "Can you still teach normal American history?" When I received the latter question from an acquaintance, who knew I specialized in the African American past and was someone with whom I felt I was building a cautious friendship, I shot back, "The last time I checked, black history *is* normal American history." Like my "assistant" would a few years later, my acquaintance stammered, "Come on, Jonathan, you know what I mean." And much like I would do at UCSD, I simply responded, "Yes, I know what you mean." In this case, I'm fairly certain that she missed the double-edged acknowledgment of her intent—that I knew she meant no real harm but was completely unaware of how her question was overburdened with privilege and amnesia.

Even though my acquaintance didn't wonder out loud if I were "legitimate," both of these instances reflect a larger crisis of legitimacy that is woven into the histories of black scholars and black studies more broadly.[1] Just as teaching the history of the United States is about creating a narrative out of the country's long-held and forgotten pasts, thinking about the history of black scholars and black studies invites a consideration of a broad set of memories: personal, traumatic memories of Jim Crow; professional memories of denied opportunities; and communal memories of the black experience that manifest themselves in complicated feelings of racial obligation. Reading "legitimacy" through these memories shows us that black scholars' experiences and the disciplinary development of black studies have been negotiated over the very charged questions of what could be known, who could know it, and who is allowed to bear witness. This chapter explores these issues, all the while wondering what it has meant to the individual when the legitimacy of that person and that person's past is questioned. Further, since so many black scholars' access to the academy has been connected directly to the development of black studies, the questions that relate to the individual extend themselves into this particular field of study: What does it mean for a discipline when it grows out of traumatic memory?

LEGITIMACY AND HISTORY (OR, WHAT CAN BE KNOWN)

These questions and issues were not yet on my mind during my freshman year at Stanford. Too concerned with navigating the typical transitional challenges from high school to college, I was only vaguely aware of the controversies surrounding law professor Derrick Bell, also in his first year at the university. Bell, who had been the first black to earn tenure at Harvard Law School, had come to Stanford after serving as the dean of the University of Oregon School of Law. Bell was known for working at the vanguard of Critical Race Theory, an approach to legal thinking that, among other things, pointed out the centrality of race (racial disavowal, racism, colorblind policies with disparate racial impact) in the construction of legal systems designed to benefit the wealthy and powerful. Because Bell did not hesitate to link even the most basic concepts in his constitutional law course to the precepts of Critical Race Theory, students began to complain that he was too political and narrow-minded in his approach to studying and teaching law. Dissatisfied students complained that Bell's theories about race informed his obfuscating approach to constitutional law, thus the law's core concepts. Several professors supported the students, allowing them to audit their own law courses and then helping to organize (with the support of the dean of the law school) a series of public lectures on constitutional law. These lectures were open to the student body; that they were created to help compensate for Bell's perceived deficiencies was a poorly kept secret.

When the Black Law Students Association protested the first lecture and pointed out the racist logics that drove the series, the law school canceled the lectures, and the dean immediately apologized for his poor decision to support the remedial talks. Despite the fact that the lectures did not proceed, the episode was an abject lesson in humiliation. Even though Bell was known for being unflappable in the face of the abiding presence of racism, he was clearly stung. In a personal reflection published immediately after the controversy, Bell did not hide his pain:

> I find myself remembering with feelings approaching fondness the occasional Southern judge, who, to insure that I did not miss his disdain for both my competence and my cause, swiveled his chair and faced the wall when I approached the bench to argue a civil rights case. Back then, the racial hostility was patent and the insult expected. [By contrast] I accepted the invitation to visit Stanford as something of a reward for a decade and a half of "proving myself worthy" to teach at a prestigious school. . . . As a guest welcomed with smiles at the door, I must confess that I simply was not prepared for what happened after I thought myself safe among friends.[2]

Bell's experiences may be somewhat unusual for the very public way in which the entire episode transpired, but they were not unique to him. Around the same time that Bell was suffering his indignities at Stanford, another black law professor, Patricia J. Williams, was being called into the dean's office at her university because students were upset by her penchant for narrative: "They are not learning real law, they say, and they want someone else to give them remedial classes."[3] Williams's students took action on this particular occasion because she was talking at length about economic rights and civil liberties as they are illustrated by events in the New York subway system. They were particularly unhappy with her lingering story about the structures of class politics that informed her failure to assist a homeless person in dire need. The dean told Williams that these kinds of stories weren't "law," that he saw them as personal stories that were veering toward the polemical.[4]

Fundamentally, Bell's and Williams's clashes with their students concerned narrative and memory. Whose narrative mattered most? Whose memories, individual or collective, counted? Even though these are stories from the 1980s and '90s, they also happen to be part of a longer history of racial policing that revolved around issues of who could teach what and how it could be taught. One of the most powerful declarations against this sort of thinking was offered in 1963, when eminent historian John Hope Franklin wrote passionately about the deficits to the store of knowledge caused by racial thinking that was about questioning the legitimacy of black scholars.

Likening the situation of black scholars in the academy to a "dilemma," Franklin angrily lamented the loss that defined black scholars' lives. In the late nineteenth and into the twentieth century, Franklin observed, black academics had to fight against a social Darwinist ideology that deemed them incapable of coherent thought in the first place. While not confined solely to writing in a reactive mode, black intellectuals still had to overcome political, social, economic, and cultural barriers that severely limited their professional opportunities and conspired in such a way that they had to carry a heavy burden of proof that they were capable. Franklin's anger and sorrow were clear: "It must have been a most unrewarding experience for the Negro scholar to answer those who said that he was inferior by declaring: 'I am indeed *not* inferior.'"[5]

Franklin continued:

Imagine, if you can, what it meant to a competent Negro student of Greek literature, W. H. Crogman, to desert his chosen field and write a book entitled *The Progress of a Race*. Think of the frustration of the distinguished Negro physician C. V. Roman, who abandoned his medical research and practice, temporarily at least, to write *The Negro in American Civilization*. What must have been the feeling of the Negro student of English literature Benjamin Brawley, who forsook his field to write *The Negro Genius* and other works that underscored the intellectual powers of the Negro? How much poorer is the field of the biological sciences because an extremely able and well-trained Negro scientist, Julian Lewis, felt compelled to spend years of his productive life writing a book entitled *The Biology of the Negro*?[6]

Franklin was speaking to a broader set of experiences for black scholars working behind the color line in the first decades of the twentieth century. But the battle over legitimacy didn't end when blacks started teaching at historically white institutions. A closer look at the experiences of one such individual, literary scholar J. Saunders Redding, illuminates just how challenging the terrain remained. Redding was one of the first black scholars to integrate the faculty at a historically white research university, and his autobiographical account contextualizes the effect of systemic racism on the personal and professional lives of black academics.

Redding was not the first black scholar to break the race barrier on college faculties. One of the crueler ironies of this situation is that black colleges did not offer Ph.D.'s at this time. Black graduate students went to schools like Harvard, Columbia, and Chicago for their doctorates but could not teach in the same institutions upon completion of the degree. In 1941, the Julius Rosenwald Fund, one of a handful of philanthropic foundations that dedicated millions of dollars to all levels of black education in the first half of the twentieth century, discovered that there were only two blacks, neither of whom held teaching positions, on the faculty at the nation's white colleges and universities. Determined to change that situation, the Rosenwald Fund arranged for prominent sociologist Allison P. Davis to be appointed at the University of Chicago. The school was willing to hire Davis because the Rosenwald Fund subsidized his salary. In short, the university paid nothing, or close to it, and received a leading scholar on the sociology of race and community formation in return. This "arrangement" spoke volumes about the resistance white schools presented to the integration of their faculties, particularly regarding the use of scarce resources in service of what many considered a political agenda.[7] Perhaps a result of the Rosenwald Fund's arrangement with Chicago or perhaps a manifestation of the pace of a changing tide, within three years, fifteen blacks taught at white colleges. Redding was part of this tide.

In some ways it is unsurprising that J. Saunders Redding would live his life at the leading edge of racial change. Born in Wilmington, Delaware, to parents who prized education, civic engagement, and activism (his father was the long-standing secretary of Wilmington's local branch of the NAACP; a sibling, Louis, was the first African American to pass the bar in Delaware), Redding started college at Lincoln University but completed his studies at Brown. He performed with distinction there and earned Phi Beta Kappa honors. Even though he graduated from college in 1928, the honor society and/or Brown did not see fit to admit him until 1943, after he had already become a nationally prominent writer and literary critic.[8]

After teaching for a few years at Morehouse College, Redding returned to Brown, where he completed a master's degree in English and American literature in 1932. He secured positions at a variety of black southern schools over the next three decades. Redding spent two of those three decades at Virginia's Hampton Institute, where, in his last nine years there, he served as James Weldon Johnson Professor of Creative Writing.[9] In 1949, however, he broke this pattern of employment and served as a visiting professor at Brown. There are scarce details about the terms of his appointment or his personal experiences while there, but today there is little doubting how Brown assesses Redding's relationship to the school.

In a special 2000 edition celebrating its 100th year of publication, the *Brown Alumni Magazine (BAM)* presented a digest of what its editors and a survey of Brown alumni deemed the 100 most important and influential people, broken down into categories from biochemistry to graphic design to zoology, to graduate from the Providence school. The editors of the magazine declared that Redding was one of four alumni who accomplished great things in the field of history. Ignoring the fact that Redding was not actually a historian, his *BAM* entry pointed immediately to his groundbreaking credentials: "He was the first black member of an Ivy League faculty, the first black to serve as a Brown fellow, and the first black to have his portrait hung in Sayles Hall."[10] What is not mentioned here is the brevity of his appointment to Brown: He taught there for only one term.

Of course, by their very nature, alumni magazines are celebratory glossies dedicated to sustaining open connections between a school and its graduates. But given the highly contested pace and nature of change regarding race relations on college campuses, it is clear that *BAM*'s commemoration is a racial celebration and a powerful example of how institutions remember. (As it happens, one of the other four historians honored in this special issue is black: Spencer Crew, Brown class of 1971, then director of the Smithsonian's National Museum of American History.) Post–civil rights celebrations of diversity are not unusual, but their contextualization, understanding the history of struggle behind the celebration, is always important. Redding's history is profoundly revealing, especially in light of the circumstances surrounding his eventual full-time move to a white campus in 1970.

Redding was a prolific writer whose fiction and nonfiction prose appeared in essay and book form. By the time he published his memoir *On Being Negro in America* in 1951, he had already produced four other major works: *To Make a Poet Black* (1939), *No Day of Triumph* (1942), *Stranger and Alone* (1950), and *They Came In Chains: Americans from Africa* (1950). It is his memoir, however, that best reflects how the combination of institutional racism and personal acts of racial antagonism amounted to a daily, low-level psychological battle with which black scholars like Redding found they had little choice but to engage.

Redding opened his memoir with a wild swing at Richard Wright and his 1941 book, *12 Million Black Voices*. Redding spoke with outrage that Wright sought to describe blacks via the Farm Security Administration photographs portraying black folklife in the Great Depression:

This [memoir] is personal. I would call it a "document" except that the word has overtones of something official, vested and final. But I have been clothed with no authority to speak for others, and what I have to say can be final only for myself. I hasten to say this at the start, for I remember my anger at the effrontery of one who a few years ago undertook to speak for me and twelve million others. I concurred with practically nothing he said. This was not important in itself, but when one presumes to speak for me he must reflect my mind so accurately that I find no source of disagreement with him. To do this, he must either be a lack-brain parrot or a god.[11]

While Redding did not mention Wright by name and thereby softened the blow—after all, Wright did pen the introduction to Redding's *No Day of Triumph*, in which he heartily praised the book—Redding's opening words speak to his frustration that whites as well as blacks too quickly reduced the diversity of black America into a single type or form. They also make plain the extent to which race and racial thinking overdetermined the life chances for all black Americans. The frustration seeped through the pages: "Though there are many lack-brains, historic and present circumstances prove that there are no gods dealing with the problem of race—or, as dangerous to the American ideal and exhausting to individual Americans as it has been for three hundred years, it would have been settled long ago. Else the gods are singularly perverse."[12]

Raised in a family of civil rights activists, Redding articulated a sense of self that acknowledged racial differences but insisted on the fundamental "Americanness" of black culture, that black and white were inextricable. This is an ideology that would become unpopular with the black militants of future decades, but in 1951 Redding's personal ideology, manifested in such a way that the individual was ascendant, was not unusual. However, this integrationist ethos, a call to respect the individual in each person, was undermined at every turn by a system of seeing race and imbuing it with constant meaning. Throughout his memoir, Redding insists his "right" to speak on his views of race does not extend beyond his self. Clearly wanting to avoid the trap that he suggested Wright fell into when he claimed to speak for all blacks, Redding also took this stance because he wanted to personalize the psychological trauma that blacks and whites incurred by racial thinking. He saw in his memoir a quest for "a purge, a catharsis, wholeness."[13] By claiming expertise in the personal, Redding then felt comfortable extending beyond himself, drawing connections to his private quest for a god of reason to larger phenomena that frustrated him and other like-minded seekers.

Redding saw his memoir as "the epilogue to whatever contribution I have made to the 'literature of race.'" Although John Hope Franklin did not mention Redding in his 1963 essay on the black scholar, it is clear that Redding experienced the same sense of personal loss and bitterness that Franklin identified: the frustration with the expectation that black scholars spoke for the race or to the race in order to be heard. Redding announced his desire to "get on to other things. I do not know whether I can make this clear, but the obligations imposed by race on the average educated or talented Negro (if this sounds immodest, it must) are vast and become at last onerous. I am tired of giving up my creative initiative to these demands. I think I am not alone."

Redding continued this line of reasoning by citing the experiences of a famous singer who lamented the constant expectation to sing spirituals in every concert. Although she sang them well, "she was weary of the obligation of finding a place for them in every program, 'as if they were theme music' wholly identifying her." She, like Redding, felt arrested in what Redding termed "ethnocentric coils." Drawing from his own experiences and that of the unnamed singer, Redding then made a declaration about his memoir's value:

> The specialization of the sense and talent and learning . . . that is expected of Negroes by other members of their race and by whites is tragic and vicious and divisive. I am tired of trying, in deference to this expectation, to feel my way into the particularities of response and reaction that are supposed to be exclusively "Negro." I am tired of the unnatural obligation of converting such talent and learning as I have into specialized instruments for the promotion of a false concept called "race." This extended essay, then, is probably my last public comment on the so-called American race problem.[14]

Although the memoir would not be Redding's final public comment on the race problem, his anger at the forces that inspired such a sentiment run throughout his book. His heart is "sickened at the realization of the primal energy that goes undeflected and unrefined into the sheer business of living as a Negro in the United States." Further, he spits that the black scholar has a "thankless task. . . . In pure self-defense he has had to try to set the record straight."[15]

After Redding's short stint at Brown, he returned to Hampton, continuing to write weekly book reviews for the *Baltimore Afro-American* in addition to his more scholarly work in the form of books and journal articles. During his quietly productive years, the scope and tactics of civil rights reform and the kinds of questions being asked of society changed in critical ways. Redding remained true to his integrationist ideology that fell out of favor with many college-aged youth as the civil rights movement morphed into its black power phase. There is no doubt that his strong adherence to the integrationist ethos made him the object of desire for university campuses that became serious about diversifying in the wake of early 1960s civil rights triumphs.

Redding's path to a just society must have seemed almost quaint in the wake of student-led occupations of administration buildings that began to sweep the country in the late 1960s. Among other things, the students called for curricular reform that would introduce the black experience into their studies, and they called for an increased diversity of the student body, administration, and faculty. In most places, these demands were articulated with relative calm. On a few campuses, however, quite the opposite happened. In 1969, the protesting students at Cornell University embodied the most extreme manifestation of this phenomenon when they literally took up arms and threatened to use force if their demands were not met. There is no coincidence in the fact that Redding secured his first permanent job at a white campus within months. When he was appointed full professor in Cornell's English Department in 1970, he became the first black at that rank in the school's College of Arts and Sciences as well as the first black to hold an endowed chair. Redding taught at Cornell from 1970 to 1976.[16]

While at Cornell, Redding had no official affiliation with the university's Africana Studies and Research Center.[17] Redding was certainly not the student militants' choice. Redding had maintained his commitment to integrationist policies when militant separatism was the passionate call of students. Redding's presence, however, was a valve that reduced pressure on the Cornell administration to do something that acknowledged the need for some measure of racial diversity on its campus. Redding, of course, was not alone in his newfound role as an object of desire. Beginning in the late 1960s, unprecedented numbers of black scholars began to find their way to teach on historically white campuses. With their arrival, new iterations of old questions about legitimacy emerged.

LEGITIMACY, RELEVANCE, AND RACIAL AUTHENTICITY (OR, WHO CAN KNOW)

The new desire for black faculty followed an upsurge in the number of black undergraduates at white universities. In a Ford Foundation report on the development of black studies in the nation's colleges and universities,

Harvard historian Nathan Huggins charted the dramatic growth in college enrollment as a result of the G.I. Bill and the postwar baby boom.[18] College matriculation by blacks approached 10 percent of total student enrollment by the mid-1970s, and with this rise came pressure to address the needs and desires of this relatively new constituency. But Huggins made sure to add an important caveat to this received wisdom: Black students were not the only source of pressure to change the appearance and pedagogy of white universities. New visions of the ability of universities to shape society and an increasing focus on career training prompted school administrators to rationalize the respective utility of departments. Administrators now felt freer to question, for example, the pragmatic value that a department of philosophy brought to a campus community. "Merely" contributing to the store of knowledge was being threatened by a heightened devotion to the market value of particular knowledge or its potential for demonstrating social relevance. In this new environment, the social sciences and physical sciences along with the professional schools found it relatively easy to rationalize their existence and "value" to a campus and its students. Humanities programs and departments, on the other hand, faced a steeper challenge.[19]

That the humanities would rely, in part, on their ability to address social problems related to race as a basis to justify their value is ironic, since, as a mode of inquiry, so many humanities programs had been criticized for their Eurocentric approach to culture, art, and thought. Whether it was true or not, black students criticized humanities courses for failing to speak to the circumstances of their lives and traditions. "Relevance"—real or imagined and, in fact, another way of wondering about "legitimacy"—was the catchword of the moment, and the either/or presumption dictated that one was part of the problem if one was not working toward a solution. The answer at many campuses was to hire one or two black faculty and have them teach one or two courses on topics like "black literature" or "black history." Typically, these courses were fully integrated into the standing curricular offerings.[20] But this was only one solution. The more contentious path universities followed to fold blackness into their curricula was the establishment of black studies programs and departments.

The very real threat of a violent outbreak at Cornell was the most extreme manifestation of student activism in service of a call for racial, pedagogical, and curricular diversity at a university. But the Ithaca school was not the only place where the development and then incorporation of a black studies program exposed serious fault lines between students and administrators.

The first black studies program in the country was established at San Francisco State in 1968.[21] Before the program was created and in an attempt to demonstrate its commitment to diversifying its faculty and, perhaps more truthfully, have black bodies teach black studies courses, the administration had hired G. M. Murray, a member of the Black Panther Party, as a lecturer. Murray did not have an advanced degree and was open about the fact that he was teaching classes "related to revolution." In late September 1968, word of his classes and their hyperpoliticized nature came to the attention of the board of trustees of the California State College System, which then voted 85-5 to fire Murray. This decision sent shockwaves through the campus and resulted in student strikes, violence between the community and police, and the school's temporary closure.[22]

Eventually, San Francisco State's new president, S. I. Hayakawa, managed to reopen the campus (with the security forces approved by California governor Ronald Reagan) and offered to create a permanent black studies department as a means to address black student frustrations. Hayakawa proposed hiring sociologist Nathan Hare, who, incidentally, had just been fired from Howard for his support of and engagement with striking students there.[23] The Bay Area student-activists had a different agenda in mind, however, that went much further than the mere establishment of a black studies program or department. They issued a ten-point list of demands that called for the creation of an independent black studies department and, among other things, insisted on universal acceptance of black applicants, the elimination of the ability of the board of trustees to dissolve black programs at San Francisco State and elsewhere, and the rehiring of G. M. Murray.[24] The students also demanded that Hare, who was chairing the black studies program, "receive a full professorship and a comparable salary according to his qualifications."[25]

The students' demands fell on deaf ears. This was made evident when Hare notified the students that President Hayakawa did not renew the former's contract. Clearly, Hare did little to inspire Hayakawa's trust. Hare recounted that soon after he arrived at San Francisco State, his assumption that he had been hired to "'coordinate' the nation's first black studies program" proved incorrect. This assumption "soon dissolved into deception as I discovered that I had been brought there to appease black students. I refused the role of a troubleshooter and tumult was not long in breaking loose. I could not and did not try to stop the student protest."[26] Very real consequences appeared in the wake of Hayakawa's and Hare's mutual refusals. Most immediate was the resignation of four of San Francisco State's six black administrators, who left publicly claiming that Hayakawa was a racist. A few months after the group resignation and apparently without blinking, Hayakawa threatened to disband the black studies department.

Within the year, Hayakawa made good on those threats when he "ousted" the department's faculty.[27]

The terms of these late 1960s debates most typically revolved around the establishment of black studies programs or at least a reshaping of the college curriculum such that the black experience was fairly reflected in the course offerings. That black faculty found themselves caught in this debate reveals a core aspect of the racial expectations driving the creation of these new institutional or at least curricular spaces: "Black courses" were to be taught by black faculty. If a university did not have black courses, it would hire black faculty to teach them. If a university wanted to find a space where it could point a bright light on the diversity of its hiring practices, it might create a black studies program and place black faculty in it. Undoubtedly, university administrators took many of these actions because they mitigated the anger of black students and salved their disaffection. The administrators' actions reflected a way of thinking that acknowledged the students' pain while making assumptions about who could best ease their trauma by respecting their presumptive collective memory.

At this juncture and in light of these dynamics, another philanthropic foundation committed financial resources to changing the university landscape. Paralleling the Rosenwald Fund's 1941 decision to finance the hiring of black scholars, the Ford Foundation awarded more than $1 million to twelve colleges and universities in 1969 and 1970 to help them develop interdisciplinary black studies programs.[28] Yale University was one of the institutions that enjoyed the foundation's largesse, and it initiated its own Afro-American studies program. In no small part a manifestation of this institutionally organized and external support, the history of the formation of Yale's program and the politics behind its formation are significantly less turbulent than those at Cornell or San Francisco State.

A breadth of scholars and foundation representatives point to the establishment of the Afro-American studies program at Yale—referred to throughout the literature as "the Yale Case"—as the best example of how a process that was committed to maintaining a scholarly approach to black studies (instead of a "therapeutic approach") could survive that era's complicated race politics.[29] Like other schools, the movement to start a black studies program at Yale sprang from undergraduate desire. Instead of occupying administration buildings, however, representatives from the Black Student Alliance at Yale (BSAY) met with university president Kingman Brewster in early 1968 and then with various administration and faculty representatives on a weekly basis over the following three months. By the spring of that year, students had organized a two-day conference that revolved around the question of black studies, its value to college curricula, and its anticipated role at Yale. The conference featured white and black speakers who represented the breadth of the political and methodological spectrum.

The debate between and among Yale and non-Yale faculty resulted in a publication, *Black Studies in the University*, and, a year later, the formation of the Ivy League's first black studies program. In these early days of black studies programs, Yale's was seen as the role model. Other university administrators admired if not envied what transpired in New Haven because it was done without threats of violence or even serious public displays of disaffection. Established scholars like Nathan Huggins praised the Yale model for its inclusiveness, "the constructive attitude of the university's senior faculty and the deft leadership of its administration."[30] But tangled up in this sense of good feeling were some of the same antagonistic or defensive race dynamics found in other campus communities. Conference attendees raised questions about who could teach the black past, who could access the cultures and memories that shaped this past, and what were the obligations of black expertise. Because black studies was directly linked to a determination to help black students and was imagined as a way to integrate university faculties, the conference participants began to delineate black studies as a space where the authenticating possibilities of black memory would be contested.

David Brion Davis, then in the history department at Cornell but soon to move to Yale, felt compelled to declare in his closing remarks (a summation of the conference proceedings) that black studies, if it were to succeed as a discipline, could not close the door to white scholars. The ability to interpret a racialized past could not logically be limited to native insiders' ability to interpret blackness. If blackness were to trump training, knowledge, and the freedom to explore complex and even controversial ideas, Davis warned, the university would fail in its role as a "custodian as well as an innovator." Paraphrasing political theorist Martin Kilson, another conference panelist, Davis concluded that "oppression conveys no special intellectual or moral virtues."[31] Nathan Hare countered Davis's claims to cross-racial interpretive ability. Elsewhere, he recalled his performance at Yale, "where I had the occasion to ponder the blank and (in a good many cases) open-mouthed stares of ignorance on faces in the predominantly white audience when I related how all white students given a test by a black colleague and me had fundamentally flunked, being unable to identify such commodities as hog maws, fried beans, and butter roll."[32] Hare's point was simple: Who better to know and interpret the full complexity of black culture and the black experience than black people? Hare's suggestions were not well received.

Huggins, for one, merely dismissed Hare and his fellow presenter at the Yale conference, cultural nationalist Maulana Ron Karenga, as "deeply anti-intellectual and hostile to the academy."[33] Huggins was clearly impatient with their assertions that oppression authorized special forms and embodiments of knowledge.

Huggins or Davis could have added that Hare's and Karenga's nationalist assertions also did violence to the actual history of black studies in the first place. Since at least the late 1930s, anthropologist Melville Herskovits, a student of Franz Boas and a prominent supporter of cultural relativism, had called for a sustained investigation of the retention of African cultural-isms among American blacks. Granted, Herskovits was not literally advocating the formation of black studies programs, but his work, particularly his 1941 book *The Myth of the Negro Past*, became the intellectual bedrock for future black studies advocates. A child of Jewish immigrants, Herskovits was an Africanist by training but became deeply invested in advocating the "Afro-American tradition." A people without an acknowledged history were a people denied their own humanity, and *The Myth of the Negro Past* (the myth being that blacks had no past) set out to correct this conscious oversight. It is unclear if Hare and Karenga would have been dismissive of a white Jew like Herskovits who dedicated his career to the "espousal of the solidity and authenticity of a distinguishable Afro-American culture," but Nathan Huggins clearly thought they should have known the history of their own field better.[34]

If one did not want to fault Hare and Karenga for failing to acknowledge appropriately Herskovits's influence on the emerging discipline, one would have been absolutely remiss a few years later to ignore the prominent role that white scholars like Herbert Gutman, Lawrence Levine, Gerda Lerner, and Eugene Genovese played in fostering a deepening awareness of blacks as active agents in making their own identity and history.[35] By the mid-1970s, an honest and less politically driven assessment of black studies scholarship would have had to confess that some of its most important practitioners were white.

Acknowledging white scholars' growing interest in or even fascination with blackness or Herskovits's foundational role in black studies did not mean that black scholars were late to come to black studies or that they only came to the field in the wake of student protests or administrative or philanthropic fiat. If one looks beyond the boundaries created by formal recognition of black studies departments, it is evident that black studies had been present far longer than most believed. In their 1980 essay "Black Studies as an Integral Tradition in African-American Intellectual History,"

James Turner and C. Steven McGann assert that black studies could trace its roots back to the young W. E. B. Du Bois and Carter G. Woodson. Du Bois created the Atlanta University Studies Series in 1913 and thus laid the foundation for black studies via the series's working papers on various aspects of the black experience. Woodson, the so-called Father of Negro History, created Negro History Week, established the Association for the Study of Negro Life and History, and founded the *Journal of Negro History* at almost the same time that Du Bois's series appeared. Taken together, Woodson's actions demonstrated the humanistic contributions of black Americans to the larger society. For Turner and McGann, Du Bois's and Woodson's actions constituted the intellectual structure upon which later black studies programs were built.[36]

Related to the diverse means by which they became institutionalized on college campuses in the late 1960s and early 1970s, black studies programs represented a range of political and theoretical approaches to the budding discipline. A few programs were methodologically traditional as far as the disciplinary questions they entertained by linking new black studies programs to established humanistic fields like English, history, and philosophy. Many more focused large aspects of their curricular agenda on constructing bridges between the campus and community. Still other programs were explicitly race-first in their consciousness, determined to reserve black studies for black people. Disciplinarily traditional, community oriented, and militantly political, these programs' modes and styles reflected the individuals who were hired to run them. But no matter where they happened to find an institutional home or how they defined it, black studies programs and their teaching staff constantly lived on the edge of controversy.

Figures such as the ubiquitous Nathan Hare often seemed to do what they could either to seek out or to provoke controversy. More than once Hare declared that he thought black studies, if done right, represented a vanguardist movement that could revolutionize the university and society. This was education in service of a larger political goal. "To solve the problems of the black race," Hare announced, "Afro-American education must produce persons capable of solving the problems of a contagious American society. To solve the problems of American society, Afro-Americans must first blackwash—revamp—the existing educational system, and revolutionize America's youth—black, yellow, brown and white."[37] This "blackwashing," in Hare's opinion, was the work of black studies departments and the black faculty who should staff them.

Theologian Vincent Harding, who attempted through his leadership of the Institute of the Black World (an Atlanta-based think tank established in

1969) to find ways to connect scholarship directly to the needs of the black community, was much more explicit in his declaration that black scholars had a duty to "speak the truth" to black America.[38] While Harding allowed for the white intellectual examination of black life, he spoke about a moral calling that blacks had to heed. They had, in his opinion, the moral obligation to preserve the community's memories. Harding declared,

> The calling of the black scholar is to move insistently beyond . . . abdication, whatever its cause. Let others study us if they will . . . but self-definition is an intrinsic part of self-determination. It is *we* who must understand our families, our churches, our works of art, the schools our children attend, the economic, political, and spiritual structures which uphold—and oppress—the communities in which we live. It is *we* who must understand how all these structures and institutions are related to our oppression and our struggle for liberation. It is *we* who must painfully diagnose our own deepest illnesses and identify with great joy our most soaring aspirations towards new humanity.[39]

Taken together, Hare's and Harding's comments created the intellectual space and rationalization for black studies programs that were oriented toward either community service or political militancy, if not separatism.

Quite expectedly, white and black scholars reacted with great passion to these kinds of sentiments. David Davis politely insisted that the pursuit of knowledge be color-blind even when society, subject matter, and the politics informing the knowledge were not. Other white scholars were hardly so polite. Eugene Genovese, for example, raged on about the implications, scholarly, personal, and otherwise, of race-exclusive enclaves within academe:

> Responsible black scholars have been working hard for an end to raiding and to the scattering of the small number of black professors across the country. Among other obstacles, they face the effort of ostensibly nationalist black students who seek to justify their decision to attend predominantly white institutions, often of high prestige, by fighting for a larger black teaching staff. The outcomes of these demands is the obscurantist nonsense that black studies can and should be taught by people without intellectual credentials since these credentials are "white" anyway.
>
> . . . Few good universities have ever refused to waive formalities in any field when genuine intellectual credentials of a nonacademic order could be provided. What has to be resisted firmly is the insanity that claims, as in one recent instance, that experience as a SNCC [Student Nonviolent Coordinating Committee] field organizer should be considered more

important than a Ph.D. in the hiring of a professor of Afro-American history. This assertion represents a general contempt for all learning and a particular contempt for black studies as a field of study requiring disciplined, serious intellectual effort—an attitude that reflects the influence of white racism, even when brought forth by a black man.[40]

Using a less strident tone, but one still bristling with rage about racial politics run amok on the college campus, social psychologist Kenneth Clark expressed his dismay over the decision by Antioch College administrators to cave in to black student demands for a new black studies program. Clark's anger did not spring from the idea of such a program but from the mode of articulation in Antioch's case. There, campus officials politically and financially supported the establishment of the Afro-American Institute and an undergraduate house that was racially exclusive. For someone who had staked his career on breaking down the barriers that preserved segregation, Antioch's decision violated Clark's principles. Clark responded to this violation by resigning from Antioch's board of trustees and issuing a public statement about the proper role of race on college campuses. "The white liberal," Clark wrote, "who concedes black separatism so hastily and benevolently must look to his own reasons, not the least of them perhaps an exquisite relief. To encourage or endorse a separate black program not academically equivalent to the college curriculum generally, indeed to endorse any such program, is to reinforce the Negro's inability to compete with whites for the real power of the real world. It is no excuse to justify the deed by citing the demand."

Invoking the same language of caretaking that motivated David Davis's opinion, Clark continued, "Colleges and universities must be the custodians of the rational and intellectual approach to the study and eventual solution of complex human problems. To succumb to any form of dogmatism, to institutionalize the irrational is to fail in fulfilling this important obligation."[41]

Ironically, not quite a year before his resignation from Antioch, Clark gave a commencement address that acknowledged student anger and seemed to sympathize with their frustration with self-satisfied institutions of higher education. His language even evoked the traumas that fueled student rage:

As I understand what the new breed of student rebels is saying beneath the incoherence of their frustration and bravado, it is that they are no longer able to accept the irrelevance, the isolation, the preoccupation with trivia, the indifference and insensitivity to flagrant injustices which pass for academic objectivity and are offered as higher education.

Beneath the din and cacophony of the righteous indignation and police sirens with which they are answered, I think I hear these students saying that they want, they demand, they are willing to sacrifice their own personal comfort and future for a morally relevant, personally fulfilling form of education.[42]

This address, titled "Learning from Students," was given at Antioch's 1968 commencement.

LEGITIMACY AND SURVIVAL (OR, WHOSE MEMORIES MATTER)

It is evident that Clark was sympathetic to the black students who suffered at the hands of racist administrations, police or security forces, and racist classmates. He was also sensitive to the fact that changes were coming fast and furious—his own resignation from the Antioch board of trustees less than a year later exemplified this. By the end of the decade and into the 1970s, black students were pressing for immediate change at colleges and universities across the country.

The student protests at Northwestern were fairly representative: a sit-in at the offices of the university administration, accompanied by a set of demands, followed by a negotiated settlement. Among the students' seven demands were calls for separate housing—the kind of request that Clark considered a step backward—a boost in the numbers of blacks admitted, and a policy statement by the university in which it openly deplored any form of racism. The demands themselves are revealing for the way that they point to student trauma. The opening lines of the document speak to this issue directly: "We, the Black students at Northwestern University, have found the academic, cultural, and social conditions for us on campus deplorably limited. In order to counteract the physical, emotional, and spiritual strains we have been subjugated to, in order to find some meaning and purpose in our being here, we demand that the following conditions be immediately met."[43]

When the administration pushed back against the student demands, the students issued another, final document in which they provided richer details about the sources of their anger and pain: "Our experience in America has not been characterized by justice in any way. No white institution can right our hundreds of years of history and experience by suddenly treating us the same as white people (only at those times when it is strategic to do so) and call it justice and equality. No matter how one looks at it, idealistically or realistically, Black people know that we are still getting the short end of the deal."[44]

True to the times, students spoke with great passion about their ideals and sense of injustice. One of the most perceptive student activists on this issue had to be Armstead Robinson from Yale University. Robinson was a core member of BSAY and was one of the four students who brought the case for black studies to the university's administration. He played a major role in organizing the black studies conference and then in editing the book that grew out of that gathering. (Robinson would come to play a central role in developing black studies beyond Yale, serving as the founding director of the Carter G. Woodson Institute for African-American and American Studies at the University of Virginia. He was at the Woodson Institute from 1981 until his premature death in 1995.)

Before he graduated from Yale, Robinson sat for an interview with the *Yale Alumni Magazine* about his experiences organizing the conference and, more generally, about his experiences being black at Yale. Joined by three other student activists—BSAY members and conference organizers Raymond Nunn, Glen deChabert, and Larry E. Thompson—Robinson's answers most powerfully captured the challenges of black life at Yale. Robinson sounded familiar notes of dissatisfaction and anger when he spoke about the "whiteness" of a place like Yale and the racial erasure of black history in the school's curriculum. However, when he addressed the foundational meaning of being black at Yale, Robinson sounded wise (and weary) beyond his years. He spoke to the role of the black individual—he was speaking of students but might just as well have been speaking about faculty at Yale and elsewhere, for that matter—in a virtually all-white setting and the fierce determination to preserve a set of memories and culture that would otherwise drown in an ocean of forgetfulness:

> The basic issue here is why were we brought to Yale in the first place? I will argue that somewhere deep in the minds of the people on the admissions committee was the idea that they needed some diversity. It's sort of like when you're cooking you throw in some salt to make the food taste better. It's a fundamentally paternalistic conception, to assume that the functional utility for bringing black people here is to use them to broaden the horizons of the white students. It almost seems as if Yale said, "Let's get some Indians, a few niggers, keep the number small but have a few as spicing so you can have the whole pot taste good." I can't handle that; not very many black people can handle it either. But some people might get the idea that talking this way implies that we're retreating into a certain negativism, that we're running away because we can't deal with it. That's not so. Our fundamental thing is a positive assertion: We refuse

to be the spicing. We think there's much more to blackness than simply to make whiteness a little grey. We think that blackness in and of itself is good. We refuse to come here and lose our blackness by sort of helping out the white majority. In a sense, that would be asking a black student to come here and become deculturated. That's a hell of a process. And it's not something you ask anybody else to do. The desire for positive black identification is, quite frankly, a positive assertion that I have some identity that I intend to preserve. I'm not running away saying that I can't deal with it. It's just that if you don't ask anybody *else* to do it, then don't ask *me* to do it.[45]

For Robinson, preserving his blackness and all the memories and histories that came with it was nothing less than an act of survival.

Decades after Robinson offered these words on the eve of his graduation from Yale, bell hooks shared her own reflections about the school, but from a professor's perspective. In a chapter titled, "On Being Black at Yale: Education as the Practice of Freedom," hooks uses language that explicitly speaks about trauma and damage and, thus, implies the need for survival. Though the story she relates happens many years after Armstead Robinson and his BSAY peers spoke about the demoralizing feeling of deculturation, the challenges of being black on a predominantly white campus seem to remain unchanged:

While assimilation is seen as an approach that ensures the successful entry of black people into the mainstream, at its very core it is dehumanizing. Embedded in the logic of assimilation is the white-supremacist assumption that blackness must be eradicated so that a new self, in this case a "white" self, can come into being. Of course, since we who are black can never be white, this very effort promotes and fosters serious psychological stress and even severe mental illness. My concern about the process of assimilation has deepened as I hear black students express pain and hurt, as I observe them suffer in ways that not only inhibit their ability to perform academically, but threaten their very existence. When I told a black female student the subject of my talk, her response was "Why talk about freedom—why not just talk about sanity? We're trying to stay sane."[46]

Other black students and scholars in the postsegregated university world wrestled with an "overwhelming whiteness" and, to an unsettling extent, used the language of trauma and survival in describing their experiences. These individuals had to endure literal physical resistance to their presence on campus (a college groundskeeper threw rocks at Robert Stepto when he was a freshman; a band of white Dartmouth students pushed future literary scholar Charles T. Davis off the sidewalk, called him nigger, and spat on him).[47] They had to endure intellectual resistance to their presence on campus (a graduate school professor invited bell hooks to his office in order to tell her that he was personally committed to denying her a graduate degree).[48] Furthermore, they had to endure the internalized pain of self-doubt that they were doing the right thing for the black community. Was their work relevant? How did it serve the race? Did it tell the right stories?

Black scholars have routinely wrestled with this last set of questions, wondering how they could rationalize their "leisurely" lifestyle when so many African Americans were in crisis. A guilt born of changing circumstance as well as a perceived failure to remain connected to the needs of black America is a phenomenon that appears with frequency in black scholars' recollections. When future professor of English Horace Porter secured a scholarship to Amherst and was thus able to leave a hardscrabble southern life for the promises of the life of the mind, he felt that he had won some sort of personal lottery. When he continued on to Yale for graduate school and as his life became less recognizable to his family, he felt the pull of home in pernicious ways. Letters from an incarcerated brother pushed Porter to the breaking point, as he struggled to reconcile his guilt with his own determination to follow his dreams. The only thing that helped him manage these emotions was the knowledge that he was not alone. "Black students like me," he wrote, "were suddenly being propelled at unprecedented speed to nominal social equality. We were flying into the middle-class on the social and academic equivalent of the *Concorde*. Our survivor's guilt was inspired by the painful perception of the growing social and emotional distance between our own lives and the lives of our families, friends, and neighbors."[49]

At a different stage in his career, historian Clayborne Carson struggled with his own success in light of so many challenges that cut short the careers of other black professors. After a quick sprint through graduate school, Carson began teaching at Stanford University. He was part of the early 1970s wave of black scholars being hired to diversify the nation's campuses and teach black studies courses. Carson recalled that it was exciting to be part of what seemed to be a fundamental shift in the academy, but over time, the breadth and depth of that shift began to look less impressive and important. Carson felt that

some of the younger Black professors who came to Stanford (and to other universities) during this period sacrificed their opportunity to gain tenure by devoting themselves to administrative and teaching responsibilities. I experienced a degree of survivor's guilt when I gained tenure, but I found it easy to immerse myself in historical research about my chosen subject matter and felt fortunate to be paid to follow my curiosity. Although I came to see my scholarly work as my most appropriate contribution to a still-evolving freedom struggle, there were times when I longed for the activist role I had left behind.[50]

Part of Carson's guilt came from the fact that he succeeded where others did not. But he was also troubled because his success might have appeared to come at the expense of the black community. Was he insufficiently dedicated to his students or to building a program in black studies? Did he avoid the get-your-hands-dirty work that his black peers pursued even if it meant giving up the chance to secure tenure? Was he still relevant? Was he, by extension, legitimate?

Historian John Blassingame, one of Horace Porter's faculty mentors, certainly had an answer to these kinds of questions. When Porter confided in him that he was considering leaving graduate school to pursue a degree in law, Blassingame immediately replied, "What about your responsibility to the black community?"[51] Porter was unprepared for the question but came to understand that for someone like Blassingame, the scholar's life was a worthy investment on behalf of the community because educators, especially those working in black studies programs and departments, were building the curriculum for future generations. They were preserving and analyzing the cultural, political, social, and economic pasts that comprised the African American narrative. This was a task of fundamental importance.

Because the language of guilt and trauma and pain suffused so much of the discourse about the black experience on historically white campuses and because this discourse accompanied a cry for "relevance" in the curriculum, critics of black studies came to see the discipline as an exercise in therapy and psychological recuperation. In 1969, Princeton economist W. Arthur Lewis—a future recipient of the Nobel Prize in Economics and the first black to win the award in that discipline—wrote about his deep suspicions of the emerging field. "The principal argument for forcing black students to spend a great deal of time in college studying African and Afro-American anthropology, history, languages and literature," he wrote, "is that they need such studies to overcome their racial inferiority complex. I am not impressed by this argument." By the time a child entered his mid-teens, he reasoned, "the whites he meets, the books he reads, and the situation of the Negro in America all combine to persuade him that he is an inferior species of Homo sapiens." Stating that schools could not shape their students' fully formed personalities, Lewis concluded, "To expect the colleges to eradicate the inferiority complexes of young black adults is to ask the impossible. And to expect this to come about by segregating black students in black studies under inferior teachers suggests some deficiency of thought."[52]

If one reads past this economist's self-declared expertise in adolescent psychological development, Lewis's doubts about relevance and legitimacy are clear. He certainly did not want to see courses on the university ledger that were anything less than rigorous and recognizable to the most traditional notion of scholarship. In fact, the great majority of black studies scholars felt the same way, knowing they could not afford to appear as anything other than serious in their academic and pedagogic pursuits. Simply put, the stakes were too high: Their professional self-respect was on the line and the future of black studies hung in the balance. Also, no one in the first generation of black studies scholars had any special training in the field, per se. When these scholars began to build the curriculum, then, they were doing the work as historians, sociologists, literary scholars, philosophers, and psychologists.

Given the literal demand for material that could be taught in the classroom (many of the texts that we now consider classics had long been out of print when black studies struggled to emerge), it should come as little surprise that one of the first places to find an emerging set of materials for the black studies curriculum was in the journals that emerged across the disciplines, all eager to examine aspects of the black experience.

The most important new journal in this regard was *The Black Scholar* (first edition in 1969), coedited by Nathan Hare. Other scholarly efforts included the *Journal of Black Studies* (1970), *Afro-American Studies* (1970), and the *Journal of Afro-American Issues* (1972).[53] Like the individuals who ran them and the institutions that supported them (if, indeed, institutional support was forthcoming), these journals underscored the breadth of opinion on the theory and substance of black studies. Prefatory statements and mission statements in the respective first issues reflect their sponsors' political orientation.

The *Journal of Afro-American Issues* was the least doctrinaire. Privately published by Educational Community Consultants Associates, Inc., an organization run by education consultant and author Roosevelt Johnson, the journal merely said that it was "devoted to the scientific determination and explication of issues affecting blacks in America." The journal published essays by academics who were mostly concerned with issues regarding professional development and the social sciences. Essays with titles like "Urban

Teachers as Change Agents: Implications for a Legitimate Curriculum" and "Teaching Black Studies for Social Change" were commonplace.[54]

The *Journal of Black Studies* (*JBS*) and *Afro-American Studies* (*AAS*) were more representative of mainstream liberal arts scholarship. Instead of essays that focused on professional development, the *JBS* and *AAS* brought together an interdisciplinary collection of essays written by political scientists, historians, literary critics, linguists, and sociologists. Sponsored by the City University of New York and the University of California, Los Angeles, respectively, these two journals expounded on the pedagogical thrust and political position of black studies within the academy. At least once an issue readers would encounter such pieces as "In Defense of Black Studies," "Teaching Afro-American History," "Black Studies: Interpretation, Methodology, and the Relationship to Social Movements," "Black Students and the Impossible Revolution," and "The Significance and Challenge of Afro-American Studies."[55]

Both journals were clearly conceived as reflective and critical supplements to the development of black studies programs throughout the country. Indeed, from the very start, *AAS* made its purpose plain: "Interdisciplinary in approach and outlooks, *Afro-American Studies* serves educators and professionals in colleges and other educational institutions initiating and developing curricula, programs, institutes, and faculties in Black Studies."[56] Arthur Smith, the director of UCLA's Afro-American Studies Center and the editor of the *JBS*, was more expansive in enunciating his journal's proposed role, even though the purpose of the journal was not markedly different from that of *AAS*. Smith opened the first issue with a signed editor's message that spoke to the trauma that accompanied the arrival of black studies. He observed, "Seldom in the history of academic disciplines has an area of study been born with so much pain and anguish as Black Studies, also called Afro-American Studies. Discussions initiated, for the most part by university students, produced significant reevaluations of curricula, research, and pedagogy."[57]

Aside from the greater detail in *JBS*'s mission statement, the only aspect that substantively distinguishes the opening statements of the two journals is tone. Smith's *JBS* statement evinced a style that suggested the political militant and racial nationalist. Given the fairly traditional nature of the articles in the journal—beyond their focus on black studies, that is—it would seem that the *JBS* was trying to do two things at once: present itself in the most academically accepted ways and deploy a language that pointed to what literary theorist Houston Baker calls the "moral panic" associated with the development of black studies programs.[58] It existed at the crossroads for legitimacy: It worked hard to be simultaneously academically rigorous and recuperative.

It is this moral panic, this sense of heightened stakes for all concerned, that one witnessed in the debates and protests in places like San Francisco State and Cornell and that one heard in the anxious declarations of someone like Eugene Genovese. But no scholar was more effective than Nathan Hare at addressing and fomenting a moral panic regarding black studies. He was, in this regard, an authenticator of the trauma that led to black studies. Hare's work was published widely, and he appeared, it seemed, just about everywhere a debate on black studies was being enjoined. It is safe to say that much of his desirability as a speaker or contributor to journals grew out of his willingness, if not tendency, to take controversial stances and out of his role as cofounder of *The Black Scholar*, the premiere magazine or journal of criticism related to the field of black studies.

Inside the front cover of the first issue, an unsigned statement (either by Hare or *Black Scholar* coeditor Robert Chrisman) enunciated *The Black Scholar*'s agenda and made plain that black artists and writers had a moral requirement to embrace this agenda as well. Among other things, black academics had to "shape a culture, a politics, an economics, a sense of our past and future history." *The Black Scholar* would serve as the best space where black intellectuals could present their analyses that would attend to these needs. The authors' words were grave and absolute: "We cannot afford division any longer if our struggle is to bear fruit, whether those divisions be between class, caste or function. Nothing black is alien to us."[59]

Taken together, *The Black Scholar*, *Afro-American Studies*, the *Journal of Black Studies*, and *Afro-American Issues* accurately reflect the broad scope of possibility that defined black studies and black intellectual production despite attempts to ignore or limit the field's or individuals' development. But what does it mean that the most important of these journals and the longest lasting as well, *The Black Scholar*, based its founding premise on a moral crisis that called black intellectuals to serve a community or risk being seen as irrelevant? Was the battle over legitimacy and relevance so deeply woven into the fabric of the field? Was it too complicated or simply too unforgiving to think that black scholars ever could be fully integrated (racially, socially, culturally, curricularly, pedagogically) into the academy in meaningful ways?

Answers to these questions, of course, depended on whom one asked. Certainly, *The Black Scholar* and its brethren were not the only sources for these questions or answers. Other scholarship from the early years of black studies demonstrates that there was no shortage of individuals offering their own opinions in the debate. Two critical texts in this regard are

Joyce Ladner's anthology *The Death of White Sociology: Essays on Race and Culture* and Gloria Hull, Patricia Bell Scott, and Barbara Smith's collection *All the Women Are White, All the Blacks Are Men, but Some of Us Are Brave: Black Women's Studies*.[60] These two anthologies are valuable for many reasons, but in terms of memory, they make very clear that so much of the call to the field, the call to a method, and the call to service were articulated in ways that erased or, to be generous, forgot the contributions or even the existence of black women. In these collections we see that the phenomenon of being left behind or forgotten is laced with trauma as well.

LEGITIMACY AND FORGETFULNESS (OR, WHO CAN REMEMBER)

Ladner's *Death of White Sociology* set out to address the ideological shifts that accompanied the changing face of American universities in the 1960s, the increasingly effective student protests for a racially inclusive pedagogy, and the recognition that the long-standing exclusion of the black experience in scholarly discourses was an injustice. Ladner was not forecasting the end of mainstream sociology, but she wanted to call attention to the fact that the sociological discourse that typically branded blacks as deviants would no longer go unchallenged. While *The Death of White Sociology* was a reactive text, spurred on by the rising popularity of black deviance narratives through the 1960s, it also needs to be seen as a generative text.[61] It was generating new narratives and, thus, new ways of remembering.

In her own contribution to the anthology, "Tomorrow's Tomorrow: The Black Woman," Ladner criticized mainstream scholarship for looking at blacks as problems and called for new social science approaches that were significantly more introspective and sensitive to structures of inequality instead of outlier behavior patterns. Ladner argued that there had to be "a strong concern for redefining the problem. Instead of future studies being conducted on *problems* of the Black community as represented by the *deviant perspective*, there must be a redefinition of the *problem as being that of institutional racism*." Ladner continued, "Studies which have as their focal point the alleged deviant *attitudes* and *behavior* of Blacks are grounded within the racist assumptions and principles that only render Blacks open to further exploitation."[62]

Ladner did not invoke black studies scholarship by name, but her critique of the state of current disciplinary practice was absolutely consistent with the collective sense among academics advocating for the establishment of black studies scholarship norms. This was an advocacy that recognized the humanity in blacks and the complexity of their experience. This was also a scholarship that angrily denounced the idea that blacks were a people without a past. But as much as Ladner was in line with the guiding principles of black studies, she differentiated herself from the majority of black studies advocates by paying serious attention to the role of the black woman in the formation of a modern black identity.[63] While *The Death of White Sociology* was clearly inspired as a reaction to the popularity of social science studies that viewed the matriarchal black family structure as pathological, Ladner's work also appeared at a moment of a rising independent black feminist consciousness. In the world of letters, Gloria Hull, Patricia Bell Scott, and Barbara Smith captured much of this 1970s consciousness in their anthology *But Some of Us Are Brave*.

Like *The Death of White Sociology*, *But Some of Us Are Brave* is a work that is simultaneously reactive and generative. Hull, Scott, and Smith felt the need to act on behalf of generations of ignored black women scholars and black women's scholarship. Aside from the fact that *But Some of Us Are Brave* made an important contribution simply from the standpoint of including new voices in scholarly discourses, the book sheds valuable light on black studies by offering an incisive critique of the formative impulses behind the discipline. Hull, Scott, and Smith enthusiastically embraced the new attention that blacks were receiving in lecture halls, seminars, journals, and books, but theirs was a qualified enthusiasm. Revisiting the lead editorial in the first issue of *The Black Scholar* reveals the kind of mindset that had to infuriate black women intellectuals and give feminists pause. In that issue, the editors called for a collective black struggle for independence and recognition and highlighted the black intellectual's role in that fight. "A black scholar recognizes this fact," the editors concluded. "He is a man of both thought and action, a whole man who thinks for his people and acts with them, a man who honors the whole community of black experience."[64] Black women scholars also wanted to honor the whole community of the black experience but understood with utter clarity that racial cohesion meant gendered erasure.

Quite unconsciously, black men's blindness combined with a white feminist racism that ignored or even disparaged black women's feminist consciousness in the early 1970s.[65] As a result, black women's studies scholars were left with few opportunities in which to present work or collaborate with like-minded academics. Hull and her coeditors urged their readers to combine the best aspects of feminist and black studies scholarships in order to fashion a black feminist movement that would, in turn, "lend its political strength to the development of Black women's studies courses, programs, and research, and to the funding they require."[66] This call for a structural shift in the work of the university echoed perfectly the call made just over a decade earlier by black studies advocates like Nathan Hare and restive undergraduates. It also came at a moment of astonishing growth in the amount of attention being paid to the place of black women in society and in academia.

But even though more scholars began to think about and teach black women's history and literature through the 1970s and 1980s (when novelist Alice Walker taught her course on black women writers at Wellesley College in 1972, it was the first such course anywhere in the United States), simply enjoying the fruits of "more attention" could not ward off the collective pain of accumulating daily indignities that emerged from a logic of illegitimacy (put very simply, not all attention is good attention).[67]

The logic of illegitimacy permeated life. As Patricia J. Williams recounted, this was a phenomenon that others, perhaps professional mentors and very likely her mother, warned her about: "I was raised to be acutely conscious of the likelihood that, no matter what degree of professional or professor I became, people would greet and dismiss my black femaleness as unreliable, untrustworthy, hostile, angry, powerless, irrational, and probably destitute."[68]

Throughout *Talking Back*, a mixture of criticism, cultural studies, and memoir, literary critic bell hooks speaks to the same issues that we hear in Williams's painful recollection. Hooks addresses the abiding challenges that women, black women, and progressives face in a cultural and intellectual climate that did not approve of people rising above their station or talking out of order; she says that "black women in higher education [need to] write and talk about our experiences, our survival strategies." Because of her own negative experiences in graduate school, hooks reassures other black women pursuing advanced degrees "who despair, who are frustrated, who are fearful that the experiences they are having are unique." She writes, "I want them to know that they are not alone, that the problems that arise, the obstacles created by racism and sexism are real—that they do exist— they do hurt but they are not insurmountable."[69]

When scholars like Gloria Hull, Patricia Bell Scott, Barbara Smith, Joyce Ladner, Patricia Williams, and bell hooks called attention to the need for black studies to be more expansive, indeed, when they called for the general scholarly engagement with blackness to be more expansive, they were arguing for a reassessment of black memory. It would still be an experience rife with pain and discord, but remembering more honestly the active participants in forging that memory was a powerful and recuperative act. It was not the only recuperative work that had to be done, however.

In February 2003, the Schomburg Center for Research in Black Culture held a conference on black studies.[70] The purpose of the conference was to assess the state of black studies roughly thirty years after the field's establishment and in light of the 2000 federal census report that showed Latinos had just passed black Americans as the nation's largest minority group. Some participants voiced concern that the country's changing demographics suggested a looming crisis for black studies. Others were less worried, citing the centrality of slavery to the country's history and the tortured history of racialized struggles over citizenship since emancipation. Before the conference began, however, Howard Dodson ignited a controversy for his comments concerning the latest generation of black studies scholars.

Dodson, the director of the Schomburg and one of the key figures in the history of the creation and institutionalization of black studies programs (he was, for example, the executive director of the Institute of the Black World for much of the 1970s), declared that he was unhappy with the direction of the new black studies scholarship. He could not understand, for example, the "social utility" of scholarship that studied black homosexuality and felt that a "commitment and clear sense of direction seems to be missing" from black studies scholarship in general.[71] For black studies scholars in lesbian, gay, bisexual, and transgender studies who are convinced that they are working at the cutting edge of black studies scholarship, this comment was a slap in the face. It also amounted to a kind of intellectual policing that black studies scholars could anticipate from certain quarters in academia but were less prepared to accept from within the black studies community. Further, Dodson's comments were a declaration of sorts that black queer studies scholars had forgotten their obligation. In a strange twist, a founder of black studies was feeling traumatized because this new generation of academics possessed a memory of the black experience that did not fall into line with his.

Pre-dating the "State of Black Studies" conference by five years, literary scholar Dwight McBride wrote insightfully about the politics of straight, black authenticity and how it could silence alternative voices. McBride argued that "there are any number of narratives that African American intellectuals employ to qualify themselves in the terms of race discourse to speak for the race. And while one routinely witnesses the use of narratives of racial discrimination, narratives of growing up poor and black and elevating oneself through education and hard work . . . we could scarcely imagine an instance in which narrating or even claiming one's gay or lesbian identity would authenticate or legitimate oneself as a racial representative."[72] Although he didn't invoke memory literally, in writing about narratives and about race and about poverty and about uplift, McBride got to the core of so many challenges that have always weighed upon black scholars and students and led to the calls for a curriculum that was relevant to a set of life experiences that white scholars had chosen to forget, or to not even learn about in the first place.

Five years before McBride's astute observations were published, I was in graduate school, beginning to work in earnest on my dissertation—an intellectual history of black radical intellectuals in the New Deal era. Facilitating my progress toward a degree was the generous support I enjoyed from the Ford Foundation and the Danforth Foundation. The Ford Minority Predoctoral Fellowship and the Dorothy Danforth Compton Fellowship were designed to increase the numbers of underrepresented minority faculty on the nation's campuses by offering generous support for graduate school study and, importantly, for annual conferences where fellows could present their work in progress and form networks that would serve them well in their future careers. At the turn of the century and in the wake of third-rail politics of affirmative action, the Ford Foundation changed the terms of its program so that the competition was open to anyone who could demonstrate a commitment to diversity in higher education. Since this change is so new, it remains unclear what the long-term effect on the nature of the program and the network of Ford fellows teaching on our nation's campuses will be. Things are much more clear when it comes to the Dorothy Danforth Compton Fellowship. More than a decade before Ford changed the terms of its support, the Danforth Foundation simply ended its program.

I was sitting in the audience of what would turn out to be the final Danforth Compton fellows annual meeting when a representative from the foundation announced the termination of the program because the foundation was going to turn its focus to supporting initiatives in elementary schools. It was hard to argue the logic of the decision: Funding graduate students with the mission of diversifying the academy was, at minimum, a twenty- to thirty-year project with uncertain results. Supporting innovative programming in elementary schools had the potential for a quicker return on investment and traceable results. At the same time, learning that a beloved program was being dismantled made everyone in the room feel like they had been punched in the gut.

Tensions were high.

Indeed, this is the only explanation I have for the interaction I had later that evening with a fellow from Brown University who decided to challenge me on my racial legitimacy and my commitment to a program of supporting the diversification of the professoriate. There were three or four of us sitting around in a hotel room, talking about the announcement from earlier in the day, wondering if the Danforth Foundation truly understood the importance of the fellowship and how long such a program took to bear fruit. We were talking from a place of pain when I suddenly became the focus of this individual's anger. He turned to me with questions that were as much accusations and prejudicial observation as anything else: "What do you know about the challenges facing the black community? You have the privilege of being light-skinned, after all. What do you know about struggle? You look and sound middle class. My brother is in jail on drug charges."

Given the fact that my inquisitor was fueled by several drinks, I probably should have dismissed the comments as some outward manifestation of unresolved personal issues (some private and inescapable trauma), but perhaps my own frustration with the foundation's decision had already exhausted my patience. Also, the last place I wanted to find myself was outcast from what I thought was a gathering of peers facing similar kinds of academic, professional, and even personal struggles. I should have ignored him, but I didn't.

Telling him to get out of my face and to refrain from lecturing me, I pointed out that I couldn't help my appearance and that I should not be asked to apologize for the circumstances in which I grew up. Also, I wasn't convinced that I was any less black than he because I didn't know anyone in jail. Finally, he ought to know that my grandfather was the first executive director of the United Negro College Fund and that my inquisitor should be grateful for his work.

Immediately after these last words left my mouth I felt miserable. Just as he played a race card against me, I played some sort of uplift meets race loyalty meets race royalty card against him. And to be honest, I knew that just as I wasn't responsible for my appearance or my class background, I had no right to take credit for work that belonged to my grandfather. As for me, I really hadn't done anything yet to earn the righteous indignation I felt on that issue.

I don't recall precisely what happened next, but I do know the conversation ended quickly. I also know that I decided not to join the party that was forming next door. Most likely, I went back to my room, feeling very alone at a conference of over 100 underrepresented minority scholars, all of whom were, like me, pursuing the doctorate with a goal of becoming a professor and changing the face of the academy.

I was not proud of my behavior that evening because I recognized that I tried to make my pain and discomfort his. As I look back, in that moment we were both guilty of forgetting the traumas that described our emerging professional lives and, truly, why we were even there in the first place.

5

THE SILENCES IN A
CIVIL RIGHTS NARRATIVE

BILL T. JONES: Do you want your children to know pain?

ELIZABETH ALEXANDER: Yes, but I want to reserve the right to
throw myself in front of the car.

BILL T. JONES: Can you throw yourself in front of history?

—Elizabeth Alexander and Bill T. Jones,
DeVane Lectures, Yale University

JAMES BALDWIN: Black people need witnesses; in this hostile
world which thinks, um, everything is white.

INTERVIEWER: Are you still in despair about the world?

BALDWIN: I never have been in despair about the world, I'm
enraged by the world.

INTERVIEWER: Enraged, alright.

BALDWIN: I don't think I'm in despair. I can't afford despair.
I can't tell my nephew, my niece; you can't, you can't tell the
children there's no hope.

—Film interview with James Baldwin,
James Baldwin: The Price of the Ticket

What do we tell our children? What stories do we pass along so that they
know their history? It is unavoidable that they will learn the past that belongs to the nation, typically a mythic narrative of exceptionalism and universal citizenship. They will absorb the narratives in their school assem-
blies, through advertisements, and via the media. That past that belongs to
an aggrieved people—in James Baldwin's case and dare I say my own—is a

different narrative. While the African American past is no less exceptional than the mythic American narrative of belonging, it is crafted in an often cruel juxtaposition to that same notion of belonging. Stories of denial need to be passed along, to be sure, but it is important to ask when and how our children need to learn that the American narrative may not belong to them.

During the height of Jim Crow, black parents had to prepare their children for a life of denial. Ray Sprigle, the journalist who crossed the color line in the late 1940s in an effort to understand the black experience, saw for himself that a child's literal survival depended on this kind of education. But Sprigle also saw the way that black parents wrestled with the timing of that lesson. "When do you begin teaching your child how he is to live as a Negro?" Sprigle wondered. "When do you begin teaching him the difference between black and white—not as colors but as races? When do you begin teaching him how to live under the iron rule of a master race that regards him as an inferior breed? When do you begin teaching him that, for him, the Constitution and the Declaration of Independence are scraps of paper? Those are the questions that every Negro mother and father has to answer."[1]

Wondering when and even what to tell the children resonates differently in the early twenty-first century than it did during the age of legally sanctioned racial segregation, when the systemic cultural practice of racial demarcation (what is often referred to as "racial etiquette") flourished. Structured and informal systems of racial difference certainly still exist, but as a second generation of post–Civil Rights and Voting Rights Acts children grow up, as they see in the most simplistic symbolic way that at least a black man actually can be the president of the country, it would seem that parents have a choice they lacked before. However, because race still has the potential to strip away at any given moment all the accumulated material and political privilege that even well-placed blacks might enjoy, children need to be prepared for a narrative in which they cannot see themselves, their past, or their future. Sprigle's question from 1949, then, resonates just as loudly today: When do you tell the children?

Clearly my father believed that he was addressing this dilemma when he told me a handful of times about "the way things were" and that I always had to be careful about how I carried myself in life. But as I would come to learn, there were significant gaps in my father's stories and lessons about how to navigate this country's racial landscape. For the longest time I presumed that my father simply didn't like thinking about his own past. What I eventually understood is that my father saw his past in transactional terms: He didn't want to engage his history because he felt he could not afford to.

What happens then? What happens when silence is the determining voice in a narrative about belonging? What happens when history is pushed aside in the faith that doing so would protect the future?

DISCOVERING MY MEMORIES

Each spring I teach the introductory survey of the postemancipation black experience, African American History: Emancipation to the Present. It is a large lecture course by my university's standards, and I usually need seven or eight graduate students to cover the necessary number of discussion sections. In any given year I know most, but not all, of the graduate assistants assigned to my course. In this context, the start of the 2010 spring term was fairly unremarkable. Shortly after our first meeting, I received an e-mail from one of these new colleagues, Chris Johnson. Chris wanted to know if he had overheard correctly that I had grown up in Montgomery, Alabama. He had been raised in Lowndes County and Montgomery—both places, as it happens, that by the time we got to the mainstream civil rights history would figure prominently in the course I was about to lead. My response was fairly short but brimmed with the beginnings of many revelations:

Hi Chris,

I was just in Alabama for two years. My father was in the Air Force and taught at the Air War College in Montgomery—Maxwell-Gunther Air Force Base. We lived on Lott Drive (wherever that happens to be).

My memories of the area are slight—mainly focused upon the world view of a 6 year-old. We're talking my pet hamster, the train that ran past the end of the development around my bedtime, and walking with my older brother and sister to the local 7-11 (although it wasn't that) to get candy.[2]

Chris's follow-up was also short, but it pushed me down a path of exploration and discovery that led directly to my efforts at memoir:

It's incredible how many connections people have to Montgomery through Maxwell.

That's a nice neighborhood. One of the city's main tributaries, Vaughn Road, runs nearby. The area features some of the more expensive real estate in Montgomery—those homes that aren't locked inside gated subdivisions that is. I imagine that the neighborhood must have been newly developed then.

My father was a NY cop during the 1970s, but he would visit family in Alabama. He told me that the area near your childhood home was all farmland then, and he kicked himself for not investing when he had the chance.[3]

I read past the relatively familiar phenomenon of the less than six degrees of separation that links the lives of African Americans who pursue a career in academia. Instead, I was simply mystified by Chris's residential assessment: My family lived in a nice neighborhood? How far was our home from the air force base? Was the sundry store still there? Did trains still rumble down the tracks? We lived in a nice neighborhood?

I sat down at the keyboard, navigated to Google Maps, and typed in "Lott Drive, Montgomery, Alabama." Simple enough. While I didn't doubt that Chris's assessment of Lott Drive was correct for at least *some* portion of the road, I thought I'd see where that road traveled and if the telltale signs of railroad tracks would help me figure out where I lived along what *had* to be a long road.

Lott Drive came up immediately, and it was only two blocks long.

I lived in a nice neighborhood?

On a lark I decided to try the streetview function in Google Maps. I knew it wouldn't work, but why not try?

It worked.

Not only did it work, but the image that filled the screen was of the house in which I spent two years of my early childhood. But perhaps this wasn't the house. Yes, we did live in a two-story California stucco–style house, but there had to be more of the same in the development. It turns out that there weren't. My family lived in this nice neighborhood and owned this stylistically singular corner house. Everyone else lived in large, one-floor, brick ramblers. My first thought was that we must have been very conspicuous. As I would soon discover, we were conspicuous but not for reasons that immediately occurred to me—although they should have.

Still mesmerized by this discovery, I zoomed out and began to look for other markers of my childhood. Right there! The railroad tracks. Satellite view tells me that trains no longer run there. More likely, upwardly mobile professionals take advantage of the greenbelt for jogging. Regardless, one quick look at the tracks confirmed for me that my spatial sense was on target, though horribly skewed by a six-year-old's memory. The tracks told me where my home was, alright, but that long trek back from the break in the barbed wire fence at the edge of the tracks to my family home wasn't quite two blocks. Lots of memories were made and lost in the meadow that

Lott Drive, Montgomery, Alabama (author's collection)

separated the tracks from my bedroom window. I don't see the meadow now—just homes. For all I know, they were there all the time.

A six-year-old has no business being near train tracks and then wandering back home either through meadows or neighbors' backyards unless, of course, he was following his older brother and doing his bidding. Every so often we would go to the corner convenience store, buy some Lik-m-Aid or a *Mad Magazine* or *Cracked* trading cards, and head home. But we didn't take the path back along the streets. Instead we'd go out the parking lot to the rear of the store and walk to the train tracks. If a slow-moving freight train came along, we would climb the ladder to a boxcar and ride there to the break in the barbed wire fence. If the train was moving a lot faster, we'd put a penny on the track to watch it get flattened. The first to find the penny that had been shot off the rails in who knows what perilous direction would get to keep it. I still remember the warmth of the coin on that rare occasion when my brother let me find it. I can only hope that he let our sister or our cousins also have a fair shot at finding the penny. I'm pretty certain I was allowed to find it, since that was the best guarantee I wouldn't tell my parents where we had gone or why.

Still marveling at this flood of memories, I went back to Google Maps streetview to see if I could find that convenience store. I knew exactly where to look. A few seconds of browsing told me that the store was now gone and had been replaced either by a gas station or an Applebees. I'm pretty sure my former source of empty calories and preadolescent gross-out humor is presently the gas station.

Now fully enthralled by the marvel of Google Maps streetview function, I decided to virtually walk my way back to the California stucco I called home—the legit way, not via the train tracks. I didn't make it 100 electronic yards before I stopped in a different set of tracks. I *knew* that building. The second I saw it, I *knew* that building.

Zooming out to satellite view provided confirmation. This was the private school, Montgomery Academy to be precise, for which I took an admissions test when I was about six. For years, my memory told me that I went to take that test with a few other kids from the neighborhood and that they, or rather, their parents, really wanted them to get in. I went along for fun. A few weeks or months later, I realized that I must not have done well on that test, since I never enrolled.

Some years later—maybe as many as another six, maybe ten—I was talking to my mother about all of this, and she told me that my memory was wrong. In fact, I did quite well on the test, I had gotten in, and the school really wanted me to matriculate. For reasons that still confound me, I have no recollection of what she said next, if anything.

All of this—the coincidence with Chris, the Google Maps discoveries, the truncated memory of my school admission—was still just a neat story and nothing more. Wanting to share all of this with my brother, sister, and father—my mother had passed away four years earlier and with her went much of our family past—I sent them an e-mail and the URL for that two-floor California stucco.

Within minutes my brother responded.

My memory was correct; that was the house in which we had lived. And yes, those were the train tracks where we braved danger on innumerable occasions. After that, however, his story about those years in Alabama was markedly different from my own. We began to exchange e-mails as I discovered aspects of my family's history that simply weren't mine. The first e-mails were short; the latter, more expansive. Both sets of e-mails astonished me but in wholly different ways.

The first rupture in my narrative of Montgomery, Alabama, revolved around the school. I had known for years that I had at least taken the school's entrance exam. Until I began to share my Google Maps discovery with my family, it had never occurred to me that my siblings might also have had some interaction with Montgomery Academy. My brother's e-mail— the first in our several-days-long exchange—parted these clouds: "Actually,

I don't know if you were ever told, when you, me and Karen took that test and passed we were the first blacks ever to pass the test in get in the Academy. Made the newspapers. Too many Klan kids at the school. That's why we did not go."[4]

"I don't know if you were ever told." The words lingered like something simultaneously there and not there.

Though spectral, the story is clear: Brian assumed that I knew that we all took the school's entrance exam. This was news to me. More significant, however, was the fact that Brian, Karen, and Jonathan Holloway had been on the cusp of actually being part of "the movement." That national narrative of America exceptionalism that I always believed I was too young to have experienced was, it turns out, dramatically close to being my own lived history.

My father was a career officer in the U.S. Air Force. (Although he had turned down two commissions to West Point—something his father could never understand—my father eventually joined the military anyway.) He had lived in seclusion for weeks with his squadron during the Cuban Missile Crisis; flown KC-135 tanker-refuelers during the Vietnam War; been chased by Russian fighter pilots when his plane intentionally violated Soviet airspace; was convinced for years that he was under surveillance by the air force for reasons he never fully divulged beyond saying that he took on a lot of "extra missions" to secure better pay; and had refused to let my mother attend the March on Washington for fear of her safety and his security clearance. Throughout his career, my father was one of the highest-ranking black officers in the air force. His accomplishments and advancements were indications that a new narrative about American possibility was being written.

All of this is to say that I grew up in a family that I understood to have brushed up against pivotal moments of change and to have benefited enormously from the gains of the civil rights movement while never directly engaging it. At least this is what my own gentle perusing of family history could ever indicate. My maternal grandfather, the one who had served as the first executive director of the United Negro College Fund, had been in the struggle for decades. He was a member of Franklin Roosevelt's Black Cabinet, serving as a race adviser to Harold Ickes, the secretary of the interior, but somewhere along the line the struggle faded from view as far as the family's public engagement with history was concerned.

It was quite a shock, then, to discover that I was on the verge of being part of the movement myself, only to be yanked back to my safer world where I worried about a short-lived hamster, bought candy from the convenience store, and hopped slow-moving freight trains back home.

My brother's follow-up e-mail—the one generated by my almost frantic entreaties for more information—provided a little more detail:

> Made all the newspapers.
> It was a big deal.
> This place was a target for all civil rights activists.
> When we all passed it was a BIG DEAL!
> And mom and dad were afraid now that we were in the newspapers.
> Didn't want to become the next posters for the next Klan rally.[5]

In another e-mail, immediately following this one, Brian went on at greater length and in more evocative detail:

> It was a very weird time.
> Not steppin' in the neighbors' yard was no joke.
> Living in that neighborhood was no joke.
> You were one of the neighborhood darlings, so young, you would go up and speak to Klan folk and they got all nervous and jerky because they liked you and you were so cute.
> screwed them up.
> . . . the other kids were allowed to play in our yard.
> the only neighbors that we could visit were the ones from the military—which oddly enough lived behind us and across the street.
> we had all sorts of joy, every day.
> when karen and i went to school we would get chastised, harassed, intimidated and [ostracized] by the blacks.
> we were the only ones who did not have lunch vouchers, and could actually pay for our lunch.
> That made it worse.
> And we got on the bus with all the white kids after school.
> Trouble started when we would actually do our homework and raise our hands in class. Pretty soon, I just stopped talking.
> The biggest event in school was when Hank Aaron hit 715 HR, black teachers cried silently because it was too dangerous to celebrate. There was such a joy in all the blacks' eyes, the lunchroom servers, the janitors, etc, Everyone was smiling with their eyes and saying nothing. It was like "We did it!"
> I did not see that again, until Gramma cried when Tiger won the Masters. It was one of those moments.
> White teachers were pissed and angry.
> Never forget that day.[6]

I'm comfortable assuming my brother meant to say, "I will never forget that day" or "Never forgot that day." However, taking creative license when I read that line, I actually see my brother closing the e-mail with literal directions to me: "Never forget that day." Naturally, this assertion, even fabricated as an assertion, is an impossibility, since nothing my brother offered was part of my recollected past. Actually, I did remember the neighbors behind us and across the street. They were both in the air force as well, but I only remember them, no one else. It never occurred to me that there might have been a larger reason behind this. (It also never occurred to me that the neighbors I never got to know were probably pushed to the edge of their sensibilities because my mother likely looked white to them and they couldn't help but see my father's obvious blackness.)

I followed up with my sister and father. Was Brian right?

Karen responded that because Brian was two years older, he simply had a different set of recollections than she did. But as she thought more about it, the general ambience of the time sounded true. She wrote, "I was called names myself at Cloverdale—'oreo'—and I had no knowledge of what it meant. The military kids were definitely ostracized. You could try out for teams and stuff but there was a townie flavor to decision making. . . . I remember mom saying that it blew them away when cousins (Brian, Pam, and I) could perform at the highest levels. Unheard of!"[7]

This was sufficient confirmation for me. My father, unfortunately, was a different story all together. He has never been one to look backward. Rather, he sprinted to get ahead, desperate even, to leave his past behind.

It was worth a shot, though. Certainly he had something to say about all of this.

I remember being very excited when his e-mail arrived. The excitement lasted all of a few seconds. It took that long to read the entire note: "That was really something to view the old home and to relive all the things that happened during that time in our lives. So many things and so many moments!!!! Remind me to tell you the story of how we bought the home."[8]

That was it. But still, there was something there.

Too excited about the e-mails that kept coming in from my brother and sister and too intrigued by the closing sentence in his e-mail that suggested a powerful story about busting racial covenants, integrating neighborhoods, or engaging in some quietly subversive civil rights action, I decided to pick up the phone and press my father on the issues.

The housing story was a nonstarter. It turns out that my father went with one of the leading real estate firms in the city, Blitz and Golinsky.

The neighborhood kids in Montgomery (I am on the left) (author's collection)

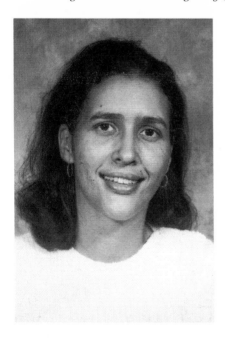

Kay Holloway, my mother
(author's collection)

(My father made the conscious decision to go with a real estate firm that had a Jewish surname. He felt that this firm would show him a full range of properties and not just point him in the direction of Montgomery's black enclaves.) To their credit, the Blitz and Golinsky realtors said they'd be happy to work with him to find him a place to buy. Shortly thereafter, he was under contract for a home three doors down from Montgomery's mayor.

Since we didn't move into that house, I assumed there was a great story to be told about race, housing, integration, privilege, and access. If the story is there (and, really, how could it not be?) it's lost to time. My father simply recalls that the sellers wanted to change the closing cost distribution after the contracts were signed. They argued that my father was getting a good deal and that he shouldn't be "bitching" about the change. Blitz and Golinsky kept at it and found the place that would become our home.

Reaching out to my father to find out what really happened with the Montgomery Academy was also disappointing. Although he recalled that we took the exam and that "something" ran in the newspapers, he insisted he had no memory of why the Holloway kids never enrolled.[9] But just when I felt I had run into a dead end with him, he started to talk in greater detail about Montgomery Academy and even the neighborhood where we lived.

"It was all part of a greater strategy," he said. "Montgomery Academy was the place where Montgomery's power elite sent their children: the bankers, the politicians, the doctors, the lawyers, and the generals at Maxwell [Air Force Base]." He continued:

> The generals at Maxwell had a plan for me. You see, I was the first black to teach at the Air War College, and they wanted to make me a general. I had been a line officer, meaning I hadn't spent my career pushing paper around on a desk somewhere but had actually risked my life time and time again. They really wanted to change the face of the air force, and part of that was finding the right kind of officer and, with him, the right kind of family. Our family was tall, your mother looked right and came from the right background, you kids were all doing well in school and could probably cut it at Montgomery Academy. The generals met with the other leaders at the school and made the case that you three should take the test and, if you passed, be admitted. That's really all I remember about Montgomery Academy. For them and their small way of looking at the world, we were the right kind of family.

But I didn't want any of that. I didn't want to be their poster child. I didn't want to be a general. I just wanted to get out of the air force. They had taken enough of me.[10]

(Later on, in a follow-up conversation, my father was more pointed, saying that he had to get out of the air force because he was "tired of killing people." My father also feels to this day that the death of his first child, David—an older brother I never met—was caused by radiation exposure at one of the air force bases where the family was stationed. All of the pilots had to walk around with dosimeters on their chests to gauge radiation exposure, but there was nothing available for the families. That the air force "had taken enough of" him reads on multiple levels, all shot through with trauma.)

When we hung up, my mind was reeling. Part of the dislocation was certainly due to the frustration that my newly imagined place in the grand civil rights narrative was being denied by a father who couldn't remember the most important detail in the story. What was more disorienting, however, is that my father could confirm the immense challenges of the era—soldiers coming home from Vietnam and suffering further degradation and isolation due to their role in that catastrophe, the constant burden of racial tightrope walking—and that all of this was news to me. Granted, I was approaching my seventh birthday when my family left Montgomery, and so, in a very real way, I should be excused from knowing these histories then. But *never* knowing these things? Never understanding that my father actually broke a color line and made a measure of military history? Never knowing that I could only remember children whose parents were in the military because these were the only people who would interact with us? How could this be possible?

A father myself, I understand the desire to protect a young child from certain ugliness in life, but erasure was a different phenomenon all together. Then, a coincidental moment came that I can only describe as cheaply cinematic. Just a few days after this part of my family's past was reconstructed, and while I was still processing why it was unknown to me, I came across a box of our mother's possessions that my brother had put together and sent to me for Christmas. I hadn't ventured near the box since it had arrived a month earlier, avoiding the emotions that were going to accompany opening this archive.

Perhaps emboldened, perhaps excited, I opened the box and started tracing my own childhood through report cards, pictures, and crude art projects my mother had kept. And then I stumbled across a document that I had

*Lt. Col. Wendell Holloway, my father
(author's collection)*

never seen before. It is dated July 4, 1968, and addressed to "My dear son."
I wasn't quite one year old at this point, so I knew that I wasn't the "dear
son" in the letter.

July 4, 1968
My dear son,

   You recently questioned me as to "why" I would take the time to fight
for America when this same America has placed so many troubles in the
path of black men. I know that my answer has been long in coming but
your question was so honest, so full of deep, pointed thought! I must

confess, an answer seemed very hard to find and even harder to express. But as I worried about your throwing fire crackers against my orders and reflected on my thoughts of the deadly "firecrackers" we Americans are using to kill and wound an enemy, I found your answer. I only hope that you can understand a little of what I am saying and wishing for you in my "answer."

Son, I am here because I belong here! The black people of America have *been there* during all of the many crises that have faced this most magnificent, most lovely, most confusing country! We have shared these crises with our blood and our strength. It is our continuing heritage to be a part of the building of America, and a part of her strength. We must share in her hope of freedom for all men, everywhere!

I believe that through my sacrifices this year, I can guarantee a little better chance for you to realize the *full* benefits of a free country! Just as I eagerly joined in the fight for the right to vote, to have a chance to cast my *free* ballot, freely, so too must I fight for the right of other men to cast their ballot. And son, the thousands of other black men here realize too, that this fight for a free ballot is equally a fight for a free country. To fight for one, you fight for the other . . . guarantee one, and you guarantee the other! We know that the sound of free ballots being cast is the beautiful sound of freedom that we so want for our children and the children of all people wherever they might live.

You must realize that the sacrifice you are making in having your dad away and the sacrifices of the thousands of other black men *and* white men are forcing the dream of freedom forward.

Yours in love and understanding,
Dad

Having recently discovered how Google Maps could refresh my own understanding of my family past, I went straight back to Google and began to enter in phrases from this letter. I knew it wasn't Baldwin, but it was in the tradition of the letter to his nephew that prefaced *The Fire Next Time*. Nothing came up, no matter how many different ways I searched for the original author. And then I found myself coming to an inescapable if unbelievable conclusion: My father might be the author of the letter.

My brother, the best family historian we have left, wasn't sure of this himself. It seemed right to him, given everything that was going on in the world and in our home, but he didn't remember the letter. I called my father back, and he confirmed, without going into any details, that it sure sounded like a letter he wrote. He didn't recall giving it to Brian, though, but I simply had to understand that his memory wasn't what it used to be and, after all, it was such a challenging time.

I was left with one question: Whose father was this? I now understood that he broke barriers at the Air War College and that the generals there wanted him to break even more. I had long known that he didn't want his family, especially his wife, to be too conspicuous for fear of some sort of professional or political backlash—a fear that was substantiated by the fact that immediately after he left the air force, his taxes were audited for five straight years. But, in the privacy of letters that he wrote and maybe never sent, was my father some sort of militant patriotic race warrior? Was his personal silence on these issues something that he felt the need to pass along to his children? Is that what made us the right kind of family? And, if so, what were the costs of being that kind of family? What did we give up, if anything, by living a life of structured silences?

Yes, I lost my (highly romanticized) chance to be a civil rights warrior like the brave souls in Little Rock, but really, since I had no idea that this was even a possibility, I never felt any sort of remorse or loss about this when I was growing up. But now that I know about it, what am I to make of it? The clinical assessment might be that my father insisted on letting the movement's frontline activists pass my family by and that my family simply rode the activists' coattails to a life of material comfort and advantage. Being the right kind of family certainly allowed for that kind of advantage-taking.

But maybe I should make of this something that is much larger than a single narrative of a single family in the civil rights era. Since Chris Johnson asked me if I grew up in Montgomery, I have had many occasions to ponder the significance of this found history. Putting aside the exceptionalism that the Montgomery Academy represented and that the air force generals desired, what we are left with is a fairly typical story of a family struggling to find a way to fit into a viciously poisoned social and political climate. It is, perhaps, a mundane story of parents working hard to protect their children in the way they thought best, hoping to leave for them a better future than the present and past they had known. Put another way, it is a story of not telling stories with the faith that being the right kind of family would pay dividends that extended beyond a child's ability to imagine a heroic past.

Thinking about my own discovery of my family's past—not my past as it turns out, but theirs—compelled me to think with greater breadth and depth about those family memories that were mine either because I had experienced them firsthand or because they had been given to me in such a compelling fashion that they became mine. One thing I realized is that so much of my upbringing was about behaving properly. Until now, I had not stopped to wonder what else might be involved in that training, beyond the need to have good manners. Truly, the logic of being "the right kind of family" was a constant in my life, even though I can only ever recall the phrase coming from my father, and then only in the context of how the military wanted its leadership cadres to look. There have been innumerable moments in my past when I simply knew I had to act in a certain way. I suppose some might simply call this being "raised right" (and I still do smile when older women—and it's always older women—say that my mother clearly raised me right). But, in truth, it was all learned and acculturated behavior.

Thinking about the absence of the Montgomery Academy history inspired me to pursue other dimly recalled moments from my heretofore idyllic childhood. When I did, a fairly predictable thing happened: The more I considered my past with greater care, the more discoveries I made. Further, the more discoveries I made, the more I realized that so many of them were easily categorized into "types." While there is a wide range of ways to parse the different elements involved in making the right kind of family, there are a few phenomena or processes that stand out when I reflect on my own experiences. We struggled with fitting in, respected our inheritance, and noted generational changes and the challenges that accompanied them. All the while, of course, we had to keep up appearances.

FITTING IN

It feels safe to suggest that the vast majority of blacks who belong to the right kind of family have endured accusations of acting white or of behaving like an Uncle Tom (if male, that is). I was no different.

Beyond the initial shock and hurt feelings of the "Uncle Tom" comments, I never paid much attention to them, since even then I could tell that the people who offered them were only cool in the moment. My plan (not that I could always articulate what it was at any given time, but I knew I had one, as delayed gratification is a touchstone of my upbringing) would take longer to realize, and I was confident that I would end up okay. I did not understand the "acting white" comments, since it never occurred to me that white folks had a monopoly on good manners, doing well in school, and being well spoken. But perhaps that was a myopia that was ingrained in me from the earliest years. When I was younger, I simply didn't understand that some black folks felt that whites claimed this monopoly and that some white folks absolutely believed they had earned it. Over time, I came to realize that there were subtleties to this belief system that added texture to what, exactly, blacks and whites felt about the cultural monopoly on good manners and a proper raising. Among whites, for example, it became clear to me — and I confess that it took me decades to see it in focus — that there were more than a few bleeding hearts who found their near-monopoly on good manners to be a national tragedy in which they were not in the least way implicated. The presumption, of course, was still there, and I could hear it when people marveled at how articulate I happened to be. I also discovered over time a range of self-confident possession among African Americans. There's really no surprise here, but there have been more than a few occasions in my life when it took a while for the obvious to exert itself.

The funny thing, however, is that the "acting white" and "Uncle Tom" comments weren't part of my childhood. As far as I can recall, I was always in very diverse classrooms. This is another way of saying that I wasn't the only person of color present, although I was often one of only two or three black children in the room. In high school I found myself in a two-track environment where my "gifted" or "advanced" classes were overwhelmingly white and Asian and my extracurricular commitments in track and football meant that I was around many more African American students. It only took being teased once for "talking white" for me to learn how to code switch. The switching, as it happens, was so successful that I wasn't even aware I was doing it until my mother started chuckling when I was talking on the phone to one of my best friends from the football team — it had to be either Keith or Eric Dove, cousins, and the folks with whom I spent virtually all of my free time.

Although unaware of it, apparently I was completely comfortable linguistically moving between my black and white worlds (even though I would never have thought of them in that way — my friendship circles simply intersected in some places and not at all in others). I carried this sense of comfort with me to college. But in that cauldron where young people exploit their opportunities to remake themselves in ways that they believe will arm them for the world, I somehow became someone who acted white and, in a moment of true humiliation, was dismissed as nothing but an Uncle Tom. There was a measure of cultural confusion here for me, since the peers who leveled these accusations at me were, from what I could tell, pretty much just like me. We were all students at Stanford, and most of us came from a class and cultural background where we shared much more in common than not.

I didn't get it then, but the taxonomy of elite college representational politics did not leave an obvious space for me:

- I did not belong to any Jack and Jill Club (or its correlates) growing up—my mother didn't care for those kinds of elite black groups—and so I lacked the proper cultural references when I moved to Palo Alto.
- I wasn't a black radical revolutionary in high school and didn't see the need to become one in college.
- I was "light-skinned" and didn't have a hang-up about it.
- I did not know what a step show was when I was invited to one my freshman year (I'll confess that I am still absolutely mortified by this fact).
- I am not even sure if I was or was not a member of the Black Student Union, even though it was one of the few groups I checked off to receive my portion of student activity fees that Stanford "took" from us at the start of each quarter.
- I was too terribly shy to attend any of the social mixers sponsored by Ujamaa (the themed residential dormitory at Stanford that focused on the black experience).
- I thought the "controversial" T-shirt the Black Student Union selected one year that said, "It's a Black Thing, You Wouldn't Understand," was really clever, but I felt I hadn't done enough to earn the right to wear it myself.
- And then, in the final blow, when I had the opportunity to pick my housing as I headed into sophomore year, I moved into the Delt House.

Technically, this was the house for the national fraternity Delta Tau Delta. In reality, it was a jock house. The guys who lived there were a mix of varsity athletes: some baseball players, a few wrestlers, and some football players (mostly linebackers and interior lineman, a virtually all-white group at the time). We were also on probation with the national fraternity, since we actually didn't do anything that defined us as a chapter. The national wanted a presence at Stanford, and this particular group of disaffected student-athletes wanted a place to live away from the geeks who didn't like them in the first place. I wasn't disaffected at all when it came to academics and was basically geeky myself; but my best friends wanted to live there, and so I joined them. What this meant, though, is that I lived solely with white people and I did so by choice. In my junior year this decision was detailed in the *Stanford Daily* by future memoirist and *Newsweek* and *International Herald Tribune* editor Marcus Mabry. The article was about African Americans who lived in white fraternities and was accompanied by a photograph of me standing on the Delt house lawn with two of my "brothers." A few days after the article ran, I discovered that I had been labeled an Uncle Tom.[11]

I was caught entirely by surprise. I know that I talked to my father about this and remember that he offered what he felt to be a consoling statement: It was just a matter of time before I ran into this kind of intragroup racism. He said he had been called all sorts of names when he went to college and then even more names when he went to Officer Candidate School. When he started OCS, he was one of a group of blacks in his cohort, and they all had to deal with a series of good ol' boy superior officers and systems of structured denial. Having been targeted for failure and on the verge of washing out, the black officer candidates wanted to band together and pursue a complaint up the chain of command. As it happened, my father demurred, because some of those good ol' boys took a liking to him and moved him along. I do not know what my father did to earn this protection beyond being willing to party with his superiors, but he had earned it and he wanted to keep it. Because he has always strategized about the future, I could sense no evidence of bitterness about these episodes when he recalled them. His choices, as he liked to point out, so clearly worked in his and then his family's favor. If my father wasn't called an Uncle Tom by his black classmates, the equivalent or the misplaced worse was certainly leveled on this or other occasions.

I understood that my father shared this story with me as one of those painful life lessons that parents share with children. This was an attempt, no doubt, to gird me for further disappointments along a racial line. Knowing the history and pattern of our interactions, I can't imagine what else he could have said that would have felt real to me, but I clearly recall being disappointed that the best advice I was being given on this occasion amounted to needing to have a stiff upper lip. My father definitely did not take this occasion to tell me in finer detail that this was the sort of thing I had to be prepared for, as emotional blackmail was native to the place where the right kind of families resided. But, upon reflection, I can tell that these life lessons, whether they came from my father, my mother, or a grandparent, all accumulated in such a way that I understood that part of being the right kind of family meant living a life of privilege and policing. This was not a Du Boisian double-consciousness, even though that certainly made sense to me when I first came across it in graduate school, but something that had become so seamless and ingrained that it became presumptively real or true. Quite simply, it was what it was.

INHERITANCE

Of course, getting to the point of something simply being "what it was" took years if not generations of hard work on both sides of the color line and hard work along class lines as well. And if you're like me and grew up in an environment where self-reflection did not come naturally, so much of this hard work was just a manifestation of life. You muddled through, focused on the task at hand, bit your tongue, and kept moving ahead.

My maternal grandmother was a case in point. A fair-skinned woman with "good hair" who certainly could have passed for white should she have ever been inclined, Viola Trent, née Scales, was not to the manor born, but she came from a family of material resources, at least within the confines of the black community in Winston-Salem, North Carolina. Her father, William Scales, was an entrepreneur in the truest sense of the term. At various times (mostly overlapping) he owned the local bank, the mortgage company, the bail bond office, the movie theater, the pool hall, the bus company, the funeral home, and a few restaurants. He also had a place out in the country where my mother, her sisters, and their cousins would gather during the summer and experience a simple independence (lots of sitting on the porch after doing morning chores or running around the farm without an adult's eyes monitoring their movements) that still brought a light to their eyes in the retelling fifty and sixty years later.

In 1928 my grandmother went off to Howard University, where, as far as I can tell, she had one heck of a time. She still chuckles (present tense noted; she is 101 at the time of this writing) about going out after curfew, climbing over the walls that kept boys out and girls in, and driving around the streets of Washington, passing bottles of alcohol from one car to another. After graduating from Howard in 1932, she returned to North Carolina. That fall, she was working as a timekeeper for a basketball game between Winston-Salem State and Livingstone College and found herself sitting next to the Livingstone scorekeeper, William J. Trent Jr. Viola became so immersed in conversation that she failed to call time properly, allowing Livingstone to win the match. Whether or not Livingstone's victory played a role in it, a courtship followed, and in 1934, Viola Scales and William Trent married. That union brought together the material resources of a family who owned just about everything that black Winston-Salemites could want or need and another family who had a tradition in

Vi Trent, my maternal grandmother (author's collection)

education, not wealthy by any stretch, but definitely possessing middle- to upper-class social status.

William J. Trent Sr. was the president of Livingstone College at the time of his son's marriage to Viola Scales. Before returning to his alma mater as its president in 1925, the elder Trent had helped establish the Atlanta Urban League as well as the Atlanta School of Social Work. For his part, William Trent Jr., Bill to those who knew him, graduated from Livingstone and then pursued an MBA at the Wharton School of Finance. When he earned his degree in 1932, he was one of the first African Americans to do so. Despite this accomplishment, the twin facts of the Great Depression and my grandfather's race meant that he was unable to find a job. Thankfully, first Livingstone and then Bennett College in Greensboro, North Carolina, provided professional shelter. In 1938, Bill Trent began working in the federal government and then, in 1944, helped to establish the United Negro College Fund. Education and access were the family business along that branch of my tree. These are lines that would continue uninterrupted into my own life, even though it would take me years to understand that what I considered routine was anything but.

Eventually, I realized that being part of the right kind of family relied on decades of practice and acculturation. As I imagine my grandmother's young adulthood and then her married life with three daughters, I see a life of relative material privilege and of real social and cultural privilege. I also see a world that must have been very small. It would have been small just because there weren't that many people who shared her social opportunities. It would have been small because the space in which she could operate without offending sensibilities that grew out of racially constructed social norms or, in many cases, law was already so constrained.

In the African American world, all of this privilege could be stripped away in a moment of Jim Crow humiliation, but rebuilding cultural capital would have been a larger and more complicated construction project. Indeed, there was at least one member of my family—on the maternal side with the fair skin and good hair—who simply got tired of not being able to find a job because of the color line. As it turned out, being from the right family didn't help at all when it came to securing a job as an engineer, a job for which he had trained and secured the appropriate degree. Either the accrued cultural capital didn't mean enough to him or he was just too impatient, and he left the family, hopping a train out of town and reappearing somewhere with a new name and new race. That branch of the family tree isn't even dead. It's simply gone.

My mother told me this story only once, during nightfall and in hushed tones, as I remember it, although that might be my dramatic imagination at work. It didn't take any imagination, however, to understand that this was a world of privilege and policing. While it would be insensitive, at best, to bemoan such privilege and the attendant social expectations of how one had to comport oneself, I felt dislocated when, as a teenager, I saw for the first time the accumulating effects of enforced propriety.

Given what I recall of the décor in the family room—the mutlicolored (brown, orange, and cream) heavy shag rug and the very large, velour, umber, sectional L-shaped sofa—I had to have been about fifteen. My maternal grandparents were visiting, and the holiday season was fast approaching. My grandmother had stated more than a few times that she really wanted to watch a movie on television after dinner. I didn't know the first thing about the film beyond the fact that it wasn't in color, and so I wasn't interested. At some point after it began, however, I joined my grandmother on the couch. From what I could tell, she was enjoying the movie.

I recall a grand song-and-dance number. It was a scene filled with Hollywood glamour: huge set, flowing dresses, champagne, and all the glitter and shine a black-and-white celluloid print could muster. Louis Armstrong was onscreen, playing his magnificent trumpet and showcasing his incomparable entertainer's skills, really giving it his all because that's what the audience desired.

And that's when my grandmother had had enough: "Nigger, shut your eyes and close your mouth!"

Silence.

I literally had no idea what to do. I assume my mouth dropped open and my eyes popped—upon reflection, not entirely unlike Louis Armstrong's but certainly with a different inflection. I had never heard this sort of language from my grandmother. In fact, I had never heard anyone in my family call anyone else a "nigger," even while in the grips of playing the dozens. What to do?[12]

I knew that this was the season of joy and giving. I knew that this was a classic Hollywood film. I knew that it played every year and that I had never heard anyone complain about it before. When I went back to recover this story for this book, I found out that the movie was *White Christmas*. I remember perfectly that the mood in the living room was considerably darker and less charitable than the title implied.

I never asked my grandmother about her comment in the moment or after. In fact, she sat through the rest of the movie and never said another word. Also, I never heard my grandmother give that kind of command to characters on a television screen (or anywhere else) again. It was almost as if the moment never happened. It was a moment when she lifted Du Bois's veil or, perhaps more appropriately, when she yanked it up just long enough to speak her honest opinion. It was a moment that had, after a fashion, simply passed. But the thing about such passages is that they aren't ever truly forgotten, just as members of the family who leave aren't ever truly forgotten, even if their names are never spoken.

In my grandmother's case, I think back to the context of her life: enjoying real comfort, but always perched precariously, and carrying along silently so many different burdens that accumulate with time and the attendant adult responsibility of having to act a certain way and not say certain things. I was too young to use the words, but when I sat with my grandmother and watched *White Christmas*, I bore witness to a world that, while terribly privileged, was also filled with profound sadness and a simmering anger for the lifetime of things that could not be said, at least not without facing troubling consequences. For me, this, too, was part of being the right kind of family: You take that bitter pill even though you know another one is bound to come.

GENERATIONAL CHANGE

Aside from the two years in Montgomery, my childhood years were not spent in the Deep South. From my lived experience, I knew that my paternal grandmother lived on the border of the District of Columbia and Maryland, and that my maternal grandparents lived in New Rochelle, New York, and then, upon retirement, Greensboro, North Carolina. And although I haven't lived in Maryland since 1993 and have never lived in North Carolina, when I'm asked where I'm from, I'll answer one of the two. (If an older black person asks me where I'm from, I always answer the latter—since that's where "my people" are from, where I was raised being an entirely different issue.) Virtually every moment of my conscious life, then, transpired in a place other than the "true South." You'll have to trust me when I say that growing up in suburban Montgomery County, Maryland, one of the most diverse and highest-per-capita-income counties in the country, did not feel like growing up in a truly southern place, even though there are many places in Maryland, to the north of where I grew up, in fact, that definitely felt and still feel southern.

That I am not southern doesn't mean that I am a stranger to the nuances of how one had to live along the colored line. We, the people, have been consumed by race and the significances of its boundaries even before the idea of this country was articulated. But the older I get, the more evident it becomes that it has always been significantly more difficult for us to talk about class differences in constructive and honest ways. Things could become complicated for those who were defined as a racial other but who enjoyed material privileges that few others in the country could enjoy. When obvious class differences appeared, the familiar lines drawn by racial etiquette began to smudge and blur. Real life is lived between the blacks and whites of life, but it's also true that a lot of danger, sometimes figurative, other times literal, lurks in those smudged areas where grey is the defining color.

One of my clearest memories of how dangerous it could be when class and race became confused in this way occurred when my mother's side of the family gathered for a reunion in Montgomery. It was the summer of 1981, and my brother was the hit of the weekend. He had just completed

Jannifer Scales, Brian Holloway, and Pam Pryor at the Scales family reunion (author's collection)

an All-American football career as an offensive tackle at Stanford and was drafted in the first round by the New England Patriots. An electricity surrounded him that made him seem invincible. Tall, muscular, and completely fit, Brian was an imposing presence. The most famous picture from that reunion had him in the center holding up two of our cousins—both of whom who were also his age—in the crooks of his arms.

Calling my brother an imposing presence in the family is saying something. For starters, we are all tall—my mother was six feet, and my sister is the "short" one at five feet, ten inches—and we were a family of accomplishment. At the time of the reunion, the middle generation had in its number a corporate lobbyist; a federal civil rights attorney; a private attorney in an old-line, white-shoe law firm; a professor of political science; several machine politics operatives (the kind for whom fellowships and buildings are eventually named); and primary- and secondary-school educators. The host family, the Pryors, were major figures in black Montgomery and perhaps even all of Montgomery as well. Julius Pryor was a very successful surgeon in private practice and had a huge house in Montgomery and a lake house somewhere nearby to prove it.

We gathered during the day at the Pryor house in the woods. The parents did whatever they were doing, and the kids spent their time flitting around Brian and then getting reacquainted by playing various games. I was a young teenager and was thus even more socially inhibited than what I consider my usual way. It didn't help that my cousin Jonathan Pryor, with whom I had often played when my family lived in Montgomery, had become significantly more cool in the intervening years. He knew how to drive a car (they start extra early in Alabama), he knew music I didn't, he knew handshakes I didn't—he just knew things in general. I was having a good time, I think. I was also powerfully self-aware of everything around me as I tried to sort out where I fit in.

In the evening, stuffed with a homemade feast that concluded with trays of peach cobbler, the out-of-towners retreated to the local Marriott. It was a very nice hotel, and since this was 1981, we could stay where we wanted. On this particular evening, some of the local young cousins joined us so we could all go swimming together. The parents remained inside, opened the doors between hotel rooms, and continued the reunion. Being young and relentlessly energetic, we were making all kinds of noise. Probably Marco Polo, probably my brother taking turns throwing people into the deep end of the pool, definitely lots and lots of cannonballs.

It was dark out. We felt free and uninhibited without our parents around. And then 1981 vanished.

At that moment an overweight, stuck-like-a-pig sweating, night-shift assistant manager with a head that looked too small for his body came out and started giving all of us grief for the noise we were making. I remember thinking this actually was reasonable, and I remember it because the last thing I ever wanted to do at that age was to bring attention to my awkward self. However, the man with the small head—it was probably balding as well—then sized up who was really in his pool. We were not the normal clientele for his Marriott.

His irritation quickly turned to anger, and he said the pool was reserved for guests and that we had to get out immediately. Although my brother wasn't the oldest cousin present, he was the biggest, and so he took it upon himself to represent the gathered children of lobbyists, political operatives, professors, attorneys, educators, and doctors. The assistant manager refused to believe my brother's assertion that we belonged and then restated that the pool was reserved for guests. His voice was raised now, and even though it was dark, I swear I could see the red move from his neck to his jowls and then to his forehead. We, the cousins, didn't know what to do. The precedent set by our families' memories of similar encounters was very clear: We needed to abide by the demands of the assistant manager. But this was a different time, and we, well, we were a different people. Also, our parents wanted us out of their hair, and we really wanted to be in the pool. Even if it was a cool night, it was still summer in Alabama.

The assistant manager's body language declared all would be right in the world if folks just listened to him. But since we still weren't moving and perhaps because he thought the ground might be shifting beneath him, he added a new requirement: We all had to prove our right to be there by bringing out room keys or he was calling the cops. The police! My brother conferred with a few cousins, and they went back to our parents' rooms to collect keys. (I don't know what they told the parents, but it couldn't have been the truth, since none of them came out to solve this problem. And, looking back, I can't believe we all didn't leave the pool at that moment.)

When the keys materialized, the assistant manager saw that there were more people than the rooms allowed, and he reasserted his edict: Only people staying at the hotel could be at the pool. One of the local cousins, too angry to take this any longer, pointed to the poolside sign that made it clear that hotel guests could bring outside guests of their own. While technically true, this wasn't helpful in the moment.

That's when the police pulled up.

All I could conclude is that the assistant manager already knew we were in the pool, or rather, he knew what kinds of folks were in the pool, and had called the police in advance, hoping to wave them off when he dispersed the crowd via his obvious authority.

Now that the cops had arrived, the balance to the whole evening was uncertain. Was this 1981 or some other, earlier time? Was this the Montgomery with a long tradition of a strong black middle class that would have been recognizable and generally tolerated by white-owned businesses?[13] Or was this the Montgomery that had handcrafted "Welcome to Klan Country" signs along the highway that my siblings unsuccessfully hid from my view as we hurtled past en route to the reunion? I'm not sure that any of us knew in that moment which Montgomery we were in.

You could tell by the confidence that now flowed through his burly frame that the assistant manager knew. He apprised the officers of the situation. My brother spoke to the officers as well. (Not to give away the story's conclusion, but this fact alone should have told us that we were fortunate enough that the responding officers understood that at least some things had changed. Older Montgomery cops were not known for paying too much attention to the black side of the story, even if the people telling it were well educated and middle class.)

Then, to our collective shock, the lead officer gave the keys back to my brother and the other cousins and told us to keep the noise down in the pool. He also pointed out that the pool closed in a half-hour and that we had to get out then and return to our rooms, per the hotel rules. The assistant manger looked fundamentally betrayed. As we watched this unfold, we knew enough to keep our collective trap shut. However, one cousin, and I'm pretty certain it was Jonathan, had a different plan and muttered, we all thought a little too loudly, "Dumb cracker." Butch, Jonathan's older brother, immediately shoved him underwater as the police and the so-designated assistant manager walked back into the front office. Whether or not it was 1981, there's simply no way they heard Jonathan's comment, since we all got to enjoy that pool, quietly, until 10:00 P.M.

We all knew that Jonathan's comment was flat-out stupid, even if it was on target. Even the out-of-town cousins knew as much. But Jonathan was a child of a different South. The old rules were still there, and they were embodied in that morbidly obese, balding, night-shift assistant manager who felt we didn't belong. But there were new rules for the children of my generation, particularly those of my generation whose families were well positioned to take every advantage of the civil rights battles of the previous decades. It was the already present black middle class, after all, that had sufficient education and the proper bearing to appear "safe" to those white southerners who were resigned either to change or to the strange progressives who actively sought it out. In short, those of us who hailed from the right kinds of families were permitted to register at the local Marriott without any problem.

There was no doubting that the Pryors were part of that group, and although I don't know about any of the terrain that Julius Pryor had to navigate as he built his medical practice, the fact that Jonathan had learned how to drive in the family's Mercedes sedan and that he almost gave his mother a heart attack when he came close to sideswiping the neighbor's Rolls Royce is telling. Even though one of our family matriarchs might have felt comfortable telling Louis Armstrong's screen persona that he had to stop acting like a simple nigger, the privileged blacks in my generation felt that we could be a little bit more obvious in our disdain for the old rules. In saying this, I don't want to overstate the scope of change. Sure, we could stand our ground when confronted without feeling that we were high-minded civil rights activists, but we still assumed that we would lose many more battles than we would win. But whether we lost or won, we were sufficiently self-confident in our (parents') station that we were not about to listen immediately to someone beneath us, even if he was white and presumptively had the police at his back. We believed we were of a better sort—our accumulated lived experiences told us as much—but, damn, we were still nervous as hell while we remained in that pool, treading so much more than mere water.

The historian in me looks back at the moment and wonders aloud how much change could have actually transpired that the young cousins won that small skirmish in the pool. How foolish were we? Indeed, in the early 1990s, when I started diving deeply into my dissertation research and came across story upon story of how racial thinking overwhelmed so many instances where a class-based analysis of a problem made more sense, I found my own antennae more attuned to the persistence of racial thinking. I also found myself increasingly skeptical and, on bad days, cynical that things would ever change. Working with undergraduates who, like me, not quite a decade earlier were navigating the shoals of racial identity politics further heightened my notion that while some things had obviously changed, as a society we were stuck.

During those dark moments, I occasionally flashed back to an experience with my father when he slowed down long enough to share with me some of his family history and, even more, drew direct links between his past and my present. In his story I heard small hints of my own experiences growing up, but much more important were the dramatic differences in our youths and in the narratives that determined our futures as African American men interacting with and within larger social and cultural forces.

My father had been raised in the District of Columbia, but according to his sister, my Aunt Virginia, he couldn't wait to get away. He left for Ohio Wesleyan for college in 1950, entered the military, and truly only returned when my family moved back to the district's metropolitan area in 1974. That was the year that we left Montgomery, Alabama, for Montgomery County, Maryland, more specifically, Potomac. When we moved to Potomac, we lived at the area's outer edge of development. At the end of the block, Korean farmers tended small plots, and one mile down the road you'd find either cow pastures or, not infrequently, horses. I turned seven soon after we moved to Potomac, and by the time I left for college, the pastures were gone and the mansions had begun to appear. The Julia Bindeman Suburban Center for the Washington Hebrew Congregation—a massive Hebrew school and cultural center—had replaced the Korean farmers when I was still in elementary school. When it was under construction, the building site made a great place for my friends and me to play for hours on end after the crews had left for the day.

I had one of those idyllic childhoods that involved going to very integrated, academically advanced public schools and spending long summers that involved the neighborhood kids rallying on our bikes and doing who knows what until lunch at someone's house and then more who knows what until the streetlights came on, at which point we had better be home. We were mostly latchkey kids whose mothers and fathers still found the time to dote on us when they came back from their law offices, medical practices, universities, the National Institutes of Health, or Congress.

My high school was still very integrated, but I saw less of my elementary and junior high school friends as I began to figure out or perhaps pursue my racial identity. Still, I traveled broadly within the high school subcultures, finding friends or at least folks who knew me and welcomed me wherever I happened to go. My college culture turned out to be much more difficult to navigate. The first dose of bitter reality came when I discovered that I wasn't the fastest, strongest, or most talented football player. Indeed, I was rather average (if that) among my new teammates at Stanford. The second dose came when I saw that I was surrounded by more than a thousand other people my age who also had done well on their SATs, graduated near the top of their high school classes, and were their respective teachers' pets. In short, I was far less special than I was accustomed to being. The final dose, and I wonder to this day if it were homeopathic, came when I realized that I wasn't black enough for my most vocal African American classmates. Nor was I militant enough. Nor was I angry enough.

I came back home at the end of my freshman year with all of that baggage and spent a strange summer trying to unpack at least some of it. Fortunately, I had work to do that distracted me from too much introspection. My father, using the connections he had nurtured during the four years he had worked as the chief of staff for Representative Yvonne Burke (D-CA) and then another eight years as a corporate lobbyist specializing in federal affairs, secured a very fancy internship for me. I was the chair's intern for the House Committee on Standards of Official Conduct—the Ethics Committee.

On the first day of my internship, my father decided to take me to the Ethics Committee offices himself. I felt a bit patronized by this decision, since I was eighteen and generally capable, but as we traveled further into the bowels of the Capitol, I began to feel grateful, since these offices would otherwise have been nearly impossible to find. I assumed it was my father's adult familiarity with the halls of Congress that allowed him to find this office so easily.

If this was like other trips to the Capitol, my father and I didn't really have much of a conversation. He was too busy working the corridors, saying hello to Capitol police, greeting House and Senate staffers, and giving a quick handshake and literal or figurative slap on the back to representatives or senators who also clearly knew him. To his credit, I was always introduced and offered my quick but quiet hello. I couldn't match his public persona, so I didn't bother trying.

When we approached the doors to the Ethics Committee offices, however, his whole demeanor changed. We slowed down (I always struggled to keep his pace, even though I was now the taller of the two) and my father became very serious: "You know," he said,

> people always complain that there hasn't been any progress. And, sure, you can look around and point to all kinds of problems. But, son, if you look closer and if you think about the past, you'll see that there's been tremendous progress.
>
> Beyond these doors are the offices of the House Ethics Committee. You aren't some random, unpaid intern, but you are working directly for the chairman of the committee [Rep. Julian Dixon, an old friend of my father and someone who was also black, which was directly related to the point my father was making]. When I was your age the only way someone who looked like us could cross the threshold is if he were pushing a cart of food.

We were standing still at the moment, the only people in the cavernous, subterranean hallway. In that moment I finally realized exactly why my father insisted on walking me to my first day on the job. This walk was akin to the morning car ride on my first day of high school when my father gave me a quick lecture about the inequities associated with fighting and presumptive guilt that ran along racial lines. But it was also more than that, since it took me years to tease out my father's personal motivation for warning me, and earlier, my brother, about not getting into fights. This time, when my father told me about racial progress, it marked the occasion when I was finally able to piece together different fragments from my father's past.

I understood suddenly, for example, why my father was able to find his way to the Ethics Committee door without so much as looking at a single directional. It wasn't that he had worked in Congress or that he had been a lobbyist for so long. Rather, it was because he had played in these hallways growing up.

Even though the Capitol had long since been built when he was running free in its hallways, its labyrinths provided the same kinds of adventures for him as the Bindeman Center had done for me. It's worth pointing out, of course, that I was horsing around in the Bindeman Center in the afternoon after the site was deserted for the day. My father was playing in the Capitol when Congress was in session. This would seem utterly exceptional if it weren't for the fact that my father actually had reason to be there, since his father, John Holloway, was a headwaiter in the Capitol Dining Room. My grandmother Fannie (known to the grandchildren as "Ginga") also worked—she was an elementary school teacher—and so there were days when they needed to find someplace to keep young Wendell occupied, since there was no one else to look after him.

These were both plum positions, made even more so because they were secured during the Great Depression. But my paternal grandfather never wanted to admit that he was a waiter. This wasn't his professional ambition, and he felt humiliated for being stuck in that job. It did, however, allow him great access to members of Congress, and through one of the relationships he fostered, he was able to secure an appointment to West Point for my father. (This was one of two appointments my father received. Much to his father's horror, my father accepted neither. My father earned the second one because in his senior year he was the commander of the black Junior ROTC in the District of Columbia—a culturally and socially prominent position and something that came with an automatic appointment to the academy.)

As we stood outside the Ethics Committee offices and I thought of my paternal past, I recalled as well my father saying on other occasions that he was always in trouble at school. In part this was due to the fact that my father loved "getting into things," but also because his father was so proud. At the start of every year, district students were supposed to fill out forms that proved their residency, provided their parents' occupations, and related other basic information. The schools knew that my grandparents lived together and that they both held jobs, but my grandfather refused to fill out and sign the form because he would have had to put "waiter" on the sheet.

Unlike my maternal grandfather, who was allowed to complete his graduate education, John Holloway never received the law degree that he believed until his death that he had rightly earned. He attended Howard Law School when it was still a two-year program, with courses held at night, since the students had day jobs. He was in the class that got caught in the lurch when the law school moved to secure full accreditation. One of the

*John Holloway, my paternal
grandfather (author's collection)*

*Fannie Holloway, my paternal
grandmother (author's collection)*

most important standards the school had to meet was the creation of a more traditionally structured curriculum. This meant three years of legal education and day classes. My grandfather's classmates, all of whom had just met the graduation requirements that were in place when they started the program, banded together to assert their claim to the degree. My grandfather felt he literally could not afford to fight for his rights, given that he was recently married and that finding any job in the early 1930s was more than a challenge. Thankfully, an old friend helped him land the job in the Capitol Dining Room, and with that, sadly, a life of unmet professional ambition and blank forms for his children began.

While there's no shame in securing a good job and helping to keep one's family sheltered and fed, it's also easy to sympathize with the intense frustration that accompanied my grandfather's denial. While he may not have been able to envision the progress that would allow his grandson to walk into the Ethics Committee's office as the chair's intern and that a black representative would be the chair, he knew enough of the world in which he lived to understand that there would never be enough progress in his time that would allow his family to be considered "the right kind." He would know instead about sending delivery boys into the Capitol's hallways pushing carts laden with food for members of Congress, all of whom were likely self-possessed with the knowledge that they came from the right kind of family or had gained access to that status once they were voted into office.

In the end, I suppose, it is a testament to some kind of progress that just as my grandfather may have been determined that his son would never push one of those carts, my father wanted to make sure that I even knew about them in the first place. This was a truly rare instance in which a silence in my past evolved into a proper history with a recognizable beginning, middle, and end.

KEEPING UP APPEARANCES

Although it does a disservice to my grandfather's sense of self and frustration and even of history, thinking about my grandfather's pride in terms of how it may have been intimately connected to appearances is helpful. Being socially advantaged, after all, is not just about one's sense of self-worth but also about the projection and consumption of that worth. Appearance and desire are united in this way. According to my father's logic, this relationship was deeply embedded in the generals' thinking when they sought out my family to integrate the Montgomery Academy in the early 1970s. It was a phenomenon that my father talked about happening in other times and places as well. Indeed, I can't recount the number of occasions when my father launched into his philosophy of what made a great leader. Looking right was part of it; being tall and having broad shoulders was also critical; and being involved in a married relationship with a supportive wife sealed the deal. It was nothing less than a Central Casting notion of the world.

To hell with being the right kind of family and looking or acting the part. "What about ideas or values?" I often challenged.

Those were important as well, he would answer, but he was talking about the "entire package." This was a phrase that was important to my father, and it could be used to understand his approach to professional advancement. The other phrase that I began to hear more as I moved out of graduate school and into my first assistant professorship was "golden résumé." Having that golden résumé was part of the entire package, but it wasn't really relevant until I finished my academic training; I can only guess that that's why I didn't hear much about it before.

Going to Stanford for college and then to Yale for graduate school was, in my father's way of seeing the world, a perfect plan, since it maximized the breadth of my growing professional network and gave me exposure to the social, political, and cultural worlds of both coasts. This made perfect sense to me, although it had nothing to do with why I applied to both schools. My brother and sister had gone to Stanford before me, and when I was a young teenager, I got to hang out with them for a couple of weeks by myself when they stayed at Stanford for the summer. To me, then, Stanford represented freedom, and it was a sensation for which I, like any other adolescent, had an insatiable desire. Yale was my graduate school of choice simply because my advisers told me that I should go there if I happened to get in. Yale had a huge history department, and there would be someone on the faculty who could support my still-unshaped notion of what I wanted to study. Even though there was a tremendous amount of hard work behind these educational opportunities (and privileged access to resources to facilitate that work), for me, at a conscious level, applying to college and graduate school really was as simple as that. Luckily, my choices also fit into my father's notion of how to gain advantage in this competitive world. Experiencing the best academic opportunities the East and West Coasts could offer meant that the lectures—my siblings and I would roll our eyes when they began and even made up numbers to go along with them ("Oh, here we go, lecture 31A on how to be a success")—would abate.

They wouldn't stop, however.

As I was wrapping up my dissertation, I had the great fortune to land a position in the Department of Ethnic Studies at UCSD. Although I had "only" been trained in history, I knew that this was the premiere department in the field, and I was overjoyed with the idea of returning west and building a career. It seemed I wasn't in the job for more than a hot minute, and I'm pretty certain that I hadn't yet gotten around to hanging my diploma on the wall, before my father started talking about other career possibilities. He was particularly focused on a White House fellowship.

Still very much a creature of D.C. and its fairly insular logics, my father knew a good number of past White House fellows, and he noted that they went on to occupy a range of leadership positions in public service, the private sector, and academia. To that end, he always managed to bring up the fact that his old friend Colin Powell had been a White House fellow. When I told my father that my work wasn't oriented toward public policy, he said it didn't matter. When I told him that I didn't want to work in the White House, he said that the fellows worked in various parts of the Executive Branch. When I told him that I just got this job and I wanted to see it develop, he said that it was only a one-year program, and my job would be there when I completed the fellowship. What he didn't say on these occasions but what I heard loud and clear was that the job would be there *if* I wanted to go back to it.

Even though I viewed a job in ethnic studies at UCSD as a major feather in my professional cap, I began to discover that my father didn't share the vision. Most obvious was the fact that he didn't know what to make of the very idea of "ethnic studies." It wasn't a traditional discipline that he could recognize, and so he concluded it had diminished value in the marketplace. He also seemed unable to remember where I taught. I understood the confusion about ethnic studies—I expected as much from him—but his inability to remember that it was the University of California, San Diego, and not the University of San Diego or San Diego State University drove me up the wall. There were significant institutional differences between the three schools. Some of the differences were material—time off for research, teaching load, resources—but I have to admit that it really bothered me that my father didn't recognize the difference in appearance. I felt that UCSD was the most prestigious of the three schools, and my pride was wounded that my father didn't understand this.

The discussions on this topic (the White House Fellows Program mainly, my current place of employment to a lesser extent) kept repeating themselves, but at least they were familiar ground, since they lined up so neatly with the various lectures to which I had grown up victim. This was terrain I knew from my childhood and through my adolescence—a terrain of heightened expectations that always left me feeling that merely doing well was insufficient. Things veered dramatically off course, however, when the large white envelope appeared in my campus mailbox. It was the application to the White House Fellows Program. Not an information packet, not a brochure, but the application.

I called my father.

"Dad!"

"Hey, just look it over. I think we could make it happen for you." I had no idea who the "we" actually were, but I didn't doubt that a first-person plural existed out there and that my father was just dying to invoke it.

"But I told you, I'm not interested in applying for the program."

"You don't get it, son. You don't have to apply. Just having the application come to your department mailbox was important."

I just stared at the receiver dumbstruck. How in the world did this ever make sense? For my father, though, it was perfectly logical: It wasn't about what one wanted to do, but what it appeared one could do. "Appearance" was wrapped up in the politics of possibility.

While my father never went so far as to send me another copy of the White House Fellows application, he did remind me on an annual basis to look into it, if only to weigh my future options. With each iteration of his plea to consider the possibility of applying, I began to see more clearly that the fellows program was about more than appearances. I concluded that my father must have felt there were material consequences to my stubbornness and that I was throwing away a major opportunity. (Was this a case of son being like father being like son? Was my refusal to apply akin to his refusal to accept his appointments to West Point?) When, during yet another one of these conversations, I challenged his persistence and reassured him that I was doing fine at UCSD, his too-quick reply told me the answer was intrinsic to his worldview: Becoming a White House fellow would give me a golden résumé. He recounted that I already had the East and West Coast training at the proper schools but "this" was the only thing missing from my vita. Once I had "this"—the thing that the undivulged "we" could probably make happen—then I could open any door that I wanted. He was unrelenting on those occasions.

A few years went by, and then I found myself back at Yale, this time as an untenured assistant professor. I had a joint appointment in the Departments of History and African American Studies, with a courtesy appointment in American Studies. I was as surprised as anyone else that I was at Yale, but I knew that it was going to be a great jumping-off point if I were unable to earn tenure. I remember being shocked—it's the only word that actually sums up my feeling—when my mother, the one who always knew I taught in ethnic studies at UCSD and the one who evinced no great desire to reaffirm the social status that was her birthright, given her parents' respective backgrounds, expressed such joy and pride that I was teaching at Yale. I honestly didn't think it would have mattered to her where I taught, but something different had transpired when the job offer from Yale came through. She was glowing over my new position. Was I now in the "right" place for someone of my background? Could her approach to belonging to the right kind of family be so low key that it failed to register with me? Was her own inherited privilege so familiar to her that it need not be named or even acknowledged?

Even though I reaped the benefits of professional privilege via my affiliation with Yale, I also have to confess that being at Yale only increased certain social anxieties. As much as I didn't like to encourage it, it was evident to me that the "Yale label" had a transactional value different from that of UCSD. The fear of being discovered as a fraud who really didn't know that much about the topics he was hired to teach only increased when I moved to New Haven. The fall from grace would be that much more painful. Having said that, however, I would be lying if I claimed to have never used this affiliation to my advantage. I never played the card at an academic conference or when visiting a different university, but when my father consulted his annual to-do list and saw that it was time to remind me about a White House fellowship, something in me said "enough."

"Dad. You've been on my back for years about a White House fellowship. I understand what the program is about and I understand how it can do great things for a career. But I'm not interested in working in the government. It's not for me."

"But, your résumé . . . it's the golden ticket."

"Dad. I have a degree from Stanford, a degree from Yale, I taught at the best ethnic studies program in the country, and now I teach at Yale in the best departments in my fields. People would kill to have my job. I actually think I've done okay for myself. What is it that I'm not doing well enough for you? What more do you need me to accomplish?"

Perhaps it was my father's turn to stare at the headset dumbstruck, because it was several beats before he replied, "Son, forgive me, I just want you to have the best things. I just want you to be able to do whatever you want in life. But you're right, you've done well. I'll do my best to leave you alone about this."

I confess to feeling great relief that I had finally won his approval, since I took my father's persistence about the fellows program to be a suggestion of an unmet potential. But in his admission that he merely wanted every option in the world available to his son, I felt a measure of real sadness that I couldn't see his efforts for what they were: a father trying to help his child along and then paving the way for a future generation to enjoy even greater opportunities. This, in the end, is all he wanted for all of his children, even if he expressed this aspiration in ways I had a difficult time understanding or seeing.

My father wasn't alone, of course, in thinking about the embodiment of his future in his children and grandchildren. Now that I have children of my own, this seems like the most natural thing in the world. I want them to enjoy comfort and the freedom to find their calling, and I want them to secure these things on their own terms. I also want to nudge them along as best I can at every opportunity. In short, I want to hoist my daughter and son on my shoulders so that they can have a better view. As my father drilled into me, being tall helps you get noticed.

As I reflect on these past moments and wrestle with the decisions that my wife and I make for our children and for the family's future, I believe I'm correct when I say that I never once consciously pursued being "the right kind of family." However, when I am fully honest with myself, I am curious to know how much of my father's aspirational lectures and how much of my mother's very quiet familiarity with privilege made their way into my subconscious. At the time of this writing, I am a tenured member of the Yale faculty and the master of one of the school's twelve residential colleges; I walk around the campus and feel that I know almost everyone I see (and, importantly, that they know who I am); I feel perfectly at ease in the various intersecting circles that include the campus police, the dining hall and custodial workers, faculty, students, staff, and senior administrators; and because of our family's profile on campus, my wife and I make great efforts to teach our children how to "act right" in public. I still think there's a measureable difference between raising them to be the right kind of children for the right kind of family and simply raising them to act right, but there are times when I simply have to wonder about the extent to which I am blind to my own privilege. I still don't know when I will tell my children so many of the family stories that can prepare them for the challenges and bitter pills that surely are in the offing. As I have already learned myself, the silences in a family's past can serve their purposes by facilitating, say, the preservation of social standing in a community, but they also come with the risk of too little memory, of not knowing the value of sacrifice that enabled a better future in the first place.

6

HERITAGE TOURISM, MUSEUMS OF HORROR, AND THE COMMERCE OF MEMORY

10:00–10:15 Opening Ceremony
10:30–11:00 Annapolis Marching Band
12:00–12:45 Annapolis City Wide Gospel Choir
 1:15–2:00 The Band Belief (R&B/Hip Hop)
 2:20–3:05 The David Arthur Project (Jazz)
 3:20–4:05 Nazu & Company (African Dance)
 4:20–5:05 Earth Wind and Fire Tribute Band (R&B)
 5:20–6:05 The Clones of Funk
 6:20–7:05 Sankofa Dance Theater (African Dance)
—Performance Schedule, Kunta Kinte Heritage Festival,
Annapolis, Maryland

Let's face it, baby, your heritage is nothing but a
bunch of raggedy-assed spirituals and some grass huts!
—George to Beneatha, *A Raisin in the Sun*

Roots was one of the most important cultural phenomena of the late 1970s. A twelve-hour miniseries dramatizing Alex Haley's 1976 best-selling novel *Roots: The Saga of an American Family,* the show was not expected to pull in strong ratings. The series historicized (in Hollywood fashion) the slave trade and the making of an American family—a story in which blacks were noble and whites were villains. It was certainly not the kind of material that a "mainstream" American audience typically consumed. ABC executives safely anticipated that black Americans as well as sympathetic whites would watch the show, but they were not prepared for its tremendous popularity. The series would become the most watched television event in history up to that time. The viewership would remain steady or increase for the eight consecutive nights the show aired. Over half of the nation's households would watch the final episode.[1]

From January 24 through January 31, 1977, the day after each episode aired, offices, classrooms, and everyplace in between became a site of recapitulation and reflection. The post-episode public performances were worthy of their own documentary. Many whites were astonished, not wanting to believe that "we" would treat "them" so horribly (I was never sure what to make of the pronouns when I heard these observations). Many blacks who weren't astonished self-righteously declared that they would have never let themselves be treated in the same manner as the slaves (of course, pointing out the fact that in many cases this anger was a condemnation of their ancestors' survival would be a bit pedantic). More than anything else, though, there was a lot of absolution going around, since we as a nation had come so far from those difficult days. That week in January was a moment—one that could never be repeated today in our world of endless channels and digital video recorders—in which a nation collectively watched a dramatization of its history and found itself having to make sense of this new narrative of the American past.

As a memoir, Haley's book was a mixture of fact and fiction—and, indeed, discerning the exact mix of the two became increasingly difficult as revelations of inaccuracies, impossibilities, and plagiarism bedeviled Haley's assertion that it was a truthful record.[2] Unsurprisingly, the television show took greater liberties with the story's facts for the sake of entertainment. Regardless of the story's veracity, the importance of Haley's accomplishment cannot be diminished. In testament to this, Haley's childhood home in Henning, Tennessee, the place where he listened to his grandparents narrate his family's history while they whiled away the time on the front porch, was listed on the National Register of Historic Places in December 1978.

I was not sitting at my parents' knee when the miniseries about Alex Haley's life aired, but I was in the room with them all the same. I don't recall whether my brother and sister, respectively, a senior and junior in high school, were there as well, but my memory tells me that we watched the miniseries from beginning to end as a family. Like so many black families, we were riveted to the TV set not only because of the dramatic quality of the show but also because finally (finally!) there was something on the television that spoke to a part of our collective history. Watching *Roots*, then, was not just about getting the opportunity to stay up late for eight nights in a row (no small issue, since I was in fifth grade at the time); it was about bearing witness to an important moment in the mythic national black family's present through the country's engagement with its past.

All of this is true, but beyond the opportunity to stay up late, this recollection of my personal engagement with the *Roots* experience fails to acknowledge the most enduring memory of watching *Roots*: Beginning January 24, 1977, and lasting through much of the remainder of the school year, I was referred to as Kunta Kinte more times than I could possibly count.

Given the fact that I was the only black male in my classroom and that we lived in the kind of politically liberal town where parents (of all colors) likely made their children watch *Roots*, I suppose this made a measure of ten-year-old sense. I do not recall if this naming game was intended to be humiliating, but I do know that I consciously decided to take pride in it because Kunta Kinte and I were both incredibly fast (although someone smarter than my ten-year-old self could have pointed out that Kunta Kinte wasn't quite fast enough on one occasion). When my friends—and they were my friends, I have no doubt of that—called me Kunta Kinte, I embraced the naming.

My other main recollection about *Roots* was not about a character, per se, but about how I experienced watching *Roots* with my family. In 1979, the sequel, *Roots: The Next Generation*, was quickly produced and aired. It followed Haley's family from the 1880s to Haley's return to Kunta Kinte's village in modern-day Gambia. Just as I had done two years earlier, I was sitting in the family room with my parents, watching the miniseries. Toward the end of the series's second hour (of fourteen), Colonel Warner, the patriarch of a large family and the most powerful man in Henning, suffered a heart attack while walking through town. His mixed-race grandson, a child of the younger son he disowned for marrying a black woman, was a doctor and ran to assist his grandfather. Even though this grandson was the only one there with the knowledge or skill to save the colonel's life, the commitment to a racial order was so intense that he was pulled away from his grandfather and prevented from providing life-saving care. Although this was a particularly overdramatized moment, there was enough truth to the exchange to move my father to action.

Before I could process what was happening, my father was on his feet, loudly cursing the dying patriarch and then his racist elder son, who made sure their young black relative stayed in his place. But the tongue-lashing was not really directed at the actors onscreen. While my father may have called the patriarch and his son "racist assholes," his harangue was really focused on those white fathers in the black family tree who refused to acknowledge their children—that is, if they didn't own them outright. I didn't think this at the time, but later, when reflecting on this moment, I found myself confused. One would be tempted to connect my father's outburst to some deep well of emotional damage from a white father or grandfather on his side of the family who did not respect the family name or his obligations. But my father's side of the family was the dark-skinned side. No one I ever met at family get-togethers or reunions was anything other than very obviously black. Further, I never knew my father to be all that concerned with his own family history in the first place. No, as far as I could tell, his was a harangue against the moral failings of white America.

At some point in my mid-teens I would discover that my father's outburst might actually have something to do with his side of the family. The details are still murky, but there was a white man on the maternal side of my father's family tree. He produced a family of mixed-race children, but because of the social sanctions of the day, he could not marry the woman he loved—one of my great-grand aunts or mothers. At least, this is the way I recall being told the story. For all I know it may be completely true; it may also be the kind of fiction you tell your children when you do not think that they are ready to understand the complexities of their world, much less their own family tree.

The uncertainty of my own family tree carried forward well past my teens. I recall making a declaration to a long-ago girlfriend that we were one of the rare black families in which there weren't any slaves. Well, there weren't any black slaves. There was a full-blooded Cherokee woman a couple of generations back who was a slave, but she emancipated herself. The long-ago girlfriend refused to believe the story and mentioned some version of my declaration to my father. Later that evening I was mortified (1) to hear my father point out that I was wrong and (2) to have him do so in such a pointed fashion. As if I weren't even in the room, my father merely said, "Jonathan doesn't know his family history." I'm embarrassed now about the shame I felt upon discovering that there were slaves in my family past, but it was not until I began this project (some two decades after my father's observation) that I could stake any claim to knowing much more about my family history.

I now know that my great-great-great grandfather on my father's side was a white plantation owner who had twelve of his own children and owned sixteen slaves. I now also know that it was my great-great-grand aunt who was Native American, though she was Iroquois, not Cherokee. However, I have no way of knowing about the love that was or was not there, and I do not know if all of Hampton Cook's children were white. Family histories can tell us something about our past, but they are simultaneously unyielding. One's imagination and determination to secure dignity in the present (on whatever terms are personally important) fill in the blank spots.

More recently, I learned that there were at least two slaves on my mother's side of the family as well: America Scales and her daughter Hannah Scales, respectively my great-great-great grandmother and my great-great grandmother. Since the popularization of DNA tracking that allows individuals to investigate their matrilineal past, I have learned from two different relatives who had their genetic background mapped that America and Hannah were likely Masa or Hausa people who hailed from what is modern-day Cameroon *and/or* that their ancestors hailed from eastern Africa 150,000 years ago.[3] While these details do not significantly clarify my roots, from the various resources at my disposal I know that I have enough information to discover even more of my family tree. However, I am largely satisfied with knowing what I know. During the course of this project I have wrestled with the significance of this satisfaction. Am I simply not that curious? Am I content in investing meaning in the uplifted family history? Am I concerned that I might discover something that is simply too painful to want to know? Whatever the source may be, I know that I do not yearn to search for horrors in my own family past. My family is intact enough for me.

Despite my own reluctances, it is clear that black genealogy owes a major debt to the popularity of both *Roots* miniseries, especially because they suggested the possibility that blacks could locate an ancestral home beyond U.S. shores. However, investing faith in locating a home in Africa meant that one was pursuing a history of horror. Given so much middle-class commitment to remaining mute about the "ugly" aspects of the black present that extended backward, silencing one's African heritage or enslaved past, the post-*Roots* desire to discover slavery and even to talk in more honest terms about the racial slights and degradations that accompanied life in Jim Crow America marked a new and important phase of a public conversation. However, the fact that people were newly willing to talk about the horrors of the family past did not mean that the traumas associated with that past, or even the powerful temptation to erase them, were mitigated.

A decade before Haley published *Roots* or the miniseries aired, historians had already turned their attention in new ways to pre-emancipation America. In the late 1960s and early 1970s, one book after another appeared that examined slavery in the United States. Increasingly, as the "new social history" took hold—exploring history from the bottom up so that we could learn how immigrants, women, common laborers, and even nonwhite

Americans lived their lives—the interest in the slave past moved from the institution to the actual people who were subjected to it.[4] By the early 1980s, academics who embraced the new social history and felt no shame in exploring and talking about slavery and its effects on, for example, the black family and community were now accompanied by a mass fascination with the black past. And just as the television industry discovered a new audience to which it could market content and thereby sell advertisements, publishers, public historians, and city and state governments began to see the possibilities of an emerging cottage industry dedicated to heritage tourism. But before African Americans could spend their money visiting sites of remembrance, before this industry could flourish, individuals' memories had to be shared, a heritage had to be identified and narrated, museums had to be built, and guides for all of the preceding had to be written.

MAKING GUIDES

In the mid-1950s, gadfly journalist and folklorist Stetson Kennedy wrote *Jim Crow Guide: The Way It Was*. The book was a satiric attempt to share with an imagined tourist, a visitor to our nation as a museum, a sense of what to expect when traveling in the United States. Kennedy's guide had all the subtlety and grace of a sledgehammer. He intended it to be a harsh wake-up call to a white American public that was determined to embrace a "take it slow" approach to the desegregation of the society: "While there are many guides to the U.S.A., this is the only one which faces the fact that despite the affirmation of the American Declaration of Independence that all men are created equal, in America, in reality, some are more equal than others." Kennedy continued, "Ever since Europeans first arrived on the North American continent five centuries ago it has been public policy that this was to be a white man's country. This policy has found expression in a four-fold programme: 1. *Extermination* . . . 2. *Exclusion* . . . 3. *Segregation* . . . 4. *Discrimination*. . . . And so you see that other guides, irresponsibly recommending hotels, restaurants, tours, entertainment, and so on, without taking into account the existing taboos, can actually get you killed."[5]

Throughout the majority of the book's 200+ pages, Kennedy offered not so much a guide as a history of injustice: a cataloging of who could marry whom, who could hold what jobs, who could vote, and who could live where. For people who were paying attention to the rising chorus of civil rights agitation, Kennedy's was a familiar narrative of a systemic and structural denial that fostered a second-class citizenship for anyone who did not have the privilege of white skin. Calling the book a guide, then, was an act akin to a performance with the notion that a curious public would consume a guidebook more easily than a book of political and social commentary informed by a close reading of history.

No matter how one interprets the book, there is one more important fact worth knowing: *Jim Crow Guide: The Way It Was* actually wasn't. Kennedy was unable to find a publisher in the United States and had to shop the book to international publishers. Eventually, Jean-Paul Sartre helped secure its first publication in 1959. It did not earn a domestic release until 1990, and then by the University Press of Florida, which was republishing Kennedy's books as he was being acknowledged as one of Florida's treasures. Ironically, *Jim Crow Guide* only appeared on the American conscience—if it registered beyond the University of Florida catalog or (progressive) Florida folklorists—as an artifact of a different era. The very document that was written as a mock tour guide to help visitors understand America's racial ways turned out to be, by the sheer possibility of its own existence, a perfect reflection of America's racial ways. In this way, *Jim Crow Guide* was an interpretive resource that was simultaneously projected and received, a museum guide and an exhibit bound in the same cloth.

That Kennedy could not find a publisher in the United States tells us much about the context in which he was writing. There is no clear indication of when he started writing the book. Was it before the Supreme Court issued its landmark decision in *Brown v. Board*? Was it before the Montgomery bus boycott catapulted Martin Luther King Jr. into the nation's consciousness? It was very likely in process when nine black teenagers fought to integrate Central High School in Little Rock, Arkansas. Even though we can't be certain about when Kennedy started putting pen to paper, we do know that he was writing in a moment of incredible racial turmoil.

Decades later, when Kennedy was preparing his book for its actual publication, he added a concluding essay that offered a look backward at the years between when he originally wrote the book and the collapse of legalized segregation. Recalling that moment when businesses began to throw out their markers of racial difference, Kennedy wrote, "I raced around to dumpsters, collecting discarded 'White' and 'Colored' signs, thinking they would be of some interest to posterity in a Museum of Horrors. Alas, I stored them under my house where termites got them, which may be just as well."[6]

Even though the termites destroyed his cache of racial horrors, Kennedy's phrasing is thought-provoking. Since the 1980s, many museums chronicling the nation's racial past—from slavery to civil rights—have opened, and some, but certainly not all, have prospered. The tourist trade that is undoubtedly part of the equation when local boosters and historians begin to collaborate on the idea of opening a new museum continues unabated. For some, these museums are triumphs, institutional manifestations of a region's or a nation's complex history finally coming to light. For others, these memorials are nothing less than Kennedy's museums of horror. How the museums—or churches, or statues, or cemetery markers—are received and experienced depends on how they are interpreted on-site and, before that, how they are narrated in the expanding library of tourist guides that introduce sojourners to the black past.

In the opening of *Weary Feet, Rested Souls: A Guided History of the Civil Rights Movement*, Townsend Davis tells the consumer how to read his book:

> For this book to make sense you have to imagine the world before air conditioning. Imagine having finished a full day's work and approaching a wood-frame church by a dirt road at night. The church is like a lantern against an inky sky, with the shadows of a few people hunched and sitting on the inside window ledges. As you approach, you can see it is packed with people. A slow and fervent humming already has begun. Perhaps you packed some food and have it hitched under one arm. If the church is big enough, bare lightbulbs are blazing in the kitchen out back.
>
> Once inside and blinking from the light, you take your seat on a scuffed pew. If it is any time other than the dead of winter, it is hot. The air is alive not just with hymns and prayers but with the continuous swish of fans, stiff paper squares on sticks provided by the local funeral home that bear the face of a bearded white Jesus. You join in the slow, measured singing of melodies well known and get ready for a night of testimonials, prayers, incessant appeals for money, and most of all, talk about freedom.[7]

Davis's purpose, of course, is not merely performative. He is writing with a goal that any historian would be bound to respect. Citing the destruction wrought by "urban 'renewal,' white flight, interstate highways, and emigration," Davis understands that communities have been left without their own historians or that sites of remembrance have been abandoned or that a new generation of citizens simply are not ready to revisit their ancestors' and neighborhoods' pasts. Davis is not alone in feeling moved to act. The stunning, recent growth in the civil rights travel guide literature is testimony to the importance of remembrance and the urgency of this call to recollect. Just to cite a sampling of the literature of the last few years yields the following books: Jim Carrier published *A Traveler's Guide to the Civil Rights Movement* in 2004. In 2008, Charles E. Cobb Jr. wrote *On the Road to Freedom: A Guided Tour of the Civil Rights Trail*, and Henry G. Lefever and Michael C. Page offered *Sacred Places: A Guide to the Civil Rights Sites in*

Atlanta, Georgia. In subsequent years Steve Cheseborough released *Blues Traveling: The Holy Sites of Delta Blues*, and Frye Gaillard authored *Alabama's Civil Rights Trail: An Illustrated Guide to the Cradle of Freedom.*[8]

Jim Carrier's *Traveler's Guide* opens in a very different way than Davis's *Weary Feet, Rested Souls*. Both books, organized by region, reflect their authors' desire to help illuminate the remarkable story of the civil rights movement. But where Davis evokes the sacred and communal space of the black church and invites readers to project themselves backward into that space by imagining a night scene filled with the textures of the day, Carrier opens by taking the tourist to contemporary Washington, D.C. There are, of course, many sites in the district that are centrally important to the nation's civil rights history. Carrier, however, makes a move that strikes at something more fundamental than the particularist narrative of civil rights. The very first stop he suggests is the National Archives, effectively the repository of the country's memory, to see the Declaration of Independence, the Constitution, the Bill of Rights, and the Emancipation Proclamation. This starting point underscores the fact that civil rights is a national story and that just as it was written by the brave men, women, and children who risked their lives for change, it was also written into the country's most important documents.

Congressman John Lewis's introduction to Carrier's work affirms this sentiment. It discusses the common ground that we all share in the making of the country's history and the preservation of its place: "We must know our history as a nation and a people. We must study and visit its birthplaces. . . . For better or worse, our past is what brought us here, and it will help lead us to where we need to go. Our forefathers and foremothers came to this land in different ships, but we are all in the same boat now."[9]

Lewis adds, "*A Traveler's Guide to the Civil Rights Movement* takes readers on a journey to the memorials, museums, battlegrounds, and sacred places that tell the amazing story of America's continuous struggle for freedom and justice, a struggle that reached its zenith during the nonviolent revolution for civil rights."[10] This is, admittedly, an innocuous quote, but it reminds us that memory work happened in many places and is recorded in many ways. For example, in *Sacred Places: A Guide to the Civil Rights Sites in Atlanta, Georgia*, Harry Lefever and Michael Page recast all of the different sites one might visit in Atlanta—colleges, homes, YMCAs, restaurants, and churches—as sacred spaces. It is as if the movement is so fundamental to black Atlantans' or, really, to all Americans' souls that every site of protest in the name of civil rights justice is also a site of struggle for spiritual salvation—the mundane significance of an everyday site has become transformed into something that exists only where faith can take you.

Whether one is moved by Townsend Davis's romantic projection into the black past at a moment of organizing for freedom, by Jim Carrier and John Lewis's invocation of a common ground conducted in a multiplicity of places and forged in founding documents, or by Harry Lefever and Michael Page's reconstruction/invocation of sanctification or spirituality born out of struggle that called for extraordinary commitments by ordinary people, one cannot help but recognize that all are part of an industry, albeit one of best intentions. These travel guides seek to evoke a particular history at the same time that they encourage consumption that can turn people into better citizens while resuscitating local economies that have suffered in the decades since the movement was in its prime.

Taken together, these contemporary guides exist apart from the scathing assessments in Stetson Kennedy's *Jim Crow Guide*. When we consider the fact that Kennedy couldn't get his book published until 1990, and thus it was relegated to being an artifact of an earlier time, we can easily see that while these post-*Roots*, post–civil rights books acknowledge a past that so many wanted forgotten, they simultaneously offer some sort of psychological reassurance about change, progress, national belonging, and a desirable authenticity. There is no humiliation to be found in these guides. Neither is racial genocide part of their collective script. One could say that these guides are committed to rehabilitation, if not quite reconciliation. They are a reflection of a more literal transformation in how we see our past. Taken together, they seem to be telling us a new story about belonging to a national myth.

When we think about the post-emancipation African American experience, there is no single figure who better embodies reconciliation, belonging, and national mythology than Martin Luther King Jr. Given this, it is worth pondering the deeper meanings behind the fact that the country's most successful civil rights museum—a place mentioned in all of the civil rights tour guides—happens also to be the place of King's assassination. Exploring how the National Civil Rights Museum wrestles with the devastation of King's murder while it celebrates the civil rights achievements of African Americans illuminates the complexities we encounter where tourist economies, heritage, and horror intersect.

MAKING A MUSEUM (MEMPHIS)

The sky was spotless as I made my way through what seemed to be a gentrifying arts district of Memphis. I wasn't far from my destination, but I was already finding it difficult to imagine a different era, since it was clear that so much had been cleaned up in the last handful of years. Even the trolley trundling past didn't look authentically old, since it was so clearly new. The place even verged on being antiseptic—the sidewalks seemed devoid of foot traffic. Granted, it was a midmorning weekday in late summer. It is likely the neighborhood's character changed in the evening when the bistros and restaurants began to fill up for happy hours and then again on the weekend when the city's farmer's market, located just around the corner, opened for business.

I wasn't there, however, to go on a pub crawl or to shop for local produce. Where was the museum? I should be close. And then, one block down, I saw it. Not the museum, but the hotel.

For anyone who studies the African American past and, likely, for most people who pay even the slightest attention during Black History Month or in their high school social studies units, you could not help but notice the sign. It seems silly to say, but it looked just like it did in the photographs. Granted, there wasn't a crowd of men, frozen on the balcony, pointing across the street to where James Earl Ray had fired his rifle, but they didn't need to be there to provide the effect of the moment.

I literally gasped, and my stomach dropped.

This was the Lorraine Hotel.

Of course, the museum was also the hotel, but the stagecraft of the museum was such that—even the vehicles parked immediately in front of the hotel were vintage cars similar to those in the parking lot when King was murdered—when you pulled up to the front of the museum, the only thing you could process was the fact that you were staring at the hotel where King spent his final moments, the hotel from all of the textbooks and documentaries, the hotel you knew even though you had never before stepped foot in the hotel, much less Memphis.

Opened in the 1920s as the Windsor Hotel, the building was purchased and renamed by Walter and Loree Bailey in 1945. The Lorraine Hotel became known for its high-profile guests who were performing a block away on Beale Street, the heart of Memphis's black community and the incubator of so many of the country's blues performers. After the shock of King's murder— and it literally was a shock, as co-owner Loree Bailey died of a heart attack after running out into the parking lot and seeing that King had been shot— the subsequent years of urban decline, and then a postsegregation renewal that meant that black visitors could stay in other, more modern facilities, the Lorraine faced foreclosure in 1982. It had become a long-term, low-income apartment complex when local activists and business leaders came together to purchase the space at auction with the intention of turning it into a civil rights museum. The museum opened to the public in September 1991.[11]

The museum is much more than a tribute to the civil rights movement's greatest leader: It aims to present a richly historical narrative of what historians now call the long civil rights movement. The museum's curators follow a straightforward chronological narrative, but they stretch the boundaries of the movement far beyond its typical start in the mid-1950s. By plotting great triumphs in the civil rights struggle along a 400-year timeline and by pointing out that slave revolts in the 1600s were nothing if not battles for civil rights, the exhibits force visitors to reimagine the familiar terrain of civil rights. The familiar is still there, however, as visitors see authentic Ku Klux Klan robes; sit in the kind of bus (and listen to the sneering remarks of an imagined bus driver played over hidden speakers) that black Montgomerians boycotted for over a year; and walk past a replica of the Birmingham jail where King penned one of the great documents in the American canon.

As they pass by other exhibits that share the history of other, less-well-known moments in modern civil rights history, visitors may be unaware that they are slowly but steadily moving up a gently sloping walkway. Until, that is, they turn a corner and are bathed in the natural light from the windows that overlook the second-floor balcony where King was shot. The museum effectively pulls you into that small space by having you walk between two hotel rooms restored to how they appeared in April 1968 when King was there. Tourists who originally saw the iconic hotel and then immersed themselves in the museum "experience" for over an hour are whipsawed back to the fact that they are in the hotel, mere feet from where King slept on April 3, mere feet in a different direction from where he collapsed on April 4.

It is a very quiet space even when it is crowded.

The final exhibit space in the museum is across the street and brings the visitor to the spot where James Earl Ray spied King through his rifle's sight and pulled the trigger. Although this exhibit is theatrical in its clear attempt to broker an emotional response, it is hard to find fault with the effectiveness of the curators' decision to re-create these scenes in this progression. Here, in the course of about two hours, visitors receive a very thorough recounting of an expansive civil rights narrative and experience the emotional trauma of bearing witness to a great tragedy. But the curators' efforts to re-create a scene of horror so that visitors could make a deeper, visceral connection to the site and to the history was not met with universal praise.

Jacqueline Smith, a longtime resident of the Lorraine after it became a low-income boardinghouse (in some accounts she is listed as a cleaning person who happened also to have a room at the facility), refused to leave the building when it was sold and being prepared for the renovation that would convert it into the National Civil Rights Museum. Smith stayed in her room after other residents had moved out, after a court order declared she needed to vacate, and after her water and heat were shut off. Finally, on March 2, 1988, two months into her illegal occupancy, four Shelby County deputies forced open the door to her room and carried her and her belongings out to the curb.

When she first announced in January that she would not leave despite the court order, Smith said that "Dr. King would have wanted me to stay here. He said he didn't want any memorial, but he wanted to help the poor." On the morning of her eviction, a sobbing Smith declared that she had no place to go: "This is wrong. You people are making a mistake."[12] Smith sat on the sidewalk among her belongings and refused to leave. More than two years later, Smith was in the same spot when another court order forced her to move. This time she was accused of trespassing on a construction site. After she ignored the order, her possessions were placed in the street, and she was moved, while sitting in her lawn chair, to the sidewalk opposite the museum. When asked by a reporter for the Associated Press why she was opposed to the museum, Smith reasserted her sense that King wanted to serve the poor—and that is exactly what the Lorraine was doing until it was closed and she was evicted. For Smith, the Lorraine—and King's legacy— were being desecrated: "This sacred ground is being exploited."[13]

More than twenty years have passed since this second forced move.

Jacqueline Smith is still there.

Smith maintains this protest vigil, urging visitors approaching the museum not to go inside. The museum, and the neighborhood gentrification that has accompanied it, she avers, has destroyed the area by making it unaffordable to longtime residents like herself. The whole neighborhood was now reserved for tourists; it was turning into Disneyland.[14] Even in Memphis's unrelenting late summer sun, Smith stands at her corner opposite the museum, behind two tables filled with copies of newspaper articles relating to her eviction. In front of one of the tables is a banner with a large counter tracking the years and days "since I began my personal protest to speak on behalf of the disadvantaged and displaced." Beneath this statement is a website where the tourist (who likely hadn't bargained on this part of the excursion) can go to learn more about Smith's efforts. Smith's website, fulfillthedream.net, presents a timeline of King's life but largely focuses on Smith's arrest and vigil and the museum's shortsightedness and crass devotion to the tourist dollar. The site does not mince words: "The National Civil Rights [Museum] has from day one, considered the ghoulish needs of the mass tourist market greater than the real need to educate and inform."[15]

In many places throughout the site, Smith invokes religious language and equates the museum's work as a "desecration" of a "sacred" space. Indeed, she faults the entire project for how it goes about the work of recording civil rights history, wondering aloud if this is the best use of a nation's memory:

> The National Civil Rights Museum exists to educate the public about the history of the Civil Rights Movement and to promote Civil Rights issues in a proactive and non-violent manner.
>
> Sadly, it fails to live up to these ideals. The truth is that the museum has become a Disney-style tourist attraction, which seems preoccupied with gaining financial success, rather than focussing on the real issues. Many people have criticized the "tone" with which information is portrayed— Do we really want our children to gaze upon exhibits from the Ku Klux Klan, do we need our children to experience mock verbal abuse as they enter a replica bus depicting the Montgomery bus boycott. Do we have so little imagination, that we need to spend thousands of taxpayers dollars recreating a fake Birmingham jail, to understand that Dr. King was incarcerated?[16]

With one exception, the museum does not recognize Smith or her protest. It invests in the seriousness and integrity of its educational work and is equally determined to honor King and his legacy and to tell the larger story of civil and human rights struggles in the United States and beyond. The museum does acknowledge Smith's presence, however. On the "Frequently Asked Questions" page for the museum's website you will find the following at FAQ number eight (of twelve): "Who is the protestor outside? Her name is Jacqueline Smith and she has protested the museum since ground was broken in 1987—though she has never been inside the museum."[17]

Even though the museum recognizes Smith's protest, if only barely, her vigil tells us something valuable about the production of history, the sanctification of certain experiences over others, and the interplay between an individual and an institution. Here, a single person with a particular set of memories and a determination to remember a figure of such importance as King in a specific way finds herself facing an institution with a public commitment to remembrance that has become the individual's horror.

MAKING A MUSEUM (GREENSBORO)

There are no protesters outside the International Civil Rights Center and Museum. The building, located in the heart of downtown Greensboro, North Carolina, is the site of the former F. W. Woolworth Company.

Unlike Memphis, Greensboro cannot be interpreted as a place where the civil rights movement died. In fact, the lunch counter sit-ins that began at Woolworth's on February 1, 1960, are generally understood as the seedbed for change, as they sparked a nationwide wave of similar protests against racism and segregation that ultimately led to the formation of the Student Nonviolent Coordinating Committee, one of the most influential national protest organizations for most of the decade. Locally, the sit-ins fostered, at least among black Greensboro citizens, a sense of a new beginning in that city's seemingly polite yet still complicated racial landscape.[18]

While it may seem that creating a memorial and perhaps even a museum on the site of King's assassination was an obvious step in the country's progress toward having more open and honest conversations about the horrors in its racial past, the determination to memorialize the Woolworth's lunch counter was a less certain affair. One of the significant differences between the sites is that the Lorraine was an independent operation and its owners lacked the capital to do much more than scratch out an existence. The Woolworth's in Greensboro, on the other hand, was part of one of the largest convenience store chains in the country. As such, the company had much greater flexibility in how it wanted to respond and recognize its own role in the civil rights struggle.

Clarence Lee "Curly" Harris, the local Woolworth's manager, acknowledged from the very beginning that the company's decision to integrate its lunch counter was as much a nod to a basic sense of decency as it was a recognition of the financial bottom line.[19] The store needed the money and could no longer afford the negative publicity. Indeed, with the passage of time, the Greensboro Woolworth's made a point of honoring the events of February 1. On the twentieth anniversary of the sit-ins, for example, Woolworth's vice president Aubrey Lewis served the four men who started the sit-in movement at the same lunch counter that denied them service when they were in college. That same day, a state historical marker was placed outside the building acknowledging the events that transpired in 1960.[20] On the thirtieth anniversary, a plaque with the four protesters' embossed footprints was placed in the sidewalk in front of the store, and the street beside the store was renamed February One Place.[21]

A moment of reckoning arrived in 1993 when the Greensboro Woolworth's closed and the national company announced plans to tear down the original building, which had been there since 1939. The company was financially imperiled, and the downtown Greensboro store was easy to slate for closing. Further, the city's downtown core had been in decline as the area's textile mills began to close and jobs and manufacturing moved out of the area and then overseas. But closing a site whose historical importance did not diminish with capital flight and corporate globalization made for a more complicated situation.

A local radio station organized a petition to save the site. It garnered immediate and widespread support. Emphasizing the fact that the Greensboro Woolworth's is hallowed ground for black Americans, only three days after the station's petition began—much less time than it took the protesters to integrate the lunch counter thirty-three years earlier—the Woolworth company announced that it would preserve the site while financing was arranged to purchase the building to turn it into a museum. Two local politicians, Melvin "Skip" Alston and Earl Jones, founded the Sit-In Movement, Inc., with a goal of buying the property and establishing a museum honoring the sit-in and that moment's role in the broader civil rights movement.[22] Years passed before the museum was able to open its doors.

I had been visiting my grandparents in Greensboro since they returned to their birthstate in the mid-1970s to retire. They lived in a quiet, integrated, upper middle-class neighborhood west of downtown. There isn't much to my memories of Greensboro beyond their house, my grandmother's gardens, the local K&W Cafeteria with its incredible bargains and endless sweet tea, and the Krispy Kremes store five minutes away on Battleground Avenue. There were a few occasions, however, when I was put into the car—probably bribed with the promise of stopping at Krispy Kremes on the way home—to go on an errand downtown. I recall virtually nothing about those trips beyond the unrelenting heat (we always seemed to visit the grandparents during summer heat waves), the sheer emptiness of the business district, and on one occasion, my grandmother pointing out the "famous Woolworth's." We weren't stopping in the five and dime, so as quickly as she mentioned this historic site, my mind was probably off on something else, likely wondering if the red light signaling hot, fresh doughnuts was going to be on at Krispy Kremes when we got there.

My first adult memory of the Woolworth's building came decades later when I took my daughter downtown to visit the city's impressive children's museum. I could not quite recall where I needed to turn—I had left the map at my grandmother's home—so I was approaching each street slowly in order to read the street signs. Spring, Edgeworth, Eugene, Greene, Commerce, Washington—all perfectly unremarkable street names that did little beyond giving me a measure of confidence that I was getting close. Then I crossed February One Place. February One?

Only when I made a series of lefts to correct for a wrong turn did I find myself at February One Place again and, thankfully, waiting at a stoplight.

And there it was: the future home of the International Civil Rights Center and Museum. By sheer coincidence I had returned to the intersection where my grandmother had pointed out the famous Woolworth's at least twenty years earlier. The long sign on the marquee above the street was still there, but it had faded so much that you didn't notice it. However, the collection of historical markers—there were at least three at the intersection then; there are more now—as well as the signs in the window indicating future plans for the museum made it clear where I was.

When the museum finally opened, fifty years to the day after the sit-ins began, it was clear that the curators and architects were determined to do more than narrate the triumph of the sit-in movement. To be sure, they did not miss the opportunity to point out the heroic past, but they didn't shy away from the horrors that motivated the students to protest in the first place.

In most museums, the informal, self-guided tour of the building and its exhibits is common practice. In Greensboro, however, the museum's curators were unable to find a way to allow such a casual visitation with the past. Due to some extreme subject matter and a determination that museum visitors not misinterpret curatorial intent, guests could only enter the exhibit spaces on guided tours.[23]

Excluding passageways such as the Hall of Courage that are lined with narratives of excellence in the long history of civil rights, the museum consists of six main spaces: a gathering room where a video puts the struggle for full civil rights into a larger context of American exceptionalism, a small theater where one watches a reenactment of the decision-making process that led to the Woolworth's sit-in, the actual lunch counter where the sit-in was held, a series of rooms filled with artifacts that narrate the injustices of racial discrimination, and a final space that turns the visitors' attention to the fact that the domestic battle for civil rights was part of a much larger and ongoing global struggle for full human rights. These spaces are informative, performative, captivating, and even inspirational. These also happen to be the spaces that everyone can visit. There is a sixth space, however, that is so challenging that a separate, circumventing passage is provided for children under the age of twelve. This is the Hall of Shame, and it immediately follows the contextualizing video that welcomes visitors to the exhibition space.

A pitch-black room that feels simultaneously cool and claustrophobic, the Hall of Shame shows iconic images from the civil rights movement in light boxes that seem to turn on and off randomly. But these are not images of iconic moments of triumph. They are, in fact, quite the opposite: the burned-out bus that the freedom riders had to flee in order to save their lives; southerners in Klan robes; victims of mob violence—those who survived and those who were staked and then burned or lynched; the unrecognizable Emmett Till in his coffin. Further, the light boxes are not neatly ordered rectangles, each containing its own image, but jagged, angular boxes with single images spread across three or four screens that cumulatively invoke the shattered windows so typical of moments of extreme race hatred when bullets, bricks, and bombs flew into living rooms and bedrooms.

It is an overwhelming and wrenching space whose effects are only mildly mitigated by the tour guide, who calmly offers a very nuanced and historically rich interpretation of the images and the contradictions embedded in the fabric of the triumphalist narrative of American exceptionalism. It is also a space that without this narration leaves itself open to being little more than a site of horror that runs counter to what is ultimately the museum's message of triumph in the face of ongoing challenges. It is for this reason, and seemingly this reason alone, that visitors must be accompanied by a tour guide. The narrative of horror, then, is very present, but one is led to it and then away from it.

Indeed, after exiting the Hall of Shame, museumgoers find themselves turning a corner, seeing a re-creation of the students' dorm room at the North Carolina Agricultural and Technical State University, and then watching a gauzy reenactment of the students' decision to march to Woolworth's the next morning. Since the visitors know that this story becomes heroic and that the students were not physically harmed, the brutality of the images in the preceding room begins to fade. This effect is magnified in the passageway from the dorm room and video that heads to the lunch counter. That passageway is titled the Hall of Courage, and in very traditional curatorial fashion (large, two-dimensional head shots of famous individuals, with narratives describing their accomplishments) reminds visitors of the great, constructive work that has defined so much of the struggle for civil rights in the United States. In their own very intimate way, the experience in the Hall of Shame and then the exit from it into the subsequent spaces figuratively amount to a process of truth and reconciliation.

Just as in so many southern cities that were sites of famous civil right struggles, issues of truth and reconciliation were never so clear in Greensboro. Even though the city long prided itself as being a beacon of progress in the history of race relations, according to some local activists the city has never come to terms with a spectacular moment of violence and seeming racial horror that happened as the city approached the twenty-year anniversary of the sit-in triumphs.

On November 3, 1979, the Communist Worker's Party (CWP), a group made up primarily of activists from outside Greensboro, organized a Death to the Klan rally and invited members of the Ku Klux Klan to attend and respond to the CWP's critique. The Klan, joined by members of the Nazi Party, took up the CWP's challenge and, after an altercation with CWP marchers, opened fire on the activists. Five protesters were killed in the shootout, and many more were injured. Most Greensboro citizens were horrified, and their dismay only increased when nine months later an all-white jury acquitted the defendants despite overwhelming evidence that the accused had killed the marchers.[24]

In the heat of the moment, city leaders declared that the violence was coincidental to Greensboro itself, since virtually none of the individuals involved were from the greater Greensboro area. The CWP knew it could garner attention for its struggles to organize workers in the local textile industry while addressing what it viewed as the linked problems of racial and economic injustice by invoking Klan racism. In this way, CWP activists understood that race continued to be a live wire in the post–civil rights South. Although they certainly did not seek out the violence that resulted, the labor organizers knew it would be easy to goad the Klan into some sort of confrontation. So much of the South was built on these kinds of horrors.

Twenty years after the November clash, a coalition of progressive Greensboro activists called for a truth and reconciliation commission—the first in the United States—in order to answer the questions, "What if America's cities—especially Southern cities—stopped ignoring the skeletons in their closets? What if they were inspired by the potential of the truth & reconciliation model as demonstrated in South Africa, Peru, and elsewhere, to help them seek life-affirming restorative justice and constructively deal with past incidents of injustice?"[25] Although the subsequently formed Greensboro Truth and Reconciliation Commission (GTRC) had no subpoena power and could not redistribute resources or reallocate justice, the GTRC believed it important to address the festering pain of the shooting, the subsequent trial, and more fundamentally, the long-term silence in the community about racial, economic, and social injustice that led up to and then followed the violence.

The commission clearly believed its work was productive, even if in the process old wounds reopened. When it published its final report in May 2006, the GTRC used the words of legal scholar Martha Minow as the lead epigraph: "Failure to remember, collectively, triumphs and accomplishments diminishes us. But failure to remember, collectively, injustice and cruelty is an ethical breach. It implies no responsibilities and no commitment to prevent inhumanity in the future. Even worse, failures of collective memory stoke fires of resentment and revenge."[26] The GTRC recognized that the scale of atrocities that called other truth commissions into being was different from what even the most skeptical and hardened activist would claim in Greensboro, but the GTRC hoped that its work remained a timely reminder "of the importance of facing shameful events honestly and acknowledging the brutal consequences of political spin, calculated blindness, and passive ignorance."[27]

Although the efficacy of the GTRC report is unclear—some local business and civic leaders still think the violence in 1979 did not reflect Greensboro's social interactions and core values, and they also feel that the GTRC only stirred up trouble for the sake of stirring up trouble[28]—it appears that the spirit of the report is at least figuratively found in the International Civil Rights Museum's Hall of Shame. That room, with its jagged and searing reminders of the ugliness in our recent past, and the Hall of Courage that follows soon after remind us that the fight for a just and better world cannot happen without a sincere and thorough engagement with the past.

While the museum still wishes it enjoyed greater foot traffic, it has played a pivotal role in the redevelopment of the downtown business district. The blocks of empty streets and stores integral to my memory of downtown Greensboro have been reenergized, and there is a growing nightlife in the city. Local bars and clubs anchor the southern end of the development district, while more family-oriented facilities—the Greensboro Children's Museum, active green spaces and parks, the first-rate downtown branch of the city library system, and an intimate minor-league baseball stadium that is home to the Greensboro Grasshoppers—define the northern boundary. The museum is in the geographic center. In this regard, it has fulfilled at least one of the goals of its founding leadership. In a June 2001 press release that announced a staffing reorganization and offered an update on the planning process for the museum, David Hoard, the newly appointed chief executive officer of the museum project, declared, "This is a unique opportunity for all involved. We are working together to open a Civil Rights Center & Museum that will document some of America's greatest victories. The International Civil Rights Center & Museum will highlight history and will positively affect economic development downtown as a tourist attraction."[29]

Greensboro leaders saw the development of the International Civil Rights Center as at least in part an investment in the city's tourist economy. In this regard, these leaders are no different from those in other southern cities and towns who viewed their complicated racial histories as present-day opportunities to attract and inspire African American visitors.[30] Without a doubt, this modern faith in the commerce of memory has plenty of antecedents. The perfect manifestation of this phenomenon would surely have been realized if the Walt Disney Corporation had been able to build its theme park, Disney's America, adjacent to Civil War battlefields in Manassas, Virginia. Disney's plan ignited a firestorm of protest from historians and preservationists for a variety of reasons, chief among them being that Disney would simplify and sanitize American history, and that Disney's crass commercialism was an offense to the adjacent grounds where thousands of Union and Confederate soldiers died. As Disney discovered, there are limits to the commercialization of the sacred.[31]

MAKING MUSEUMS (WILLIAMSBURG)

Colonial Williamsburg occupies a curious place in this continuum. Conceived in 1926 by local Episcopal rector W. A. R. Goodwin and oil tycoon John D. Rockefeller Jr. as a "shrine to the spirit and values of the American Revolution," Colonial Williamsburg still imagines itself a "patriotic institution charged with conveying fundamental American values."[32] In the wake of the turn toward social history in the early 1970s, the private battles historians always have about how to interpret the past became very public at Colonial Williamsburg as the institution's curators increasingly advocated an approach to history that recognized the past as a site of contestation and not merely celebration. Put another way, Colonial Williamsburg's internal debates concerning how to represent the past turned into a very public struggle about the very history and memory it was selling.

My sole visit to Colonial Williamsburg preceded these public debates, but the challenges of sharing a history that wasn't part of my literal and figurative family's memory was apparent even to my fourth-grade eyes. For me, the moment of clarity came when I saw a door to a pew.

It was 1976 or 1977, and my class was heading south on a three-day field trip to Williamsburg and Yorktown, Virginia. It was an era of national celebration: Two hundred years of freedom! Two hundred years of the perfection of liberty! Two hundred years of independence!

Beyond using my brand-new Kodak Instamatic camera with a rotating flash cube on top to take tons of pictures—many, it would turn out, were pictures of my friends taking pictures of me, and many would prominently feature the tip of my finger in the frame—I mostly remember two things about that trip: the walking tour of Williamsburg and the church pew.

The visuals from my walk in Colonial Williamsburg still spring to mind clearly: the crushed, tan gravel under my feet; the old buildings with rippled

My Colonial Williamsburg stockade keepsake photograph (author's collection)

glass windows; and the craftsmen who showed us how our ancestors made paper, shaped candles, or smithed iron. I would be lying if I said that I began to think that something wasn't quite right about the day's narrative while I posed, smiling, standing in the stockade outside the legislative chambers. No, I'm sure the idea didn't sneak into my brain then. The stockade photo opportunity was too cool, after all. But I do know that at some point between the blacksmith and the stockade I noticed that there weren't any black people working at Williamsburg—anywhere.

Williamsburg had yet to wrestle publicly with the issue of how to portray the enslaved past to the tourists who flocked to its manicured grounds. The curators of this fascinating outdoor museum had not yet resolved how to tell a story about a broader narrative of what it might mean to talk about "our" ancestors in a new way. The whitewashing of our nation's past—in a year of celebration, no less—didn't strike me then as a deliberate attempt to fashion a script of who belonged to the American narrative. But something in me stirred while standing on that stage, something that spoke to a different past.

Soon after, and by freakish coincidence, my hope was answered, but not in a way that I could ever have imagined.

At our last stop on our field trip, the tour guide directed us into a church. I can't tell you much about the building except that it was a gorgeous co-lonial affair—all brick and white outside and row after row of white pews inside. I recall the guide going on about how the wealthiest people paid for church pews and, in recognition, had their names carved into the doors by a skilled craftsman. There is a lot of history to be found in those doors, she said. We can tell a lot about who lived in Williamsburg just by looking at those pew doors.

I was bored and was leaning into my mother (a trip chaperone), wonder-ing how much more we had to endure before we could get on the bus and go home. And then, at the moment when all interest had flagged, a classmate poked me in the ribs. His eyes were wide as he pointed toward the pew door. It took me a moment to process what I was reading. I mean, I knew the words immediately, but the significance took a few more beats. I leaned into my mother with a true purpose now and pointed to the door. I can't begin to calculate the odds, but we were seated in a pew that had been paid for by none other than John Holloway.

Given how well-documented *some* of our ancestors are, I am confident I could easily find that church today, find that pew, and find out more about John Holloway. But if I did, what more would I know about myself, my family, or my past?

My people were from North Carolina—that's what I had always known. In time, I learned that there are a lot of Holloways in Virginia Beach and southern Virginia, in general. So, perhaps the odds weren't as long as I imagined them to be.

But what is worth knowing about this memory is the way I remember how my body tensed up when I saw my name—even though it was spelled differently—on that pew.

Those doors told us a lot about who made Williamsburg. They told us about our ancestors; they told us about our home; they told us about who belonged in one of our national monuments to freedom, to independence, to liberty. And yes, they told us something else about who belonged. Some-thing else entirely.

The tension in my body was telling me something also. I look back and recognize that my visceral knowledge—my tension—was the physical man-ifestation of an absence that could only have been constructed by a systemic attempt to deny me (and my people) a knowledge of my memories and history.

Granted, the great majority of the visitors to Colonial Williamsburg wouldn't find anything physically unsettling or even noticeable about the narratives that presented themselves to my fourth-grade mind—even before I encountered that pew door that set my brain spinning. But historians and museum curators were increasingly unhappy with the very gentle portrayal of the colonial past that hewed too faithfully to Goodwin and Rockefeller's wish for a patriotic accounting of American history. While even in the mid-1970s a visitor could find the occasional black reenactor walking the grounds in Williamsburg, that same visitor likely left the site not knowing that over half of Colonial Williamsburg's population was black and enslaved.

In the late 1970s—a few years after my visit—the Colonial Williamsburg Foundation began the process of addressing this lapse in earnest. It established a Department of African American Interpretations and Presentations. The department set about collecting and reinterpreting artifacts found in the various archaeological sites at Williamsburg, and in so doing debunked the longtime curatorial consensus that the slave experience could not be reconstituted because insufficient physical material related to slavery survived.[33]

By the early 1990s, curators felt that they had enough evidence and that they knew enough about the slave experience in Williamsburg that they could make a bold statement about the colonial past. In 1994, they decided to hold a slave auction. This decision was a reflection of the department's dual commitment to be as historically accurate in its work as possible and to encourage visitors to reflect upon the meaning found in the horrors of slavery. This sensibility is embodied in the department's mission statement: "To preserve, recreate, and interpret the community and lives of Virginia's 18th-century Africans and African Americans; to engage and inform our audiences about the diverse Africans who endured the horrors of slavery and formed new kinships and networks for survival; and to compel (encourage) people to examine their perceptions of the African-American past, the legacies of slavery, and understand the significance and contributions of Africans to the American character."[34]

There is little doubt that slave auctions were a regular part of Williamsburg's past, but it was far from clear that visitors—tourists, really—had any desire to learn any more about Colonial Williamsburg than I had in fourth grade. For example, prominent black betterment organizations were desperately anxious about the plan, and leaders of the local branches of the NAACP and the Southern Christian Leadership Conference showed up on the day of the auction to protest it, although they did not try to stop the auction from proceeding. Even for those who did not protest, there was no racial consensus on the event. One African American mother brought her daughter to the auction to show her that "black people had nothing of which to be ashamed," while a local editor of a black newspaper, the *New Journal and Guide*, argued that the auction trivialized the "African holocaust in America."[35]

However, if one were to believe R. Emmett Tyrell Jr., conservative journalist and editor of the *American Spectator*, one would think that the auction was a desecration of the tourists' right to an experience that offered wholesome portrayals of the past. When Tyrell heard about the plans for the auction, he wrote a blistering editorial that ran in the *Washington Times*:

> Unpack my bags! The family's summer excursion to Colonial Williamsburg is canceled! The politically correct uplifters have just brought their gruesome hallucination of American history down on once-charming Williamsburg. No longer is it a fit place for family outings. Perhaps if one's family is composed of neurotics and hysterics, Williamsburg is worth a visit. But cheerful, discerning families had best pursue more intelligent recreation.
>
> Not long ago mom and dad could pack the children into the family gas guzzler and drive off to Williamsburg for a pleasant—albeit idealized— immersion into a facsimile of America's 18th Century Colonial life. Standing on nearly 178 acres are nearly one hundred reproductions of Colonial homes and shops. Jolly women in bonnets and hoop skirts trundled along tidy streets. Friendly men in vests and calf-high stockings worked the blacksmith shop and other buildings. Whites appeared with blacks, some blacks being freemen, others being slaves. Visiting families could purchase Colonial fare in the shops and very good restaurants.
>
> After an entreating and mildly educational day, family members could return home, their imaginations aglow with visions of the American past. Doubtless those of a skeptical temperament entertained normal questions: What of disease, of poverty, of slavery and the generalized harshness of the Colonials' more severe mentality? The politically correct uplifters may find it difficult to believe, but intelligent Americans visiting Williamsburg have over the years thought about such things.
>
> Yet now the heavy hoof of the uplifter has transformed this pleasant family tourist stop. Today's visiting family returns home having been put through an emotional wringer during which many of man's meaner passions have been dramatically displayed. Skits put on by Williamsburg actors depict cruelty, racial bigotry and slavery, at their worst, right before the family's eyes.

Tyrell then sadly imagines a car ride home in which shocked tourists, traumatized by their visit, try to make sense of this new national story. He continues:

All this is the baleful consequence of new skits obtusely referred to as "Enslaving Virginia." One Harvey Bakari, development manager of Williamsburg's African-American program, explains that such distressing skits as a slave auction, the harassment of a pathetic black pedestrian by a "slave patrol" and a discussion by slaves about joining forces with King George's Red Coats are attempts to get tourists "to confront the reality of racial discrimination." But is a family tourist venue the appropriate place for confronting reality in all its grimness?

. . . Frankly, this is not the way I want to spend my vacation. . . . Most Americans rather like America, which is why as the years go on Williamsburg will attract fewer normal Americans and more lunatics.[36]

Christy Matthews (then Coleman) was the director of the Department of African American Interpretations and Presentations when Tyrell wrote his screed against the curators' decision to stage a slave auction. Indeed, Matthews was the driving force behind the auction and participated in it herself, portraying a crying woman, begging (but failing) to be sold to the same man who purchased her husband. Whether Matthews saw Tyrell's rant or not, she knew at the most personal level how upset many people were with her decision.[37] In the moments leading up to the start of the auction and in the controversy that ensued, Matthews was emotionally wrecked. However, her professional judgment told her that she was doing the right thing.

Recognizing that the past is filled with all manner of horrors, Matthews observed,

In many cases, what propels the opposition is a belief that interpreting slavery or other tragedies of the American past somehow devalues our accomplishments. Nothing could be further from the truth. It could be argued that when an informed populace understands and accepts this nation's shortcomings and the sacrifices made to aspire to an ideal, a greater sense of empowerment often emerges. By delving into these harsher areas, we become more cognizant of the challenges that lie ahead and better prepared to find the solutions to problems that continue to plague us.[38]

As reasonable and rational as Matthews's observations may be, how does one reconcile that with Tyrell's argument, once you remove its excessive venom? How does one achieve a balance between a record of the past that is digestible to the greatest number of people and a record of the past that is unafraid to speak to the challenges that gave the past its true texture? These are the questions with which museums, public historians, and curators constantly wrestle. When it comes to heritage tourism, however, the institutional and professional standards that amount to a type of quality control in a museum setting are less consistently applied. Indeed, a key motivating factor behind much of the heritage tourism industry—dollars—complicates the work for those individuals who manage these sites and want to make them historically nuanced and educational. Sites of true horror—places where physical violence, cultural depravity, or moral failure made themselves known—are difficult to market, especially when visitors to these sites may view themselves as inheritors of the horror itself.

MAKING HERITAGE

By any account, the southern heritage tourism trade is booming as cities and states increasingly recognize the consumptive power of the black dollar. The attention to this market is intense. Several museums were opening in 2005–6 in Montgomery, Alabama. In 2005, the Alabama Bureau of Tourism and Travel released *The Alabama Civil Rights Museum Trail*, a twenty-four-page booklet guiding tourists to the state's main sites of racial shame and remembrance. Indeed, Alabama may have been on the leading edge of state-sponsored efforts to remember the civil rights past. In 1983, it was the first state to distribute a black heritage guide.[39] Currently, the Alabama Civil Rights Trail is one of sixteen state trails featured on the "Sweet Home, Alabama" website. From this site you can also navigate to, among others, the Food & Wine Trail, the Hank Williams Trail, the Civil War Trail, and the West Alabama Hunting and Fishing Trail.[40]

In the thirty years since Alabama produced its first black heritage guide, African American Heritage Trails can now be found throughout the country. They predominate in the Southeast but are also to be found as far north as Boston and Martha's Vineyard. The jewel in the crown of these trails, however, is the brand-new Louisiana African American Heritage Trail.

The official history of the Louisiana African American experience debuted in February 2009; it is in your pocket and at your fingertips—literally. A very basic Internet search will take you to the website for the state of Louisiana's African American Heritage Trail, a site titled "A Story Like No Other."[41] After following a few links, you can download the LikeNoOther smartphone app, and you are ready to explore Louisiana's rich black history. However, before you start using the app to browse various heritage sites, read capsule histories of these sites, bookmark them in a separate file, and then map them in order to create a personalized itinerary, two performers set the stage for understanding and appreciating the unique nature of black Louisiana's heritage.

When you navigate to "A Story Like No Other," a splash page opens with a shot of a lonesome unpaved country road at some point in the early fall or late winter. Two musicians amble in from the left side of the screen, their laconic and swaying pace keeping time with the thrum of crickets or cicadas hidden among the brown grasses and thicket of trees covered with Spanish moss in the distance. While the harmonica player calls us to attention with his keening yet comforting playing, the guitarist sings:

A governor like no other,
A millionaire like no other,
A boycott like no other,
And a coach like no other,
And the music, sweet music,
Music like no other,
When it comes to soul food, my brother,
It's like no other.
A story, yes a story, like no other.

While the guitar player sings, performing in blissful rapture, a montage of images scrolls along the right side of the screen. The viewer sees politician P. B. S. Pinchback, millionaire Madam C. J. Walker, scenes from the 1953 Baton Rouge bus boycott, legendary college football coach Eddie Robinson, musicians playing in a public square, and soul food matriarch Leah Chase. In short, the introduction is all about celebration and excellence. In this regard, this "story like no other" is strikingly similar to the opening of Townsend Davis's travel guide *Weary Feet, Rested Souls*. Like Davis's nostalgic invitation to the reader to travel back into time and become part of a church community where, amid flapping fans and appeals for donations, there was "talk of freedom," the splash page for "A Story Like No Other" invokes a backwoods scene where an authentic duo of native Louisianans encourages you to explore the natural roots of the black experience.

There is nothing wrong with or even offensive about the entreaties. In fact, they make perfect and compelling sense in the context of travel tourism. But as the tourist begins to navigate through the website or the smartphone app and assemble the planned route through the state, what kinds of history will he or she encounter? Will the memories of the long-neglected black voice be experienced, or will some state-sponsored version of history rule the day? Will there even be a distinction between the two? Or will some of Tyrell's "vicious uplifters" destroy the cherished narratives of the Louisiana past in order to satisfy a present-day political agenda?

The stakes here are considerable. Though conceived by public historians who were dedicated to getting the story right, the Louisiana African American Heritage Trail was brought to fruition because of the financial boon that could accompany it. A 2007 planning document for the trail makes explicit the connection between the history that is revealed at these sites and the market opportunity therein:

> Cultural and Heritage tourism is one the fastest growing segments of the hospitality/tourism industry. Coupled with a growing African-American travel market, a heritage trail highlighting the achievements of African Americans will have a positive impact on our state's economy by broadening awareness of Louisiana's cultural and heritage assets.
>
> African Americans represent 13 percent of the visitors to Louisiana, making the state the second most popular African-American visitor destination in the United States. Some 3.25 million African American visitors travel to Louisiana *annually*. Calculating from the average visitor expenditure, the African-American market currently spends approximately $11 billion annually on trips to Louisiana. Combined with a growing interest in heritage and cultural tourism, this initiative has immediate positive impact on Louisiana's tourist economy.[42]

A year later, in a memo to then lieutenant governor Mitch Landrieu, under whom the Department of Culture, Recreation, and Tourism and the Office of Tourism operated, it is evident that the marketing plan had evolved. The state's tourist economy—the second-largest industry in the state, after petrochemicals—and its African American history were about to merge:

> With a view towards tapping into the rapidly expanding African American tourism market and drawing attention to Louisiana's rich African American heritage, the Office of Tourism has developed a new marketing initiative that will bring the state to the forefront of national tourism trends. Louisiana's African American Heritage Trail will support tourism efforts at the local level by providing far-ranging marketing and development assistance, and will serve to complement the major festivals, such as Jazz Fest and ESSENCE, that already attract tens of thousands of African American tourists to Louisiana each year. And, as one of only two statewide African American Heritage Trails in the entire country, it cannot fail to garner national attention in the media and press.[43]

Even though potential market economies helped to justify the trail's creation, the public historians who conceived of Louisiana's African American Heritage Trail remained committed to reconstructing the African American experience as accurately as possible. As they began to develop their plan for the trail, they decided to focus on five core themes: plantation life, the history of Louisiana's free people of color, the Civil War and Reconstruction, Jim Crow, and the struggle for civil rights. Organizing the experiences of blacks through these themes made natural sense, given the prominent role these events, places, or people played in Louisiana life, but the historians remained concerned about how to excavate, literally and figuratively, the African American past, when so much of it had been ignored or silenced. With this challenge in mind, they set out to find those sites throughout Louisiana that were telling the state's history faithfully.

They had mixed success.

There were places like the River Road Museum, a small, essentially one-person operation that presented the history of African Americans in Donaldsonville, a key waypoint along the Mississippi River in sugarcane country. The River Road Museum survived on a shoestring budget while seeking support from the state government and the National Park Service for, among other things, its community gardens that simultaneously re-created what slaves would have planted around their cabins to supplement their meager rations and provided produce for the local present-day population. The suggested donation inside the museum door is $5.

The heritage trail historians also found plantations that catered to a paying, tourist economy that were slow to accept, if not flat-out resistant to, incorporating slavery and its horrors into their site's narrative. Oak Alley Plantation explained its resistance to unsettling narratives in romantic and financial terms. According to historian Jessica Adams, Oak Alley owner Zeb Mayhew believes "Oak Alley visitors, for the most part, are looking for a 'Gone with the Wind' brand of fantasy. They come for the hoopskirts, the grandeur, and the elegance."[44] This attitude greatly frustrated the state historians, who were looking for sites that were prepared to deal with a fuller historical narrative instead of a fantasy. This much is made clear in an internal memo following a conference that the state's Department of Culture, Recreation, and Tourism cosponsored with the National Park Service. The conference was about how the black past was interpreted at Louisiana's heritage sites:

> The market for African American heritage is expanding in this state, and one of Louisiana's key offerings has been, and will continue to be in the future, the state's plantation legacy. Building the opportunities for visitation to these sites is of critical importance, especially as many of the River Road sites are still at 50% or less of their pre-Katrina numbers.

Hearing the message from these leaders in black interpretation at plantation sites, then, was an important step forward in getting Louisiana's plantation sites on the right track in terms of constructing new interpretations and reaching out to new demographics. These sites can still offer the "Big House" tour, but are now beginning to offer the "quarters" tour as well, giving Louisiana's visitors even more options for expanding their knowledge of the state and its unique history.[45]

I had never been to a plantation before. Visiting relics of a "simpler" era never appealed to me. My reluctance was predictable, of course, as anyone who isn't a romantic about the antebellum South would understand. But here I was, on the Evergreen Plantation, a major stop on the Louisiana African American Heritage Trail.

About a dozen of us gathered for the walking tour. If I had to guess, most people were there to see the Big House. I was interested in this as well, but I was mainly there to see the other buildings. It so happens that Evergreen Plantation has the largest collection of original buildings from the era of antebellum plantation farming—over thirty-five buildings, in fact.

The Big House, the gardens, the pigeonairre—all of these places were interesting or lovely, but more so as a collection of still-life structures or settings. The kitchen, however, was mesmerizing, not for the three shelves of darky collectibles (mammy salt shakers and such) that had no relationship to the antebellum past but were carefully displayed all the same, but for the way the tour guide explained the daily obligations of the slaves who fixed the meals for the residents in the Big House. The ghosts began to arrive when the guide demonstrated how the heavy pots would rest over the burning wood, how the cooks would use long iron rods to manipulate those pots, how the slaves rose every day, day in and day out, to sustain those who shackled their lives.

I was dumbfounded, though, when we moved toward the slave cabins. There they were, ominously silent, down a haunted allée of oak trees. Absolutely still. Waiting for us.

Much to my surprise, I was very hesitant to go down that path. I felt I was trespassing. I was going where I did not belong. But I also admit to being confused because these weren't my people. *My* people were from North Carolina and Virginia. They weren't from southern Louisiana. The presence of the figurative and psychological connection, however, could not be denied. These *were* my people. History told me as much, even though history also told me that reducing a radically diverse population to "A People" was intellectually lazy. Nevertheless, before I walked up the steps to the

Slave cabins, Evergreen Plantation (author's collection)

first slave cabin, I silently apologized for paying $20 to buy a ticket to see the plantation and to pay for the upkeep of the Big House. I apologized to all of them: Henry White, Appollon, Ben Lewis, Joshua, John, Edmund, Tom Brown, Manuel, Stirling, Crouch, Moses, Fleming, Alfred, Robert, Terry, Georges, Benjamin Harrison, Nelson, Baptiste, Abraham, Ambrose, Squire, Aron, Jackson, Anderson, Tom, Henry, Ben, Jean Pierre, Joe, Pierre, Lenhen, Ursule, Suzanne, Geneviéve, Fanny, Cloe, Dunca, Zabelle, Hector, Eblany, Will, Ursine, Clara, Jacques, Germine, Alexis, and two children, unnamed, all of whom were listed as property.

Considering the distanced silence that accompanied the displayed porcelain grotesqueries in the kitchen; the cost per person of maintaining the Big House, which was still private property and occupied in the off-season; the fact that I was the only black person on the tour; and that some of our group arrived as part of a daylong private bus tour moving them from one plantation to another, I found myself taking deep breaths, trying to gird myself for whatever whitewashed narrative the tour guide would offer about the slave cabins.

The guide, however, surprised me. "This is hallowed ground," she said. "We don't know enough about the people who worked this land and who lived in these cabins. We do know, however, that they were skilled farmers and craftsmen and that they built everything that we have seen today."

What I found to be remarkable in the moment, as it turns out, was a noted shift in the narrative a visitor to Evergreen would have heard just a few years earlier. Then, visitors to Evergreen would still have seen the slave cabins, but the tour's focus would have been entirely on the plantation house and the other white-occupied spaces. The kitchen, now a site where one learns how slaves fed the plantation, was then merely the place where the owner hosted dinner parties.[46] Granted, the mammy figurines remain, but one can imagine they played a more interactive role during the dinner parties than in their perched gargoyle-like silence one finds today—mouths agape, frozen in what some might think is a wide and foolish grin but in what others might understand to be a primal scream. My tour guide didn't reference them at all.

There's no doubting that visitors still come to Evergreen primarily to see the plantation house, and it is likely that they may view the slave cabins as something more akin to spectacle than as a site of violence, subjugation, and loss. The tour guide's changing narrative, however, reflects an evolving sensibility about how to tell stories about the black past.

In Louisiana, well before the idea of the heritage trail took shape, public historians had been wrestling with the issues of a representational voice. In 2004, Miki Crespi, the chief of ethnography for the National Park Service, prepared a study addressing issues related to the development of the Cane River Creole National Historical Park.[47] Given the long history of the plantation's connection to the local community (laborers and sharecroppers—some still living in the grounds' slave quarters—were working the land by hand until the late arrival of mechanized farm equipment in the 1960s), Crespi conducted an ethnographic study of Magnolia Plantation to gain a better understanding of how the site registered among its white, black, and Creole populations.[48]

Crespi found that nostalgia maintained a firm grip on locals' recollections about the plantation. Whites recalled Magnolia as a "wonderful place, 'a fun place to visit.'" Whites' views of blacks were similarly platitudinous. Crespi recorded that "some whites perceived Magnolia's black community as a peaceful place occupied by relatively happy people who were well treated." Crespi continued, "From the perspective of whites, who primarily viewed blacks in public rather than private venues, it seem [*sic*] that 'no matter where you would go, when blacks were working they were always laughing and having a good time, no matter how hot it was or how hard the work was.'" Black residents, on the other hand, while less effusive in their recollections, still took enormous pride in the area, especially the quarters where slaves and then field hands lived. "'When we lived here,'" one resident declared, "'this was a superb place.'" In the intervening years, the land

Kitchen collectibles,
Evergreen Plantation
(author's collection)

had become overgrown and weed-choked, and blacks felt it was incumbent upon the National Park Service to put the place back in order.[49]

The relative unanimity about Magnolia began to break down, however, when whites and blacks were asked for suggestions about what kinds of interpretive events or activities the Park Service could provide. Reflecting a sensibility that recalled a history of happier times, white residents felt Magnolia should be a "fun place to visit with family-oriented and children's activities, including riding horses, taking buggy and surrey rides, having someone perform magic tricks for children, and providing farm machinery that children could ride." Magnolia guides, they thought, should also tell "ghost stories" about the overseer who allegedly haunted the grounds. Blacks, meanwhile, reiterated the need for the Park Service to "clean and repair the quarters, the store, and other farm structures," "teach black work songs," and "encourage events, such as homecomings and community reunions."[50] It's easy to imagine that local blacks had had enough of ghost stories involving an overseer.

In a program guide for the 2008 conference "What Are We Saying?: Discovering How People of African Descent Are Interpreted at Louisiana

Plantation Sites," a similar sentiment was captured. On the inside cover of the guide, two quotes were placed next to a picture of a gate latch. The implication is that both quotes were in reference to the functional and artfully crafted latch. The first quote was from an unnamed black man: "I wasn't raised around plantations, but I know what my old family said about them. I'd like to say I like the gate latch, that it's pretty, but all I can think about that [is that] it was just hard work for nothing." The second quote was from a white man: "You see? I look at things like that [gate latch] at these plantations I visit and it's proof to me that the slaves were happy. A sad man couldn't make something like that."[51]

Whether referring to a simple yet elegant gate latch or an entire plantation, these quotes are stark reminders of racial difference in how the past was remembered. They also underscore the difficulty public historians and curators faced as they sought a new way to narrate the past that remained accessible or even recognizable to as many people as possible. In the case of Magnolia Plantation at Cane River, Crespi wrote that the anxieties of blacks and whites about how to talk about slavery—a "painful and shameful past"—were ultimately resolved and that the local communities gave the Park Service "permission" to narrate the story. With the locals' blessing, the Park Service began to tell a "complex past on behalf of a diverse community that finds the subject too difficult or sensitive to address itself."[52]

But telling a new story about an old place was not a simple matter of writing a new script based on new interpretations. At Baton Rouge's Magnolia Mound Plantation (not to be confused with Magnolia Plantation at Cane River, a few hours away by modern interstate), for example, curators have been chipping away at older, more traditional narratives that focused on the plantation house. As late as 1999, for example, tour guides at the Magnolia Mound Plantation declared that the site did not have any records about the slaves who had worked on the plantation, and so they had to develop a narrative about the Magnolia Mound slaves based on secondary literature about Louisiana sugarcane plantation slave systems.[53]

Ten years later, and under the guidance of a new manager who also happened to be a trained archaeologist pursuing a more nuanced engagement with the past, the Magnolia Mound Plantation script had been aggressively rewritten. Previously, visitors to the site only had a structured tour of the plantation house and the kitchen house. The rest of the outside grounds were open to visitors but without curatorial guidance. (In 1998, a slave cabin was relocated to the Magnolia Mound site—the original cabins had not survived—but it was not yet woven into the guided tours of the plantation.)

In the new Magnolia Mound script, the presence of slaves is palpable throughout the tour. Every room in the Big House, for example, was a site where free and slave interacted. The tour now continued outside the plantation house, and the slave cabin was incorporated into the broader narrative about life on the plantation.[54] Archaeological digs had unearthed an entire narrative about how slaves lived at Magnolia Mound. Furthermore, genealogical research projects at the turn of the century revealed extensive records about the enslaved people who lived at Magnolia Mound. Now, tour guides could talk about Josephine, Basheba, Abram, Fanny, Dick, Harry, and another forty-five slaves who lived in sixteen cabins in the slave quarters.[55]

This did not mean that the interpretive challenges had been surmounted. Nor could they ever be. In truth, the difficult work was only just beginning. Now that Magnolia Mound's enslaved people had names and now that the curators knew how they lived, the curators' commitment to understanding and projecting the complete story of Magnolia Mound only intensified. Curators incorporated the restored slave cabin into the tour, but they made sure that they framed the cabin in a particular way. In a lesson plan targeting students from third to twelfth grade, the opening line of the tour is a serious call to remembrance: "We are about to enter the slave cabin. This is a real slave cabin. What does 'real' mean? People really lived here, not fake, nonfiction. So we need to be respectful when we are in this place. No joking or wisecracks."[56] Another serious matter curators continue to struggle with is the fact that Magnolia Mound, now a 16-acre site, used to encompass 950 acres. The size of the site isn't a problem, but the research staff is now certain that the private homes abutting the property nearest to the restored slave cabin are built on slaves' unmarked graves.

Given the fact that Louisiana's African American Heritage Trail includes many other plantations, there is no doubt that unmarked graves exist elsewhere on the tourist trail. However, due to the expansion of the inner ring of Baton Rouge suburbs, Magnolia Mound now appears as if it were built into the neighborhood instead of the other way around. That a suburban life is perched above unmarked slaves' graves is a silent grotesquerie that Magnolia Mound's curators will never be able to address unless they start buying up rows of currently occupied houses—something that is unlikely ever to happen.

Perhaps the most powerful site of mortal anonymity, however, is found on the edge of downtown New Orleans in Tremé, the city's sixth ward. Tremé is often referred to as the longtime or historic home to New Orleans's black populations, and there are several stops on the heritage trail within blocks of one another. The first-rate New Orleans African American Museum is near Congo Square and Louis Armstrong Park. Between the two is St. Augustine Church, one of the oldest churches in North America serving a largely black Catholic congregation. The history of the church itself is impressive, as it speaks to the unique relationship between blacks, Creoles, and whites in a part of the city that has been the economic, social, and cultural home to generations of blacks. But a small memorial outside the church speaks in utter silence to the horror of loss and trauma that undergirds so much of the history that tourists experience on the heritage trail.

At first glance, the memorial looks like a quaint garden with a curious set of crosses planted in it. But closer inspection reveals a powerful force at work. There are multiple small crosses of various size and design planted among the tropical grasses. Looming over them is a massive cross. It leans at a forty-five-degree angle and appears to have been made out of a ship's anchor chain. Tangled in this cross, this chain, are half a dozen slave shackles, some intact, some broken.

This site is the Tomb of the Unknown Slave.

On October 30, 2004, the St. Augustine community dedicated this site, created to honor the "memory of the nameless, faceless, turfless Africans" who died in Tremé. More than this, however, the shrine is a call to remember all slaves who lie buried in unmarked graves. The memorial plaque acknowledges that the tomb tells a story that is as boundless as its subjects are nameless: "There is no doubt that the campus of St. Augustine Church sits astride the blood, sweat, tears, and some of the mortal remains of unknown slaves from Africa and local American Indian slaves. . . . In other words, the Tomb of the Unknown Slave is a constant reminder that we are walking on holy ground. Thus, we cannot consecrate this tomb, because it is already consecrated by many slaves' inglorious deaths bereft of any acknowledgement, dignity, or respect."[57]

As a site of historical performance, the Tomb of the Unknown Slave is a powerful marker of loss, absence, injustice, and cruelty. Although based in historical fact, it is, in the end, a figurative assertion, and it is likely because of this that it does not elicit the tendentious commentary that the slave auction at Colonial Williamsburg inspired. Further, the memorial is not a "national shrine" like Williamsburg but is merely placed outside an actual shrine in a black neighborhood—one that, given the sultry New Orleans air, is too far removed for most tourists. Perhaps it is for all of these reasons— the shrine's figurative symbolism, its blackness, and its location—that the Tomb of the Unknown Slave is allowed to stand as a silent sentinel over a

Tomb of the Unknown Slave, Tremé, New Orleans (author's collection)

racial horror that is boundless and timeless, even as it also happens to be stop number two in "A Story Like No Other."

MAKING A MEMORY

The haunting absence to which the tomb alludes echoes the central themes in Toni Morrison's Pulitzer Prize–winning novel, *Beloved*. Morrison's masterpiece, a wrenching story of a self-emancipated woman's struggle to find peace for herself and her family, is a meditation on the deadening effects of memory—too much memory of some types and not nearly enough of others. In *Beloved*, we learn about Sethe, the book's central character, and her successful efforts to secure her children's escape from slavery and then her own. Once free, Sethe is haunted by the possibility of being captured and returned to her abusive owner. When he does find her and sends a crew to capture her and her children, she is overwhelmed by her memories as a slave and attempts to murder her two sons, a toddling daughter, and an infant. This, she believed, was an expression of true love—their deaths would spare them the trauma of a life not worth living. Sethe manages to kill the toddler but spends the rest of her life haunted by her act of true love as well as the ghost that returns to consume her and this love.

Beloved offers a polyphony of voices that narrate their memories of Sethe, her actions, and their pasts as slaves. It is a book riven with horror, much of it too powerful to be recalled: rape for sport and for breeding, physical and psychological assaults of all manner, lynching, and the terror of recognizing that virtually no "whitepeople" believed that blacks had the capacity for human complexity. In the book's closing pages, a chorus of narrators affirm the trauma of these memories when they speak to the breadth and depth of Sethe's lived nightmare (and their own), saying, "It was not a story to pass on," and adding, "Remembering seemed unwise."[58] In animating the inner lives that "whitepeople" believed blacks did not possess, Morrison made the narration of absence an assertion of memory. Blacks had a past, *Beloved* declares. It may well have been a horrific past, but it existed and could therefore be named.

In 1988, the Universal Unitarian Association honored Morrison with the Frederic G. Melcher Book Award for her accomplishment in *Beloved*. In her acceptance speech, she explained why she was compelled to write *Beloved*:

> There is no place you or I can go, to think about or not think about, to summon the presences of, or recollect the absences of slaves; nothing that reminds us of the ones who made the journey and of those who did [not] make it. There is no suitable memorial or plaque or wreath or wall or park or skyscraper lobby. There's no 300-foot tower. There's no small bench by the road. There is not even a tree scored, an initial that I can visit or you can visit in Charleston or Savannah or New York or Providence, or better still, on the banks of the Mississippi. And because such a place doesn't exist (that I know of), the book had to.[59]

Morrison continued that, with hindsight, she saw that *Beloved*'s concluding pages—those that declared in different ways that the African American past as embodied in Sethe's story was unwise to remember—were actually a call to do the opposite. "I think I was pleading," she said, "for that wall or that bench or that tower or that tree when I wrote the final words."[60] When we accept Morrison's own assessment of her work, the entire novel needs to be understood as an act of authorization, one that said a memory existed in the void, and that it was time for everyone to reconcile with the past. To be sure, this reconciliation was quite different from the stories of universalist triumph that one finds in the civil rights travel guides, but it was still a call to come to terms with the horrors that haunted the African American past.

When the Toni Morrison Society was established in 1993, it heeded Morrison's declaration and adopted "a bench by the road" as the group's motto. The society also heard Morrison's plea in her acceptance speech as a call to action and started the Bench by the Road Project. This project sought to install permanent benches in locations that were important but unmarked sites related to the African American past. Although museums like those in Memphis and Greensboro and monuments like those in New Orleans were opened or consecrated in the intervening years, the Morrison Society understood that there remained ample room for further discussions about the absences, traumas, and to use Sethe's own construction, "rememories" in the American narrative. The benches could do some of this work.[61]

In 2008, the first bench was installed at Fort Moultrie in Sullivan's Island, South Carolina. More than 300 people, including Morrison, members of the Morrison Society, representatives from the National Park Service, and local Charlestonians, attended. During the installation ceremony, Morrison and Thomalind Polite threw a memorial wreath into the Atlantic Ocean. Afterward, Polite, a seventh-generation descendant of a ten-year-old girl stolen from Sierra Leone in 1756 who was then quarantined with other Africans in the Sullivan Island pest houses before being sold, declared that a "circle closed" when they installed that first bench, remembered, and thereby honored the millions of unknowable people who passed through Sullivan's Island.[62]

There are now six such benches, and fourteen more are planned.[63] It is far too early to know if they will become the focus of important tourist destinations like the stockades in Colonial Williamsburg or King's hotel room at the National Civil Rights Museum in Memphis or the Woolworth's lunch counter at the International Civil Rights Center and Museum in Greensboro. It is also too early to know if they will be incorporated into the growing number of civil rights tourist guides, or if they will merit mention in various electronic state heritage tourism websites and smartphone apps. What is already clear, however, is that their very presence is a declaration that memory and horror shape the narrative that gives meaning to the African American present. In addressing what Morrison called "the hunger for a permanent place," the benches align neatly with the post-*Roots* sensibilities that speak against the absences in black memory.[64]

MEMORY IN THE DIASPORA

Africa is the birth of mankind. Africa is the land of my ancestors.
But Africa is not my home. I hardly know this place at all.
—Eddy L. Harris, *Native Stranger*

I tried to picture in my mind a chief, decked out in cowrie shells,
leopard skin, golden bracelets, leading a string of black prisoners of war
to the castle to be sold. . . . My mind refused to function.
—Richard Wright, *Black Power*

My people are from North Carolina and Virginia. Why, then, do I find myself many thousands of miles from my roots, waiting for my tour guide to
take me to Elmina Castle, the largest slave fort on the Ghanaian coast?
Why am I sitting here at a beach resort five minutes from a major axis in
the historic triangle slave trade, about to visit my second such castle in as
many days?

I've come to Ghana because sorting out the nuances and complications
of the remembered black past requires returning to The Beginning—or at
least one of the places that is now recognized by an ever-growing tourist
trade as a beginning of sorts.[1] For many African American tourists, coming to Ghana and, more specifically, coming to Elmina or Cape Coast slave
castle is about returning. Before this trip, I had never been to Africa. More
importantly, I had never imagined myself as being from Africa in any psychologically purposeful way. In traveling to Ghana, I told myself that I have
come to observe others return.

And others do return.

Beginning in earnest in the wake of *Roots* and the subsequent com-
modification of the discovery that blacks had a traceable past, African

Americans have journeyed to Africa's west coast in search of something.[2] As literary scholar Saidiya Hartman shows us in her graceful travel narrative–memoir–critical history *Lose Your Mother*, African Americans have reversed course across the Atlantic Ocean for the most mundane reasons (a love of adventure), for the most romantic (a search for a place they feel is their ancestral home), and for the most heartbreaking (an escape from the hell of their birth country).

During her research trips to Ghana and then a subsequent yearlong stay in the country, Hartman found that these last two groups—the romantics and the brokenhearted—were wrestling with different aspects of memory in the diaspora. The romantics sought a collective, figurative memory that connected them to ancestors they would never know. The brokenhearted simply suffered from too much memory, "unable," Hartman writes, "to erase the image of a fourteen-year-old boy's bloated corpse dredged from the Mississippi, or four dead little girls buried in the rubble of a church in Birmingham, or Malcolm's slumped figure on the floor of the Audubon Ballroom, or Martin's body on a hotel balcony in Memphis, or the bullet-shattered bodies of Fred Hampton and Mark Clark."[3]

I'm not entirely sure in which category I belong. I know I love the adventure of travel, but this was a business trip. I also know that I'm not a diasporic romantic. I am a citizen of the United States and am determined to embrace it despite all the reasons its history can offer to break my heart. And speaking of my heart, it's mainly agitated and bewildered, not broken. Knowing this much about myself and determined as I was to cast an unblinking scholarly eye on how the story of My People's past (not my people's past) was told, I still have to admit feeling a thrill the first time I looked at my in-flight monitor and discovered that my comfortable British Airways flight—bumped up to Premier Economy, thank goodness; it was almost a seven-hour flight, after all—was now in African airspace. Was the electricity that traveled down and back up my spine my body's way of acknowledging the true adventurer in me, or was it telling me that, yes, I actually was getting close to home? My everyday, logical self said that it was the former. Part of me, however, was left wondering.

Perhaps I am no different from Eddy L. Harris, who spent a year traveling by himself throughout the African continent, searching for answers to his own subconscious curiosity about what Africa meant to a black American. In Harris's childhood, Africa was the stuff of fairy tales, a "magnificent faraway world . . . a motherland." As an adult, Harris wrestled with powerful ambivalences about the need to know Africa. He concludes that "by going to Africa I could see the past and then get rid of it, shed myself of this *roots* business once and for all, those invisible shackles that chain us too often to the past." In practically the same breath, however, he also concedes that he is mesmerized by the continent: "I had some eerie feeling Africa could teach me about life and what it means to be human, deepen my appreciation for all that I am and all that I have, help me to find, perhaps, the face of God, perhaps even my own face, help me to step out of my cozy little world, out of myself so that I could see myself better and better define myself. Even if, as Thomas Wolfe suggested, you can't really go home again, perhaps it helps to know where home is, to know where you have come from."[4]

Whether or not I was inspired by Harris's tortured curiosity about Africa, one thing was sure: I wasn't going to get on my hands and knees and kiss the tarmac when we arrived in Accra. That kind of public display of emotion wasn't for me. But after disembarking from the plane and walking toward the waiting bus, I took the opportunity to look over my shoulder, curious to see if anyone behind me was less emotionally restrained and was bending down in order to thank (the) God(s) that they were able to return home. I admit to feeling disappointed that no one did. Regardless, soon enough I had my bag and my stamped passport in hand, and I was en route to my air-conditioned hotel. Tomorrow I was off to Cape Coast to see my first slave castle. The day after that I would visit Elmina. Sorting out my emotions could wait.

THE FACTS ABOUT HOME, I

These are the most basic facts one learns from the literature:

Originally small fishing villages, Elmina and Cape Coast grew into the headquarters for Portuguese and British trading ventures. The Portuguese were the first Europeans to arrive, establishing a trade for gold in the late fifteenth century and building Elmina Castle in 1482 to serve as a warehouse, garrison, and administrative center for their enterprise. Soon after, the Portuguese began to participate in the region's slave trade. Before the British arrived over 200 years later and took control of a different, nearby castle that they renamed Cape Coast, successive waves of European trading powers sought to control the burgeoning traffic in gold, cloth, brass, and of course, humans. The Dutch, Swedes, French, and Danes all made major inroads, building lodges, forts, and castles along what is now the Ghanaian coast.[5] Over the course of 300 years of European coastal occupation, at least eighty fortifications of various types were built.[6]

Originally designed as storage facilities for commodities such as precious metals, ivory, mahogany, pepper, and salt, the castles' storerooms were converted into dungeons when Europeans turned to human commodities. While we will never know the exact numbers, over the course of the roughly 325 years during which Europeans relied on Elmina and Cape Coast for their slave-trading efforts, it is certain that millions of Africans passed through these coastal forts and castles bound for other destinations in the slave-trading triangle: South America, the Caribbean, North America, and Europe. Based on increasingly rich and detailed histories, we know about the trade that brought humans to the West African coast. We also know where slaves were kept in the castles, how they were treated, and that if they survived the hell waiting for them in the castles, they would pass through aptly named Doors of No Return to a fresh nightmare aboard ships crossing the Atlantic Ocean.[7]

But facts on the page begin to feel inadequate when you see the castles looming over the coastline, secure on promontories above still-active fishing ports. Painted a stark white, the imposing castles flash in the blazing sun against a blue sky while ocean waves crash at their foundations; the castles are places that visually, symbolically, and literally convey power, authority, and violence. Even though the castles' cannons have long been silenced and are now thoroughly rusted, the fact that they remain on guard, pointing in all directions, only underscores the fact that valuables were stored inside.

When you enter the castles, virtually everything you have read in advance feels superfluous as the weight of centuries of racial horror press down on you. They press down when you and your tour group of maybe ten people enter the dungeons where hundreds of slaves were held. They press down as you walk through open archways that used to be closed doors. They press down on you as you struggle to adjust your eyes to the dim overhead lights—provided so you can navigate the worn stone floors. They press down on you as you look upward toward ceiling hatches, now open, that were once sealed.

The dungeons remain mentally and physically suffocating.

The scholarly literature cannot prepare you for what it feels like to see the scrape marks made in the stone walls and floors by shackled Africans. Nor can the literature prepare you for the smell that is still there—yes, still there—from the feces, vomit, and in the women's dungeons, menses that were often at calf height despite shallow drainage trenches that had been dug into the floors once the storerooms began to hold people.

The scholarly literature also cannot help you process learning about or seeing houses of worship built into the forts. In Cape Coast, a chapel used to be immediately above one of the male dungeons. (Did moans of rapture and misery mix there?) In Elmina, a chapel was built in the central courtyard just outside the windowless punishment cell where thirty slaves at a time, chained together, were forced behind a door that would remain closed until every last person was dead. It is now a museum. On the second floor of the castle and almost directly over the punishment chamber, there is a small room that overlooks the courtyard chapel. Above the threshold of the door is a wood carving that a Dutch governor commissioned. Was it a reminder to his garrisoned troops about their role in Elmina? Did he leave it so that future generations could understand their motivations? Was it some sort of epitaph? As it happens, the carving is an excerpt from Psalm 132: "For the LORD has chosen Zion, he has desired it for his dwelling, saying, 'This is my resting place for ever and ever; here I will sit enthroned, for I have desired it. I will bless her with abundant provisions; her poor I will satisfy with food. I will clothe her priests with salvation, and her faithful people will ever sing for joy.'"[8]

Elmina and Cape Coast Castles are twenty minutes apart by car—while standing on the buttress of one you can just make out the other with the naked eye. They also happen to be, if one can forgive the stunningly inappropriate analogy, the indisputable jewels in Ghana's tourism crown.[9]

THE FACTS ABOUT HOME, II

Days earlier, I had been wondering what my experiences were going to be like and how I was going to be affected. I began my journey to Ghana with a five-day excursion in England that included a visit to the International Slavery Museum in Liverpool and a talk at Oxford University's Rhodes House.

The International Slavery Museum opened in 2007 for the bicentennial of the British abolition of the slave trade. At the time of this writing, it occupies the third floor of the Merseyside Maritime Museum at Liverpool's Albert Dock, now the site of the largest collection of museums in the United Kingdom outside London.[10] The museum is divided into thirds. One end of the museum displays artifacts that one would find in a West African village. The other end of the museum examines the legacies of slavery—there, an exhibit of portraits featuring blacks in the diaspora who have accomplished great things is joined by exhibits examining current human rights abuses around the globe. The middle third of the museum focuses on the enslaved experience, from life on a typical sugarcane plantation to the journey through the middle passage itself. In the very center of the entire museum is a small, circular theater that offers what one can only call a multisensory experience about life aboard a slave ship—or, more accurately, in the hold of a slave ship. Curators refer to the space as the "Middle Passage Immersion."

The short film appeals to two only senses: sight and sound. Nevertheless, the immersion is overwhelming.

When I walked in, I didn't know that the looping film only ran two minutes, but I do not think that I even lasted that long. Feelings of abject subjugation surrounded me as I heard actors and actresses moaning, their faces caked with open sores. I watched them vomiting and then saw that vomit drop down through the slats of their shelf onto the person below. I noticed the way the shackles tore into their ankles and heard the creaking of the shipboards and the whistling of the wind. I had to get out of the theater so that I could breathe easily again.[11]

A deep sleep and a comfortable train ride the next day took me away from the "Middle Passage Immersion" and to Oxford University. I was there to give a talk on (of all things) spectacle and trauma. I had plenty of free time before the talk, however, so I took advantage of the weather and walked around the campus, visiting some of its most famous museums. I became overwhelmed in a totally different way. At the newly renovated Ashmolean, I wandered across four floors of artifacts that cataloged civilizations across thousands of years. At the Pitt Rivers Museum of Anthropology, I strolled among endless glass cases that displayed the bones, masks, feathers, arrows, and more from the natural and civilizing world. At the Bodleian Library, I had the fortune of catching the "Treasures of the Bodleian" exhibit before it closed. There I viewed, among other things, the Gutenberg Bible, the Magna Carta, a lyric poem by Sappho, Euclid's *Elements of Geometry*, Shakespeare's First Folio, the Gospel of St. Thomas from the third century, and a copy of the Qur'an from the sixteenth. Taken together, my tour of Oxford's museums was a quick journey across time and space of recorded histories. The best of what we have known, made, and thought was represented in those aptly named treasures.

The irony of it all was not lost on me. I could not ignore the fact that in twenty-four hours I would be traveling south to a different country where I would visit a different set of museums that were deeply involved in the violent erasure (once thought complete but now recognized as partial) of the memories of millions of people. I was also attuned to the further irony that my trip to Ghana was immediately preceded by my talk at Rhodes House, the administrative center for the Rhodes Scholarships, both named in honor of colonialist Cecil Rhodes, who, to be as politic as one could be, was not confident that African colonial subjects—who apparently did not have a past worth preserving—could be civilized and thus "saved."[12]

As I would come to understand in the next few days, the juxtaposition between England and Ghana was jarring in more ways than I could have anticipated. Take, for example, the comparisons one draws from the imperial seat and the imperial site. When I compare my experiences in Oxford and Cape Coast or Elmina, I could see that the seat and the site encompassed a series of museums and administrative centers that were historically about affirming (whether through remembrance or erasure) state power and, in essence, "home." What I would also learn is that when it came to the slave forts and castles, one can safely say that not until 1979—at least not in any official, state-sponsored way—did the shared imperial narratives about home begin to run on different tracks.

The fact that the castles at Cape Coast and Elmina were still standing hundreds of years after they were built could be read as an ironic insistence that the history and memory of what transpired in the forts could not be erased. As it happens, however, until relatively recently both castles were silent sentinels that harkened back to a past of some sort, but not one that was detailed by curators or guides and developed as a site for tourism. In *Routes of Remembrance: Refashioning the Slave Trade in Ghana*, anthropologist Bayo Holsey elaborates that Ghanaians who lived in the shadows of the castles were mainly curious about who would construct such huge buildings, especially when they were not houses of worship. Holsey points out that this general lack of curiosity was due to the "reticence of previous generations to discuss the slave trade." Because of this, "the castles long remained profane structures within the landscapes of Cape Coast and Elmina, appreciated primarily for their size and beauty." She continues: "While residents regularly entered the castles, they did not view them as important historical monuments, and if they were uneducated, did not associate them with the slave trade."[13]

Ghanaian sensibilities about the slave forts began to change in 1979 when the United Nations Educational, Scientific, and Cultural Organization (UNESCO) designated Cape Coast and Elmina Castles World Heritage Sites.[14] This heightened interest in the castles encouraged a more intense dedication to their preservation and an opportunity to reap the financial benefits of tourist dollars. Although this would eventually prove to be the case, debates about the very act of preservation, the nature of remembrance, and the tension between the two dominated conversations about the castles for the next decade.[15] Slowly, over the course of the 1990s, momentum began to build as first PANAFEST, a Pan-African heritage festival based at the slave castles, and then groups like the African American Society to Preserve Cape Coast Castle embraced the castles as sites of remembrance.

Predictably, accompanying this increased attention were debates about the propriety of preservation and tourism. Was it appropriate to maintain and even beautify such sites of horror? Should tours be conducted? Should visitors be expected to pay for the tours? Should the dungeons be cleaned of the centuries of accumulated filth?[16] Should they even be called castles when they were, in fact, dungeons?[17] Should there be a restaurant? (A restaurant-bar was built at Cape Coast in the early 1990s but was quickly closed as numerous groups—from tourists to local chiefs—expressed their anger over the decision. For African American tourists, building the restaurant in the castle was akin to putting a café in a cemetery; local chiefs were furious that they were not properly consulted.)[18]

In the end—and, for some, "the end" clearly meant a capitulation to the almighty American tourist dollar—Ghanaian curators, cultural figures, and politicians embraced the UNESCO designation and went to work developing a new narrative for an age of return, rediscovery, and reimagination. Part of this new narrative was literally built into the castle walls in 1992 when identical plaques were placed in the courtyards at Cape Coast and Elmina. These plaques marked a major step in a still-evolving narrative of recognition and reconciliation:

In everlasting memory of the anguish of our ancestors.
May those who died rest in peace.
May those who return find their roots.
May humanity never again perpetrate such injustice against humanity.
We, the living, vow to uphold this.

The closing paragraph of *Castles & Forts of Ghana*, a handsome photo-essay book that I purchased at the entrance to the castles, builds on this new narrative clearly: "If the castles and forts gangways leading to the slave ships once appeared to be 'the doors of no return,' thanks to the new spirit of reconciliation and the UNESCO institutionalisation of the Castle and Fort culture, now it has become 'a new Akwaaba' for the black Diaspora, the 'Gates of Return' into their second home, their real home, in Africa!"[19]

The book's final comments invite a thought-experiment about the meaning of home and return: What does it mean to come home to a place you have never been? Can you return when you have never left?

More directly, however, the closing words are an explicit reference to an Emancipation Day celebration held a year earlier at Cape Coast. The remains of two former slaves, Crystal from Jamaica and Samuel Carson from the United States, were exhumed and transported back to Ghana. Then they were passed from the exterior of the castle into the courtyard through the Door of No Return before being reinterred at Assin Manso, an upriver location recognized as the final resting stop before the slave castles.[20] As part of this ceremony, the exterior side of the door was renamed the Door of Return.

When the tour guide opened the Door of No Return and encouraged my group to go outside, we did not find some fantastic wasteland that served as a living testament to the horrors of life in the castle and the trade that justified its existence. Instead, we came face-to-face with a thriving fishing culture. Hundreds of men were sorting out their nets as they pulled canoes up from the surf. Flags of various colors flew from the canoes' prows, making the scene almost feel like a festival. As tourists—all of whom are considered *obruni*, or "white foreigner," even if they are black—we were simply part of the castle scene that the fishermen saw performed several times a day, every day. Our two groups, the fishermen and the tourists, didn't interact and, in effect, were characters in a tableau vivant. The tourists were curious, a bit dazed, but unsure of what to do except to go back into the castle; the fishermen were too busy to care. Ironically, I felt more at ease in the castle, as if I belonged there, not outside.

After walking back into the castle through the Door of Return, we were greeted by a large tile plaque affixed to the wall that read "AKWAABA." Usually, "akwaaba" means "welcome." Since the reconciliation ceremony in 1998, however, a more formal interpretation of the word was intended: "welcome home." This is where the tour of Cape Coast Castle concludes. The tour guide, after leading the group through chambers of horror—the men's and women's dungeons, the punishment cells for those who resisted their capture, the site where the Anglican chapel used to be—told us that with this gesture, Ghana welcomes its brothers and sisters home and teaches us that one of the typical responses to "akwaaba" is "maydasi," or "thank you." He then offers a "new akwaaba" to all of us, and we respond with "maydasi" in unison, on this occasion meaning more than merely "thank you" but "thank you for welcoming us home." At that point we are free to walk around the castle, ideally stopping in the castle gift shop after we finish our self-guided tour of the museum on the second floor. The entrance to the shop is immediately to your right when you exit the museum. A banner proudly positioned above the door signals that this is a stop not to be missed. It turns out that the Cape Coast Castle Museum Shop was recognized at the Eighth National Tourism Awards ceremony as the Tourism Retail Outlet of the Year, Coastal Zone.

I did not go in.

Meanwhile, in Elmina Castle, a 2011 exhibit in its museum makes clear that questions about the connections between memory and tourism are also unresolved, and ironies about the castles as renovated sites of horror and

Fishing village, Cape Coast, Ghana (author's collection)

remembrance remain. The exhibit details the renovation and preservation of the castle and captures (unintentionally?) the still-underexplored contradictions embedded in the process of renovation as well as the debates about how the sacred and profane clash at the slave castles. The final poster in the exhibit is titled, "Building on the Past to Create a Better Future."

THE FACTS ABOUT HOME, III

I was sitting in the resort's beachside restaurant when my smartphone's alarm interrupted the bizarre reverie I had been lost in since returning from Cape Coast. It was time to take my antimalarial medicine. I put down Caryl Phillips's *Crossing the River,* a curious choice to take my mind off Cape Coast, since the book begins with an African father lamenting the fact that he had to sell his three children into slavery—sending them downriver (perhaps past Assin Manso?)—because his crops had failed so miserably. When my dinner arrived—banku and okra stew (trying to eat like a local though paying resort prices)—I took my pill, and while scrolling through digital pictures of the castle, I noticed that I was humming. Since I found it more than a little inappropriate to hum while bearing witness to such horror, I paused a half-second to wonder what tune, exactly, was on my mind.

I was dumbstruck, utterly unable to process the depth of our surreal universe, when I realized I was humming along to the restaurant musician who was playing a spritely version of one of the Carpenters' most famous pop love songs on his minisynthesizer:

Everything I want the world to be
Is now coming true especially for me
And the reason is clear
It's because you are here
You're the nearest thing to heaven that I've seen

I'm on the top of the world lookin' down on creation
And the only explanation I can find
Is the love that I've found ever since you've been around
Your love's put me at the top of the world.

The next morning, I was still trying to locate some redeeming significance from my absentminded humming along with Karen and Richard Carpenter. While it would have been nice to believe that the lyrics were some sort of spiritual call from my ancestors, thanking me for returning home, I reconciled myself to the fact that soft pop treacle from the 1970s made for nice background music at an upscale, surfside restaurant at a re-sort catering to European, Caribbean, and American tourists. For me, the significance of the moment came in the recognition that I was a member of the target audience: a tourist with disposable income who would know the music well enough to be able to hum along absentmindedly. The Carpenters, not this place, represented my home.

After breakfast, I found myself back in my private car, being driven along the Trans-West African Coastal Highway, headed to Accra for a tour of the major downtown attractions. Throughout the two-hour ride to Accra I was engrossed in various sights: roadside vendors selling pineapples; trucks laden with kenkey, a fermented maize side dish I was summoning the cour-age to try; small towns that would suddenly emerge and disappear just as quickly; magnificent silk cotton trees towering like sentinels over the rest of the coastal canopy; and tro-tros (shared taxis, more like minivans) covered with stickers declaring a faith in God or Jesus, crammed with people, car-rying the occasional goat on the roof. I also kept my eyes peeled for other tourists like me. We were, in fact, everywhere, and we always stood out, whether it was due to our ubiquitous plastic bottles of water, our cameras at the ready, or our upscale air-conditioned cars or buses.

Most of all, I was hoping to run into a tour group from New York City that I knew was going to be in Ghana at the same time I was there and would be covering much of the same ground. This was a tour organized by the Brooklyn Museum of Contemporary African Diaspora Art (MoCADA) as the signature event of its fall programming. A week earlier, I had met someone who was going on the MoCADA trip. We were both waiting for our visas at the Ghanaian consulate in New York City and struck up a brief con-versation. Mid-twenties, relatively affluent (I assume, given the cost of travel to Ghana and then the tour itself) though evincing an Afro-Bohemian air, this traveler left me transfixed. Much of my fascination was driven by the fact that I already knew MoCADA had billed the trip as "A Journey Home." Was she a traveler, a romantic, or suffering a broken heart? Although she was a U.S. citizen and a resident of New York City, where was her home? Unfortunately, in that moment my tendency toward shyness overcame my scholarly curiosity and I had failed to ask the MoCADA traveler all of these questions and more.

Frustrated at myself for the lost opportunity, I scanned the tour buses we passed on the trip back to the capital, determined to ask those questions if our paths crossed.[21] Regrettably, that opportunity never came. Before I knew it, my guide pulled our car into the empty parking lot at the W. E. B. Du Bois Memorial Centre for Pan-African Culture, the first stop on my daylong tour of Accra, the site of Du Bois's Ghanaian home, and the final resting place for him and his wife Shirley Graham Du Bois.

Perhaps Du Bois's last years are a metaphor for the challenges that arise when questions of home are wrapped up in black memory. Hounded in his final decades by a reactionary federal government for his peace activities, frustrated by the fact that his passport had been held for seven years so that he could not travel freely, and despairing that America's color lines were too strong to erase, Du Bois gave up his U.S. citizenship in 1961 and accepted Kwame Nkrumah's invitation to relocate to Ghana, where he would receive state support to complete his long-dreamt-of *Encyclopedia Africana*.[22] Du Bois's Ghanaian home is now a museum that contains his private office; a room full of gifts, mementoes, and commendations from Cold War Communist leaders; and a public library. In truth, though, the place is threadbare, and the museum docent, though very pleasant, seems simultaneously disengaged and fully aware of how little there actually is on-site.

The last stop on the short tour was the mausoleum containing Shirley Graham Du Bois's ashes, which sit next to a large, marble crypt where her husband was interred after a state funeral led by Nkrumah. Ceremonial stools line the sides of the tomb and offer symbols of love, brotherhood, and harmony carved into their bases. Significantly, one of the stools also has a carving of the symbol for the sankofa bird. Represented by a bird walking to the left while its head arches up and back to the right, suggesting a circle, the sankofa bird is a reminder of the past's importance, since it is always returning even while it is moving forward.

Thinking about this, the hesitant yet emergent diasporic romantic in me cannot help but hear in new ways Du Bois's words from 1919, when he called on black Americans to rise up to the challenge of claiming their full citizenship rights in the wake of the sacrifices of their sons on the killing fields of Europe. Although dismayed, Du Bois still believed in the American experiment then. He still believed that there would come a time when black memory would be enfolded into the nation's history—even if Du Bois had to write the history himself.

Indeed, as I stood next to Du Bois's crypt, next to this Ghanaian citizen's final resting place, next to the stool with the sankofa bird carved into its base, Du Bois's words from 1919 truly sounded different: "We return. We return from fighting. We return fighting."

Despite the chills I felt while standing in Du Bois's presence, despite the evocative lure of the call, and even despite the sankofa bird's beckoning, I recognize that my trip to Ghana was not a diasporic return for me. My people still hail from North Carolina and Virginia, even though I now know in a more literal way the sights, sounds, textures, and aromas of where their people's people might have called home. Similarly, while I found it deeply moving to see piles of memorial wreaths laid in the slave dungeons at Cape Coast Castle and by the Door of No Return at Elmina Castle, I also know that it would have felt like too much artifice for me to have left a wreath. I also appreciate that my embrace of my Ghanaian memories, albeit sincere and representing a way of understanding one's place in the world, is just that: my embrace of my memories. Other African Americans who traveled the same paths—and at almost literally the same time—speak about their Ghanaian memories in very different ways.

Even though I never connected with the MoCADA tour group while in Ghana, a member of that group kept a journal of her ten-day adventure and posted a post-trip testimonial online at the MoCADA website. The testimonial underscores the profoundly different ways that diasporan memories are kept:

> Oh Mother Africa, you have welcomed us home—It's so cutting, like something opens me up and reveals more than I can handle. On Tuesday, October 18th, I wrote these words as I sat at the edge of the Atlantic Ocean after breakfast just a few hours before we would go to St. George's Castle Dungeon at Elmina. My first Journey Home was a gift in oh-so-many ways. The opportunity to travel to my cultural home . . . to spend days in the Motherland with a group of young and young at heart people who love and value art, culture, themselves, and Africa; the heat, the sounds, the rhythms, the food, the smiles, "Akwaaba!"

Her experiences were "remarkable, inspiring, beautiful, energizing, balancing, wrenching and overwhelming." Recounting how she "tearfully and sorrowfully descended to the depths of the dungeons of the castles" and felt "the torment, grief, and resilience of my ancestors who fought, endured, and survived so that I could be," she was also deeply moved by her visit to the Kwame Nkrumah Memorial Park and then the Du Bois Centre. The visit to Du Bois's home was particularly affecting: "Walking where he walked, seeing the books in his library, and being able to sit on a stool at the foot of his tomb, was surreal. As I stood at the case displaying his teacups and began to cry, I had to stop myself for fear that if I released, it would take too long to come back." She concludes her testimonial with a declaration: "I am a child of Africa. My name is vickie [*sic*], I have made my first Sankofa, and I thank God for the Journey Home."[23]

The tourist's closing thoughts are captivating. That she felt she had to restrain her emotions for fear it would "take too long to come back" invites all manner of questions. What was at stake for her in coming back? Where was she coming back from, and why would it take so long to return? Where was she going? Woven through these musings, and apparent throughout her testimonial, in fact, is the question of "home." MoCADA marketed the event as a journey home, and it is clear that at least for this member of the group, this construction was more than a clever turn of phrase. Since I visited many of the same sites as the MoCADA tour group, I feel comfortable claiming that many of my literal Ghanaian memories must be similar. I recognize, however, that my figurative memories could not be more different, even if my memories, like Vickie's, still wrestle with the meaning of home.

This, I think, leads to the crux of what is so vexing about African American memory. If memories are the narratives that tell us who we are and tell us where we belong, if memories are the creative forces behind the formation of homes, communities, and nations, where does black memory take its people? Can black memory help African Americans find their home?

As he prepared to take his first trip to Ghana (then the Gold Coast) in the early 1950s, Richard Wright wondered many of the same things. When Wright's wife and their friends encouraged him to make the trip in order to observe Prime Minister Kwame Nkrumah's efforts to put Gold Coast on the path to independence, Wright's first response was shock: "'Africa!' I repeated the word to myself, then paused as something strange and disturbing stirred slowly in the depths of me. I am African! I'm of African descent. . . . Yet I'd never seen Africa; I'd never really known any Africans; I'd hardly ever thought of Africa." Wright wondered, "Being of African descent, would I be able to feel and know something about Africa on the basis of a common 'racial' heritage? Africa was a vast continent full of 'my people.'"

Not sure if the intervening "three hundred years imposed a psychological distance" between himself and his ancestors that was so great he might not be African at all, Wright still felt compelled to go. He needed to answer certain bedeviling questions: "Was there something in Africa that my feelings could latch onto to make all of this dark past clear and meaningful? Would the Africans regard me as a lost brother who had returned?"[24]

As he convinced himself to make the journey, Wright's uncertainty did not wane. Yes, he wanted to learn more about Nkrumah's efforts, wanted to know if this black prime minister would be able to lead a peaceful decolonization effort, but Wright could not escape the nagging feeling that he should be more excited about the trip, energized by the knowledge that he was going to his figurative home. He understood that modern racial thinking suggested there should be "some vestige, some heritage, some vague but definite ancestral reality that would serve as a key to unlock the hearts and feelings of the Africans whom I'd meet. . . . But I could not feel anything African about myself, and I wondered, 'What does being *African* mean?'"[25]

Wright, of course, did go to Gold Coast and discovered while there just how Western and American he really was. His book-length travelogue is filled with instances of frustration, pride, fascination, and condescension about black African cultural, social, and political practices and possibilities.[26] Even though Wright's visit occurred nearly sixty years before the Mo-CADA group journeyed home and before I made my own trip (ostensibly to observe others return home), it is clear that we all wrestled with a wide spectrum of powerful emotions. All of us were African American, all of us were making our first trip to Africa, and all of us wondered what was in store for us in a place that was an ancestral and/or cultural home of some type.

My Ghanaian experiences have helped me understand that when it comes to so many aspects of the African American past, literal and figurative memories always and never align. For example, as much as I appreciate the emotional recollections of the MoCADA tourists, I also cannot understand them. We share the same home, but we also clearly do not. In this case, their experiences and mine point to the terrible truth in which a search for home can lead to a place where one finds there is no home worth having. After all, no one wants home to be a horror-soaked dungeon. Neither do people want home to be a place where the dictums of second-class citizenship rule the day: Get off the sidewalk, lower your eyes, don't talk back, know your place, tell them what they want to hear, act right, talk right, and most of all, be grateful for what you have.

In *Atlantic Sound*, Caryl Phillips writes, "Where a man keeps his memories is the place he should call home."[27] Phillips is talking here about memory's ability to move, reshape, and reconstitute itself until it has found a place it can claim as its own. When all is said and done, perhaps this is memory's great gift: its ability to hearken back to real and figurative events that allow people to imagine a place they can call home, even if that home is somewhere they have never been before. In such instances, "home" is a place where the possible and impossible can commingle, where contradiction makes more sense than tidy narratives that speak of unflinching progress, and where the psychological shelter of the figurative can offer protection that is as real as the roof over one's head.

NOTES

INTRODUCTION

1. Walker, *Richard Wright, Daemonic Genius*, 154.

2. Wright, "How 'Bigger' Was Born," xxvii.

3. See Grant, *Negro with a Hat*; Lewis, *W. E. B. Du Bois, 1868–1918*; Lewis, *W. E. B. Du Bois, 1919–1963*; McKay and Maxwell, *Complete Poems*; Gilmore, *Defying Dixie*; and Holloway, *Confronting the Veil*.

4. Kersten, *A. Philip Randolph*; Pfeffer, *A. Philip Randolph*.

5. Historians have argued convincingly for a reframing of the civil rights movement era such that it does not begin in 1954 or 1955 and end in 1968. They point to earlier starting points prior to World War II, referring to this new periodization as the "long civil rights movement." I lean on that construction here. For a sampling of the long civil rights history, see, among others, Hall, "Long Civil Rights Movement and the Political Uses of the Past"; Gilmore, *Defying Dixie*; Singh, *Black Is a Country*; Brown-Nagin, *Courage to Dissent*; and Hamlin, *Crossroads at Clarksdale*.

6. Douglass, *Narrative of the Life of Frederick Douglass*; Jacobs, *Incidents in the Life of a Slave Girl*; Brown, *Narrative of William W. Brown*.

7. Blassingame, "Black Autobiographies as History and Literature," 7.

8. The new memory politics I will be examining start to occur at a scale heretofore not experienced or expressed in African America. Here I join scholars like Ron Eyerman who recognize that as African Americans migrated from the rural landscapes toward the urban, they also participated in expanding ways with new spheres of technology and communication. See Eyerman, *Cultural Trauma*.

9. In an essay on change and continuity in black music, Nathaniel Mackey argues, "Underlying the great amount of attention given to changes in the black stance and situation is the deeper conviction that a continuum exists within which the threat of dilution, cooptation, or amalgamation by the dominant white culture has been and continues to be repelled. A black *position*, one of outsidedness or of alienation and resistance (which will in [Amiri Baraka's] *Black Music* come to be called 'the changing same'), becomes a kind of 'unmoved mover' at the root of black America's transformations" (Mackey, "Changing Same," 360). Similarly, in *Blues People*, his classic critique of cultural practices and racial authenticity, Baraka (then LeRoi Jones) talks about the "consistent attitudes within changed contexts" (Jones, *Blues People*, 153).

10. Blight, *Race and Reunion*, 109.

11. Wright, "Ethics of Living Jim Crow," 2. Also see Ritterhouse, *Growing Up Jim Crow*, 170–71.

12. Wright, "Ethics of Living Jim Crow," 1–2.

13. Holloway, *Confronting the Veil*, xi.

14. Ellison, "Richard Wright's Blues," 85.

15. Nora, "Between Memory and History," 285–86.

16. Earley, "Introduction."

17. Popkin, *History, Historians, & Autobiography*, 63.

18. The full quote is as follows: "Silences enter the process of historical production at four crucial moments: the moment of fact creation (the making of *sources*); the moment of fact assembly (the making of *archives*); the moment of fact retrieval (the making of *narratives*); and the moment of retrospective significance (the making of *history* in the final instance)" (Trouillot, *Silencing the Past*, 26).

19. Brundage, "No Deed but Memory," 6.

20. Wallach, *Closer to the Truth Than Any Fact*, 145.

21. Warren, *Who Speaks for the Negro?*, ix. Getting to the truth of something means relying on "facts." What a fact happens to be, however, is a matter of philosophical debate. See Howlett and Morgan, *How Well Do Facts Travel?*

22. For more on this controversy, see Arsenault, *Sound of Freedom*.

CHAPTER 1

1. The long and tangled history of blacks' battles for respectability is well told from a range of perspectives. Some leading examples include Higginbotham, *Righteous Discontent*; Gaines, *Uplifting the Race*; and Hunter, *To 'Joy My Freedom*.

2. Wright, "How 'Bigger' Was Born," xxiii.

3. See, for example, the following books: Harris and Spero, *Black Worker*; Harris, *Negro as Capitalist*; Davis, Gardner, and Gardner, *Deep South*; Davis and Dollard, *Children of Bondage*; Johnson, *Shadow of the Plantation*; Johnson, Embree, and Alexander, *Collapse of Cotton Tenancy*; Johnson, *Patterns of Negro Segregation*; Frazier, *Negro Family in Chicago*; Frazier, *Negro Family in the United States*; and Frazier, *Negro Youth at the Crossways*. Bunche and Dorsey wrote in short form. For further discussion of this era's social science scholarship, see Holloway, *Confronting the Veil*, and Holloway and Keppel, *Black Scholars on the Line*.

4. Most famously, the modern field of cultural relativism was fostered at Columbia University under the leadership of anthropologist Franz Boas. Meanwhile, at the University of Chicago, Robert Park was creating a massive sociological research agenda with a specific focus on race. Many of the leading black scholars trained at Columbia and Chicago during this era.

5. Wright, "Introduction," xviii.

6. See Wright, "How 'Bigger' Was Born," throughout.

7. Wright, *12 Million Black Voices*.

8. Sutherland, "Preface," xi, xii.

9. Johnson, *Growing Up in the Black Belt*, xxii.

10. Ibid., 77.

11. Ibid., 99.

12. Ibid., 76.

13. Ibid., 332.

14. Wright, *12 Million Black Voices*, 41.

15. Frazier, *Negro Youth at the Crossways*, 63.

16. Ibid., 290–92.

17. Jackson, *Gunnar Myrdal and America's Conscience*, 110–13, 130–33, 186–230.

18. Myrdal, *American Dilemma*, li.

19. Jackson, *Gunnar Myrdal and America's Conscience*, 27–35.

20. Ibid., 121–34.

21. Ibid., 241–45. The enthusiasm for *An American Dilemma* would wane over time. By the mid-1960s, many scholars, particularly African Americans, had grown weary of the moralism found throughout the book. One of the most influential critiques of *An American Dilemma* was written by Ralph Ellison when the book appeared. The review, however, was not published until 1964 when Ellison included it as the final essay in his collection, *Shadow and Act*. Deeply unhappy with Myrdal's contention that blacks' development was always in reaction to whites' actions, Ellison wrote, "But can a people . . . live and develop for over three hundred years simply by *reacting*? Are American Negroes simply the creation of white men, or have they at least helped to create themselves out of what they found around them?" (Ellison, *"American Dilemma,"* 315). Also see Jackson, *Gunnar Myrdal and America's Conscience*, 298–310.

22. Holloway, "Editor's Introduction," 25.

23. Myrdal, *American Dilemma*, 966–79.

24. Ibid., 963.

25. Ibid., 928.

26. Ibid., 928–29.

27. Ibid., 927–29.

28. Ibid., 929.

29. Ibid., 60.

30. Janken, *Rayford W. Logan and the Dilemma of the African-American Intellectual*, 145–66.

31. Couch, "Publisher's Introduction," xxi–xxii.

32. Ibid., xxii.

33. Renan, "What Is a Nation?," 11.

34. Wright, "Introduction," xvii.

35. Drake and Cayton, *Black Metropolis*, xiii–xiv.

36. Wright, "Introduction," xvii.

37. Ibid., xxix.

38. Ibid., xix.

39. Ibid., xxviii.

40. Drake and Cayton, *Black Metropolis*, 379.

41. Ibid., 572.

42. Ibid., 564.

43. Ibid., 566.

44. "This account of a doctor's Christmas experience is based on an actual incident witnessed by one of the authors, when he was a participant-observer in a group of lower-class households for six months, and on interviews with the physician involved and his wife. The principal characters' inner thoughts are obviously fictionalized. But

the other quoted material in this chapter, as throughout the book, has been selected from interview-documents gathered by trained interviewers and has not been subjected to imaginative recasting" (ibid., 564).

45. Ibid., 728.

CHAPTER 2

1. In his examination of cultural trauma, sociologist Ron Eyerman writes about "unifying primal scenes" in black life, pointing to the connections between the cultural legacies of slavery and the construction of a black community. Eyerman points out that many blacks feel that slavery is something "lived and living, an inherited and transmitted habitus which determines current behavior." The fact that a codified system of slavery is defunct does not matter to those for whom being enslaved was part of their family history. The lingering effects of that cultural trauma had a profound and ongoing effect on personality development. See Eyerman, *Cultural Trauma*, 194.

2. Despite his eventual claims to the contrary, Johnson never actually edited *Negro Digest*. He hired Ben Burns, a white journalist and former Communist, to edit the new magazine. Johnson was the business mind driving the enterprise. Fearful that black readers and political moderates (Johnson's target population) would reject a magazine edited by a white radical, Johnson convinced Burns to work anonymously at first. See Burns, *Nitty Gritty*, 30–31, 36–38. On the Johnson business empire, see Johnson, *Succeeding against the Odds*, 152–71, 205–9, 248–52, 324–35, 340–56.

3. The black press was a vehicle for identity construction, a means for a struggling population to ascertain its space in the American republic. Given the value and power of the black press, we are compelled to look more carefully at who produced these papers and whom the editors targeted as their reading audience. It should come as no surprise that these publications were the work of middle- and upper-class blacks. These individuals, though undoubtedly committed to uplifting the race through raising group awareness of local, national, and international events (and how these events affected their lives and social status as citizens), were also committed to the preservation of their own status as leaders in the black community. These publishers consistently sought a black middle-class public that was also committed to personal elevation and self-preservation. The black press placed a heavy emphasis on lifestyle announcements like marriages, charity events, cotillions, fraternal and sororal events, and women's service group activities. To that end, the content of the black press reinforced the bourgeois strivings of its publishers and audience and sent a powerful message of proper black behavior. But it wasn't just about reinforcing a bourgeois mentality. Striving working-class blacks could look to *Negro Digest* (and later Johnson publications) as a reservoir of black middle-class sensibilities that they could tap for aspirational purposes. See Shaw, "'Negro Digest,' 'Pulse,' and 'Headlines and Pictures,'" 33–36.

4. In his study on black graduates from United Negro College Fund member institutions, social scientist Daniel C. Thompson points to the reliance of pre-1960s black leaders on white support: "Too often black segregated leaders had to be approved by powerful white segregationists in order to get anything done for their black followers. Usually the black community suspected the more effective among them as

being 'safe,' in the sense that they would bow to white mores rather than insist upon black rights" (Thompson, *Black Elite*, 151). Nathan Hare labeled the leaders of the civil rights movement "Black Anglo-Saxons" because they were so dependent on white support: "Dignitary leaders tend to be either handpicked by the white power structure or catapulted into fame by white press coverage of some mass event. (At least two leaders were made in the March on Washington.)" (Hare, *Black Anglo-Saxons*, 1). For similar claims about black leadership's reliance on white benefactors, see Holloway, *Confronting the Veil*, and Holloway, "Black Intellectual and the 'Crisis Canon' in the Twentieth Century."

5. For examples of Schuyler's biting style and his political independence, see Schuyler, *Black No More* and *Black and Conservative*. New scholarship on Schuyler has begun to appear in recent years. See, for example, Hill and Rasmussen, *Black Empire*; Leak, *Rac(e)ing to the Right*; and Ferguson, *Sage of Sugar Hill*.

6. Schuyler, "My Most Humiliating Jim Crow Experience."

7. Jim Crow and travel went hand in hand. *The Negro Handbook*, a compilation of facts and statistics about black life in America, included a special section on civil rights that listed lawsuits that grew out of incidents of racial discrimination in different travel industries. See, for example, Murray, *Negro Handbook*, 33–34.

8. "Evict Negro Soldier Even from Jim-Crow Seat in Bus." Mitchell had just announced that he would not run for reelection, and this article was written as a retrospective of Mitchell's congressional career. The case in question is *Mitchell v. United States* 313 US 80 (1941), in which the court held that the denial of "substantial equality of treatment by an interstate carrier based on color or race is a violation of the Federal Interstate Commerce Act." This was not as much a literal victory against Jim Crow as it was a reaffirmation of that aspect of *Plessy v. Ferguson* that declared that as long as accommodations were equal, separation was constitutional. That said, Mitchell's case significantly restricted the extent to which one could interpret and then apply *Plessy*'s doctrine. See "Mitchell's Greatest Victory Doomed Jim-Crow Cars" and "Mulzac Back Home."

9. "Insult to Captain Mulzac." On Mulzac's fame, see Biondi, *To Stand and Fight*, 8, 151. A political cartoon about the Mulzac incident ran in the following week's edition of the *Afro-American*. In it, Captain Mulzac is depicted sitting down to eat a large pie. The crust is open, and there's a bare chicken bone inside—nothing else. Meanwhile, steam rises from the bone with the word "segregation" in it. On the pie pan is the phrase "Four Freedoms for Everybody." Below the picture is the cartoon text, which reads, "Sing a song of sixpence, a pocket full of rye; four gigantic freedoms baked in a pie. When the pie was opened, a bone was in the pan; wasn't that a measly thing to set before a man?" ("Nursery Rhyme for Captain Hugh Mulzac").

10. Coleman's quote reads in full, "I feel I have been done a great injustice, in that I am now in the armed forces of this great nation for the purpose of defending democracy, a democracy that has not yet awakened to the fact that any man who is good enough to offer his life for the defense of a country is entitled to a fair deal from that country; no more should any man ask, no less should he receive" ("Evict Negro Soldier Even from Jim-Crow Seat in Bus"). In Mulzac's case, when the Virginia police officer said that Mulzac had to move, the skipper reportedly replied, "I have

orders, too. . . . My Government has given me orders to fight for democracy. It seems your State Government has given you orders to fight against democracy. I'm over there fighting for you fellows over here. We are carrying stuff in the ships, day and night, watching for submarines for draft dodgers like you fellows over here who tell us where to sit" ("Mulzac Back Home").

11. Of the twenty-six "Jim Crow" essays, seven discussed Jim Crow incidents related directly to travel, and nine grew from disputes over public accommodation, chiefly in restaurants and hotels.

12. Logan, "My Most Humiliating Jim Crow Experience"; Rahn, "My Most Humiliating Jim Crow Experience."

13. Fleming, "My Most Humiliating Jim Crow Experience."

14. Frank Marshall Davis, "My Most Humiliating Jim Crow Experience," 57.

15. Ibid., 58.

16. Arthur P. Davis was, for much of his career, a professor of English at Howard University. The first black to earn a doctorate in English from Columbia University, Davis is best known as coeditor, with Sterling A. Brown, of *The Negro Caravan: Writings by American Negroes* and, with J. Saunders Redding, *Cavalcade: Negro American Writers from 1760 to the Present*.

17. Arthur P. Davis, "My Most Humiliating Jim Crow Experience," 61–62.

18. Hurston, "My Most Humiliating Jim Crow Experience," 25.

19. Ibid., 26.

20. Ibid., 26.

21. Powell, "My Most Humiliating Jim Crow Experience," 75.

22. Ibid., 75–76.

23. Hamilton, *Adam Clayton Powell, Jr.*, 115–21, 145–48.

24. Jane Dailey points to the literature that discusses the roots of the political debates about black freedom and the way that they revolved around a fear that black freedom meant an assault, literally and figuratively, on white women and womanhood. See Dailey, "Limits of Liberalism in the New South," 95.

25. Arguments linking manhood to a variety of symbolic, social, and political manifestations can be found in Gail Bederman's impressive *Manliness and Civilization*.

26. Redding was best known for such works as *To Make a Poet Black*, *No Day of Triumph*, and his collaboration with Arthur P. Davis on *Cavalcade*.

27. Redding, "My Most Humiliating Jim Crow Experience."

28. For various examples of interracial appeals, see the following in *Negro Digest*: "Our White Folks"; "Parlez-vous Francais? Da, Da, Tovarich"; "Some of Our Best Friends Are White"; "An Investment in Understanding"; "A Negro Magazine for Whites Also"; and "Bonanza for Dixie Libraries."

29. *Negro Digest*, June 1945, back cover.

30. Ibid.

31. *Negro Digest*, November 1942, back cover.

32. "Speaking of Christmas."

33. Myrdal, *American Dilemma*, 908.

34. Johnson claims to have come up with the idea for the series on his own. This claim is hotly disputed by Ben Burns, effectively *Negro Digest*'s editor in chief at the

time. As resolving this discrepancy is beyond the scope of this chapter, I refer to the "editors" when talking about Burns's and Johnson's collective contributions to the magazine's success. See Burns, *Nitty Gritty*, 35–38.

35. On frustration and bitterness, see a variety of essays that appeared in *Negro Digest* under the "If I Were a Negro" series title: Sancton, "Minority to Majority"; Spingarn, "Time Is NOW"; Borgese, "Bedroom Approach to Racism"; Field, "Color of Injustice"; Moon, "Dixie Bottleneck"; Adamic, "There Are Whites and Whites." For examples of essays that called for increased black involvement in the union movement, see Johnson, "Building a Brave New World," and McWilliams, "Economic Roots of Race Hate."

36. Zara, "Coming Days of Glory."

37. Johnson, "Whites are Individuals Too."

38. Ibid. Emphasis added.

39. Matthews, "My Most Humiliating Jim Crow Experience," 61.

40. Kevin Gaines offers a critical assessment of this uplift ideology in *Uplifting the Race*. See, especially, Gaines's introduction.

41. Villard, "No Time for Pessimism."

42. Stegner, "Common Cause of Color," 59.

43. In a scathing exception to the entire series, jazz critic Leonard Feather opined, "If I were a Negro I'd resent the vague idealism and lack of specific detail that has characterized most of the articles in the '*If I Were a Negro*' series to date." Feather's essay was also unusual for its cutting satire on race and social position. The title is effectively descriptive of the essay's tone: "Wanted: A White Mammy." See Feather, "Wanted: A White Mammy."

44. Pollock, "Demonstrate Not Demand."

45. Hurst, "Sure Way to Equality."

46. Park and Burgess, *Introduction to the Science of Sociology*, 138–39.

47. Embree, "Basic Steps toward Democracy."

48. Literary critic C. K. Doreski refers to the essays in the "If I Were a Negro" series as "philanthropically inclined and ultimately condescending liberalism" (Doreski, *Writing America Black*, 95).

49. Johnson, *Succeeding against the Odds*, 118–19.

50. Clark, "On Racism and Racist Systems"; Baraka, "Black Aesthetic"; Mkalimoto "Cultural Arm of Revolutionary Black Nationalism."

51. Alexander, *Black Interior*, 91–98.

52. "Backstage."

53. See, respectively, Alphonse Heningburg, the director of Education Services for the National Urban League, and Edwin Embree, president of the Julius Rosenwald Fund, in "Letters and Pictures to the Editor," *Ebony*, December 1945 and January 1946.

54. Daveson, "Letters and Pictures to the Editor."

55. The caption of the tennis photograph speaks volumes about *Ebony*'s visual stories. Here, leisure, accomplishment, and a commitment to the race went hand in hand: "Cosmopolitan Tennis Club on Convent Avenue boasts among its members National Urban League head Lester Granger and Negro College Fund executive William J. Trent,

joshing each other between sets about waistline worries. Cosmopolitan has played host to tennis stars like Alice Marble and Don Budge" (*Ebony*, November 1946, 9).

56. Little, "Letters and Pictures to the Editor."

57. Covers from *Jet*, November 1 and November 8, 1951.

58. "Nation Horrified by Murder of Kidnapped Chicago Youth." For more information on Till's murder, public witnessing, and the *Jet* photographs, see Raiford, *Imprisoned in a Luminous Glare*, 87–89.

59. Elizabeth Alexander points to others who had reactions similar to those of my colleague's father. Anne Moody, Charlayne Hunter-Gault, Shelby Steele, and Muhammad Ali wrote about their memories of Till's murder. All were shaken by their memories, but they all remain committed to share them. "These Emmett Till narratives," Alexander writes," illustrate how black people have paradoxically had to witness their own murder and defilement in order to survive and then to pass along this epic tale of violation" (Alexander, *Black Interior*, 189–94).

CHAPTER 3

1. *Shaft*.

2. Scholars have read the black body as a site of contestation over meanings of citizenship, sexuality, power, violence, social order, and nihilism. See, in the last fifteen years alone, Carby, *Race Men*; Brooks, *Bodies in Dissent*; Young, *Embodying Black Experience*; Brundage, *Beyond Blackface*; Robinson, *Forgeries of Memory and Meaning*; and Goldsby, *Spectacular Secret*.

3. Griffin, *Black Like Me*, 11.

4. Seiler, "'So That We as a Race Might Have Something Authentic to Travel By,'" 1092.

5. Ibid., 1099–1100.

6. Griffin, *Black Like Me*, 59.

7. Halsell, *Soul Sister*, 11.

8. Ibid., 13.

9. Ibid., 16.

10. Ibid., 158–59.

11. Sprigle, *In the Land of Jim Crow*, 5.

12. Ibid., 101.

13. Ibid., 111–12.

14. DeFrantz, *Dancing Revelations*, 26–28.

15. Todd and Ailey, "Roots of the Blues," quoted in ibid., 15.

16. *An Evening with Alvin Ailey American Dance Theater*.

17. DeFrantz, *Dancing Revelations*, 38.

18. Although writing about a different set of musical vernaculars, Karl Hagstrom Miller offers astute readings on how music and musical performance aligned with presumptions of cultural authenticity in the blues and country music (black music vs. white music). Audiences did not need to know the lyrics to any Negro spiritual, but they understood the cultural signifiers that accompanied black gospel folk music—even if the signifiers were complete fabrications. See Miller, *Segregating Sound*.

19. Many thanks to Leslie Woodard for helping me understand the language of the dancers' movement.

20. DeFrantz, *Dancing Revelations*, 23.

21. Ibid., 91.

22. Ailey interview in *An Evening with Alvin Ailey American Dance Theater*.

23. The AAADT had already become something of a fixture at the Kennedy Center by the time I first saw them. In fact, they were the first modern dance company to perform at the Kennedy Center, appearing just one month after the hall opened. See Dunning, *Alvin Ailey*, 268.

24. Von Eschen, *Satchmo Blows Up the World*, 1–4.

25. Ibid., 61–64.

26. The Kerner Commission, established by Lyndon Johnson in the wake of 1967 race riots and named for its chair, Otto Kerner, governor of Illinois, was impaneled to investigate the causes of urban racial unrest across the country. See Greaves, "Interview," 356–57.

27. Bowser, "Pioneers of Black Documentary Film"; Klotman and Cutler, *Struggles for Representation*, xv.

28. Knee and Musser, "William Greaves," 15.

29. Greaves, "Interview," 354–56.

30. Knee and Musser, "William Greaves," 16.

31. Greaves, "Interview," 357.

32. Cutler, "Rewritten on Film," 154.

33. On "factness," or the mutability and fungibility of a "fact," see Nelson, "Factness of Diaspora."

34. While *Take This Hammer* was important in its own right, it was not the first "black documentary" aired by KQED. That honor belongs to the series *Where Is Jim Crow?* that was conceived of and directed by Buzz Anderson and aired just a few months before the Baldwin documentary. *Where Is Jim Crow?* examined black life in the Bay Area, with a special focus on celebrities who hailed from the region or were passing through town. It was a simple arrangement: Anderson would sit with the guest—people such as Eartha Kitt, Lena Horne, Harry Belafonte, and Stokely Carmichael—in a plain studio with two chairs and a coffee table and discuss Jim Crow.

35. Baldwin interview in *Take This Hammer*.

36. Ibid.

37. Knee and Musser, "William Greaves," 16–17. For a fine general summary of the First World Festival—the actual festival, not the documentary—see Von Eschen, *Satchmo Blows Up the World*, 150–61.

38. *First World Festival of Negro Arts*.

39. Ibid.

40. Acham, *Revolution Televised*, 42–48.

41. Ouellette, *Viewers Like You?*, 134–35.

42. Lott, "Documenting Social Issues," 75, 93.

43. Ibid., 75.

44. Bourne, "Interview," 335–36.

45. Klotman and Cutler, *Struggles for Representation*, xvi–xvii.

46. Knee and Musser, "William Greaves," 17.

47. Ibid.

48. When filmed for the documentary, Drake was teaching at Roosevelt University, where he had established one of the first black studies programs. A year after the film aired, Drake was at Stanford University, where he started that school's black studies program.

49. Drake interview in *Still a Brother*.

50. Unnamed subject interview in ibid.

51. Morris interview in ibid.

52. Jackson interview in ibid.

53. Rustin interview in ibid.

54. *Watermelon Man* marked Van Peebles's first turn directing a Hollywood studio feature film. It would become such a success for Columbia Pictures that Van Peebles was given a three-film contract. The contract never was filled, however, as Van Peebles's next film, his independent *Sweet Sweetback's Baadasssss Song*, was beyond the studio's toleration. See Van Peebles interview, *Watermelon Man* DVD.

55. It will come as little surprise that this was not the original scripted final scene. In the original, Gerber wakes up, relieved to discover his blackness was merely a nightmare. He does learn a lesson, however, and vows to be more sensitive to blacks. Van Peebles could not abide by the scripted ending that suggested that being black was a nightmare, and so he shot his own version without the studio's knowledge or permission. See Van Peebles interview, *Watermelon Man* DVD.

CHAPTER 4

1. UCSD did not have a department or program in black studies when I was on its faculty. Generally speaking, the field of ethnic studies was born of the same kind of intellectual and political struggles that defined the establishment of black studies programs across the country in the early 1970s. For the purposes of this chapter, then, ethnic studies and black studies are equivalent.

2. Bell, "Price and Pain of Racial Perspective," 5, as quoted in Kennedy, "Racial Critiques of Legal Academia," 1767.

3. Williams, *Alchemy of Race and Rights*, 28.

4. Ibid., 32.

5. Franklin, "Dilemma of the American Negro Scholar," 299.

6. Ibid.

7. Wilson, "Predominantly White Institutions," 362.

8. Redding, *On Being Negro in America*, 34–37; Berry, "Introduction," 1–2. Also see Miller, *Born along the Color Line*.

9. Berry, "Introduction," 5.

10. *Brown Alumni Magazine* 101, no. 2 (November–December 2000), http://www.brown.edu/Administration/Brown_Alumni_Magazine/01/11-00/features/history.html. *BAM*'s claim that Redding was the first black to serve on an Ivy League faculty is a close call. William Fontaine joined the University of Pennsylvania's Department of Philosophy in 1947 as a visiting lecturer. The position was renewed the next year.

Having suitably proven himself, Fontaine became a full-time member of the department in 1949. Regardless, *BAM* is certainly correct in declaring that Redding was pathbreaking. See Kuklick, *Black Philosopher, White Academy*, 1, 78–79.

11. Redding, *On Being Negro in America*, 9.

12. Ibid., 9–10.

13. Ibid., 26.

14. Ibid., 26–27.

15. Ibid., 122, 125, 128.

16. Berry, "Introduction," 8.

17. Ibid., 9.

18. Huggins, *Afro-American Studies*, 6–7.

19. Ibid., 9–12.

20. Cass, "Can the University Survive the Black Challenge?," 46.

21. See Karagueuzian, *Blow It Up!*; Rojas, *From Black Power to Black Studies*; and Biondi, *Black Revolution on Campus*.

22. Huggins, *Afro-American Studies*, 22.

23. Hare, "Battle for Black Studies," 75.

24. Ibid., 79–80.

25. Ibid., 79.

26. Huggins, *Afro-American Studies*, 23; Hare, "Battle for Black Studies," 75–76.

27. Huggins, *Afro-American Studies*, 23.

28. Bass, *Widening the Mainstream*, 7.

29. Huggins, *Afro-American Studies*, 26–27; Bass, *Widening the Mainstream*, 7–9; Baker, *Black Studies, Rap, and the Academy*, 22. McGeorge Bundy, who as president of the Ford Foundation directed millions of dollars toward the establishment and development of black studies, offered a warning, telling students, "Be careful if this is something you study only because it makes *you* feel better about yourself. . . . [In] the end, in a university the therapy that comes from a subject that is *only* therapeutic will not last. If you undertake to study a subject because of the *subject's* importance, then at least you are doing something real" (Bundy, "Some Thoughts on Afro-American Studies").

30. Huggins, *Afro-American Studies*, 26. Years later, the "deft leadership" Huggins praised was analyzed differently by Houston Baker, who observed that in Yale's case a combination of good timing and luck helped that campus mitigate the more radical impulses in black studies by formalizing the creative process of the program before black radical undergraduates came to campus a year or two later. See Baker, *Black Studies, Rap, and the Academy*, 22.

31. Davis, "Reflections," 220.

32. Hare, "What Should Be the Role of Afro-American Education in the Undergraduate Curriculum?," 19.

33. Huggins, *Afro-American Studies*, 26.

34. Mintz, "Introduction," ix, xiv.

35. See, most specifically, Gutman, *Black Family in Slavery and Freedom*; Levine, *Black Culture and Black Consciousness*; Lerner, *Black Women in White America*; and Genovese, *Roll, Jordan, Roll*.

36. Turner and McGann, "Black Studies as an Integral Tradition in African-American Intellectual History."

37. Hare, "What Should Be the Role of Afro-American Education in the Undergraduate Curriculum?," 15.

38. Ward, "'Scholarship in the Context of Struggle,'" 44–45.

39. Harding, "Vocation of the Black Scholar and the Struggle of the Black Community," 12.

40. Genovese, "Black Studies," 39–40.

41. Clark, "Letter of Resignation from Board of Directors of Antioch College."

42. Clark, "Learning from Students," as quoted in Clark, *Toward Humanity and Justice*, 46–47.

43. "Black Student Demands," 297.

44. "Still Stronger Demands," 303–4.

45. "On Being Black at Yale," 385.

46. Hooks, *Talking Back*, 67.

47. Stepto, "Greyhound Kind of Mood," 77; Porter, *Making of a Black Scholar*, 136.

48. Hooks, *Talking Back*, 57.

49. Porter, *Making of a Black Scholar*, 90.

50. Carson, "Scholar in Struggle," 34.

51. Porter, *Making of a Black Scholar*, 92.

52. Lewis, "Road to the Top," 345.

53. Other journals came into existence before and after the four listed in the text. For example, the *Journal of Negro History*, the *Journal of Negro Education*, and *Phylon* had been around for decades. Other noteworthy publications include *Transition*, *Negro American Literature Forum* (now *African American Review*), *Callaloo*, and the *Western Journal of Black Studies*. This chapter focuses on the ones named in the text for their very specific attention to the question of black studies from disciplinary, political, and pedagogical perspectives.

54. Johnson, "Urban Teachers as Change Agents"; Banks, "Teaching Black Studies for Social Change."

55. Moss, "In Defense of Black Studies"; Walters, "Teaching Afro-American History"; Cruse, "Black Studies"; Harding, "Black Students and the Impossible Revolution"; Obichere, "Significance and Challenge of Afro-American Studies."

56. "Editorial Statement."

57. Smith, "Editor's Message."

58. Baker, *Black Studies, Rap, and the Academy*, 19.

59. Unsigned statement, *Black Scholar*.

60. Ladner, *Death of White Sociology*; Hull, Scott, and Smith, *But Some of Us Are Brave*.

61. Thompson, "Reflections on Ethics in Research," 477. In her own introduction, Ladner points to the long history of the deviance scholarship—starting with Robert Park's and Ernest Burgess's "Chicago School" of sociology in the 1920s—and demonstrates how much of the 1960s scholarship relied on these old models. Ladner was speaking most specifically of scholarship like Nathan Glazer's and Daniel P. Moynihan's *Beyond the Melting Pot* that observed that "the Negro is only an American and nothing

else. He has no values and culture to guard and protect" (Ladner, *Death of White Sociology*, xxiii).

62. Ladner, *Death of White Sociology*, 419.

63. Ladner studied black female teenagers for four years and concluded, "The total misrepresentation of the Black community and the various myths which surround it can be seen in microcosm in the Black female adolescent. Her growing-up years reflect the basic quality and character of life in this environment, as well as anticipations for the future." Ladner added that "by understanding the nature and processes of her development, we can also comprehend the more intricate elements that characterize the day-to-day lives of the Black masses" (Ladner, *Death of White Sociology*, 428).

64. Unsigned statement, *Black Scholar*.

65. See Cade, *Black Woman*; Davis, *Women, Race & Class*; and Moraga and Anzaldua, *This Bridge Called My Back*.

66. Hull and Smith, "Introduction," xxi.

67. Ibid., xxvi.

68. Williams, "Alchemical Notes," 407.

69. Hooks, *Talking Back*, 61.

70. The conference was cosponsored by the Princeton University Program in African-American Studies, the City University of New York (CUNY) Institute for Research on the African Diaspora in the Americas and the Caribbean, and the Schomburg Research Center. After opening at the Schomburg, the conference moved to CUNY's graduate school.

71. Felicia Lee, "New Topic for Black Studies Debate, Latinos."

72. McBride, "Can the Queen Speak?," 376–77.

CHAPTER 5

1. Sprigle, *In the Land of Jim Crow*, 67.

2. Author to Chris Johnson, electronic mail, January 25, 2010.

3. Johnson to author, electronic mail, January 25, 2010.

4. Brian Holloway to author, electronic mail, January 27, 2010. Montgomery Academy was established in 1959, in response to the Supreme Court's decision in *Brown v. Board of Education*. From its very beginning, the academy was designed to be a haven for the power elite in Montgomery. As a private school it could follow the color line. It maintained that commitment until the early 1970s. Montgomery Academy was declared a discriminatory institution in a federal lawsuit brought by black parents challenging the school's tax-exempt status (see *Allen v. Wright*, 1984).

5. Brian Holloway to author, electronic mail, January 27, 2010.

6. Ibid., January 28, 2010.

7. Karen Holloway to author, electronic mail, January 28, 2010.

8. Wendell Holloway to author, electronic mail, January 27, 2010.

9. Despite my best efforts, I have been unable to find this article. Further, the record of my family's relationship to the Montgomery Academy is lost. Because my siblings and I did not enroll, the record of our application was purged with all the others who were accepted but did not attend.

10. Holloway interview with author.

11. Mabry, "Many Blacks in Largely White Frats Feel at Home." Mabry, it turns out, had a similar experience. In his memoir, *White Bucks and Black-Eyed Peas*, Mabry writes about his decision in his freshman year to skip the black student orientation party in order to hang out with his new freshman dorm friends: "Big mistake. From that point on, I was no longer a part of 'the community.' Not because I didn't want to be or because they didn't want me to be, but because it all seemed too difficult, too out of the way, too much of a reach. I had my clubs and they had their world. When I dated an African-American alumna after college, only one year my junior, whenever she told anyone from 'the community' that she was seeing Marcus Mabry, who had also gone to Stanford, they would ask, 'You're going with a white man?'" (Mabry, *White Bucks and Black-Eyed Peas*, 173).

12. After writing this chapter, I discovered from my brother that my maternal grandfather did not hesitate to use this racial epithet. My brother recalled feeling much the same way as I did—frozen—when he heard my grandmother utter the dreaded word.

13. Jo Ann Gibson Robinson writes about Montgomery's strong black middle class and its ability to navigate the era's segregated economic, social, and political landscapes. Blacks were still second-class citizens, of course, but the well-educated and properly stationed blacks had access to the mayor's office, could agitate (within certain proscribed limits) for change, and enjoyed certain freedoms that working-class blacks dared to dream about. See Robinson, *Montgomery Bus Boycott and the Women Who Started It*.

CHAPTER 6

1. MacDonald, *Blacks and White TV*, 215; Bogle, *Prime Time Blues*, 240–43.

2. Among many others, see Morrissey, "Oral History and Boundaries of Fiction," 42; Mills and Mills, "'Roots' and the New 'Faction,'" 3–8; Foley, "History, Fiction, and the Ground Between," 400–402; Nobile, "Uncovering *Roots*," 32; and Taylor, "'Griot from Tennessee.'"

3. According to my aunt's mtDNA testing, the Genographic Project determined that she belongs to haplogroup L1 (subclade L1b). Alondra Nelson has written convincingly about the vagaries of what I call the genetic tourism industry. The hard science is there, of course, but Nelson points out that it is built upon a scaffolding of social and cultural presumptions about what a scientific fact is in the first place. In the case of African Americans' genetic roots, the "factness" of their past is deeply connected to the "aspirations for reconciliation that animate a particular orientation to the cultures of science." See, in particular, Nelson, "Factness of Diaspora," 253–55, 264–65.

4. See, for example, Blassingame, *Slave Community*; Gutman, *Black Family in Slavery and Freedom*; Fogel and Engerman, *Time on the Cross*; Genovese, *Roll, Jordan, Roll*; and Litwack, *Been in the Storm So Long*.

5. Kennedy, *Jim Crow Guide*, 7–8.

6. Kennedy, "The Long Minute," in ibid., 234.

7. Davis, *Weary Feet, Rested Souls*, 11.

8. Carrier, *Traveler's Guide to the Civil Rights Movement*; Cobb, *On the Road to Freedom*; Lefever and Page, *Sacred Places*; Cheseborough, *Blues Traveling*; Gaillard, *Alabama's Civil Rights Trail*.

9. Lewis, "Foreword," ix.

10. Ibid., vii.

11. http://www.civilrightsmuseum.org/?page_id=92.

12. Green, "Woman Won't Vacate Motel Where Rev. King Was Slain"; Balfour, "Woman Evicted from Site of King Slaying."

13. "Protestor Is Removed from King Hotel Site."

14. Smith interview with author.

15. http://www.fulfillthedream.net/pages/mlk.boycott3.html.

16. "Why Boycott the Civil Rights Museum."

17. http://www.civilrightsmuseum.org/?page_id=484.

18. William Chafe writes that many white Greensboro citizens were deeply proud of their city's and even the state's reputation for progressive policies on racial matters. Black Greensboro citizens felt something else entirely about race relations in their city and state. See Chafe, *Civilities and Civil Rights*, 98–101.

19. Plunkett-Powell, *Remembering Woolworth's*, 159–61.

20. http://www.sitins.com/timeline.shtml.

21. Schlosser, *Remembering Greensboro*, 43.

22. Hairston, *Greensboro North Carolina*, 80.

23. When this book went to press, the curators were still struggling with this issue and were working on a plan that would allow visitors to walk themselves through the exhibits.

24. Chafe, *Civil Rights and Civil Liberties*, 251–52; "Sequence of Events on November 3rd 1979."

25. From the Greensboro Truth and Community Reconciliation Report website, accessed March 26, 2013, through http://web.archive.org/web/20070210222841/http://www.gtcrp.org/.

26. From Minow, "Memory and Hate."

27. Introduction to *Greensboro Truth and Reconciliation Final Report*, 15.

28. Author's interview with Methany, Greensboro City Council member at large.

29. "New Collaboration between Sit-In Movement, Inc., and North Carolina Agricultural and Technical State University."

30. Speaking specifically about Montgomery, Alabama, but clearly referencing the broader phenomenon, historian Glenn Eskew is critical of this impulse to mix a historical narrative with a municipal impulse to raise money. He writes, "What began as veterans of the struggle gathering to remember past events at sites of memory has become a civil rights industry that manufactures an ahistorical interpretation of the social movement as a means of promoting a new American civic religion of tolerance. Now sensing the profits to be made, Rotarians and other municipal leaders in Montgomery hustle a tourism package that embraces the Cradle of the Confederacy's dual legacy as the birthplace of the modern civil rights movement" (Eskew, "Selling the Civil Rights Movement," 196).

31. For more on this controversy, see Craig, "Historical Advocacy"; Warren, "Saying No to Disney"; Bailey, "How Washington Insiders Ambushed Mickey Mouse"; and Silberman, "Battle That Disney Should Have Won," 24–28.

32. Gable, Handler, and Lawson, "On the Uses of Relativism," 793.

33. Matthews, "Where Do We Go from Here?," 108–9.

34. Ibid., 110.

35. Harris, "We Can Best Honor the Past," 394–95.

36. Tyrell, "Stinging Portrayal of Slavery."

37. Carson, "Colonial Williamsburg and the Practice of Interpretive Planning in American History Museums," 30.

38. Matthews, "Where Do We Go from Here?," 107.

39. Walker, "Southern Heritage Tourism Luring a Growing Market of Black Americans."

40. http://www.800alabama.com/activities/tours-and-trails/alabama-civil-rights-museum-trail. Noting that the amount of money involved in these tourist enterprises is "considerable," Owen Dwyer points out that local and state governments want to "rectify their public image and attract tourist dollars at the same time. These twin motivations suggest why states like Alabama and its neighbors promote an unabashedly heroic recounting of the movement a generation after issuing pledges of massive resistance to integration" (Dwyer, "Interpreting the Civil Rights Movement," 16).

41. AStoryLikeNoOther.com.

42. "Louisiana African American Heritage Trail."

43. Memo, Chuck Morse to Lieutenant Governor Mitchell Landrieu, January 22, 2008.

44. Adams, *Wounds of Returning*, 67.

45. "Interpretation of Plantation Slavery Conference." This is not to say that the old scripts are gone. They are still around and, in fact, are thriving. If you happen to be on a Louisiana Office of Tourism e-mail listserv, you will get invitations to "Explore the Plantations of River Road." If so inclined, you will have the opportunity to take a "fall trip along the River Road . . . to antebellum mansions, lush gardens, delicious restaurants, and charming bed and breakfasts." The embedded link at the bottom of this advertisement is titled "Ride to Romance."

46. Adams, *Wounds of Returning*, 64–67.

47. The Cane River Creole was established as a historical park in 1994. It is comprised of the Oakland and Magnolia Plantations and has over sixty historic structures on its property.

48. Magnolia Plantation is part of the larger Cane River Creole Park.

49. Crespi, "Brief Ethnography of Magnolia Plantation," 61–62.

50. Ibid., 65.

51. "What Are We Saying?"

52. Crespi, "Brief Ethnography of Magnolia Plantation," 76.

53. Rose, "Rethinking Representations of Slave Life at Historical Plantation Museums," 118.

54. The following is an example of how slaves were incorporated directly into the narrative of the plantation house: "We are now in the family room. This salon or parlor

was modified during the Duplantier time by skilled slaves, free people of color or artisans. According to their wealth, planters would have had several skilled slaves, such as carpenters. In fact, the succession papers of John Joyce listed two slaves Cato, a Creole of Jamaica, and American Will, from the Coast of Guinea as 'good carpenters.' Cato and Armerican [*sic*] Will could have worked in the construction of houses like this one" (Magnolia Mound Plantation Tour Script, 15).

55. "A Day in the Life of a Slave," 1–3.

56. Ibid., 1.

57. Memorial marker, Tomb of the Unknown Slave, St. Augustine Church, New Orleans.

58. Morrison, *Beloved*, 274–75.

59. "A Bench by the Road."

60. Ibid.

61. "Bench by the Road Project."

62. Lee, "Bench of Memory at Slavery's Gateway."

63. As of 2012, the benches are at Sullivan's Island, South Carolina; Oberlin, Ohio; Hattiesburg, Mississippi; Paris, France; Concord, Massachusetts; and Washington, D.C.

64. "A Bench by the Road."

EPILOGUE

1. In his study of memory in the black Atlantic, American studies scholar Alan Rice begins in Ghana, specifically at the slave castles and their doors of no return. He identifies the doors as a cultural "ground zero" for African Americans that "almost always has to be an imagined site of ancestral departure" (Rice, *Creating Memorials, Building Identities*, 1–2).

2. James Campbell makes clear that African Americans have talked about and followed through with plans to return to all parts of the African continent for hundreds of years. The rationale for returning was always shifting, but in postcolonial Africa (essentially from the 1960s forward) the reasons for returning increasingly revolved around a touristic quest to find "home." On the general phenomenon of returning, see Campbell, *Middle Passages*; on the specifics of African American tourism, see 370–73.

3. Hartman, *Lose Your Mother*, 38.

4. Harris, *Native Stranger*, 27–28.

5. Holsey, *Routes of Remembrance*, 29–33; Richards, "What Is to Be Remembered?," 89–90.

6. Anquandah, *Castles & Forts of Ghana*, 20.

7. See, for example, Eltis, *Atlas of the Transatlantic Slave Trade*; Smallwood, *Saltwater Slavery*; St. Clair, *Door of No Return*; Rediker, *Slave Ship*; and Harms, *The Diligent*.

8. Performance studies scholar Sandra Richards writes powerfully about the inconceivable proximities of the slave dungeons and houses of worship and the surreal career of Philip Quaque, an African Cape Coast native who traveled to England as a teenager only to return as an Anglican missionary who facilitated/consecrated the English slave trade for fifty years. See Richards, "Who Is This Ancestor?"

9. James Campbell points out that part of what makes Elmina and Cape Coast Castles such successful tourist destinations is their location: "Bunce Island [in Sierra Leone] is also handicapped in the tourism stakes by the absence of an ocean view. I do not say this facetiously. Proximity to the sea is always an asset for a tourist site, but it is particularly important in African American heritage tourism. Standing on the edge of the Atlantic, gazing westward toward the Americas, one can imagine oneself standing at ground zero of African American history, the geometric point of origin from which African people radiated out into the Atlantic world" (Campbell, *Middle Passages*, 427).

10. The International Slavery Museum opened on August 23, 2007. Eight years earlier, UNESCO designated that day as the International Day for the Remembrance of the Slave Trade and its Abolition. August 23 is the anniversary of a 1791 uprising in Santo Domingo (now the Dominican Republic and Haiti) that led to the global abolition of the transatlantic slave trade. See Benjamin, "Exhibiting Sensitive Histories," 2. The museum is slated to expand beyond the third floor of its current site. The expansion was scheduled for 2012 but has since been delayed due to significant funding cuts related to the global recession.

11. The museum's curatorial team hotly debated the "Middle Passage Immersion" prior to its installation. Some team members wanted a traditional exhibit related to the middle passage that was more in line with what one might find in a museum that was explicitly neutral in its presentation agenda. Museum director Richard Benjamin acknowledged that "there is a fine line between visceral displays of such highly emotive and sensitive objects and turning the museum into what a member of the curatorial team called a 'shop of horrors.'" In the end, however, Benjamin feels the museum was right to install the immersion. The International Slavery Museum, he states, is clearly not a neutral site. It is a museum with a clear agenda, and it should not shy away from it. See Benjamin, "Exhibiting Sensitive Histories," 11, and Benjamin interview with author.

12. For an acknowledgment of the contemporary awkwardness related to Rhodes's legacy in a postcolonial world, see Philip Ziegler's recounting of the debate to create Mandela-Rhodes Foundation in South Africa to enhance educational opportunities. "The coupling of the names of Mandela and Rhodes, from the point of view of public relations, was brilliantly conceived" (Ziegler, *Legacy*, 322–28).

13. Holsey, *Routes of Remembrance*, 161. When Holsey asked locals in Cape Coast and Elmina about the slave trade, they disavowed any connection. They "insisted it was not their history, for their ancestors had never owned slaves, had never had loved ones captured, or participated in captures" (Holsey, *Routes of Remembrance*, 4). Sandra Richards has also pointed out that "various ethnic traditions forbid discussion of slavery" and that communities clearly invest tremendous "psychic energy in maintaining silence around a public secret" (Richards, "What Is to Be Remembered?," 96–97).

14. Anquandah, *Castles & Forts of Ghana*, 8. The philosophy of the World Heritage Convention (part of UNESCO) states that "there are some parts of heritage which are of such outstanding value to the world as a whole that their protection, conservation and transmission to future generations is a matter not just for any one nation but for the international community as a whole."

15. Holsey points out that the strategic plans concerning the castles' conservation were not driven by a desire to engage in a rich discussion of their role in the slave trade but to invoke "the age of exploration, a key romantic narrative of the modern age and an invitation as well of forms of connection between Africa and Europe" (Holsey, *Routes of Remembrance*, 162).

16. Ibid., 162–67.

17. On the castle/dungeon debate, see Richards, "What Is to Be Remembered?," 103–4.

18. Ibid., 96; Bruner, "Tourism in Ghana," 294.

19. Anquandah, *Castles & Forts of Ghana*, 105. In 2007, the Ghanaian Ministry of Tourism initiated another effort to link reconciliation to a potential tourist market. Abena Ampofoa Asare explains: "Named after the Biblical story of a slave whose experience of bondage led to the salvation of his entire family, the Joseph Project was an initiative that sought to remove many of the emotional and bureaucratic barriers to diaspora tourism and settlement in Ghana. One of the Joseph Project's first initiatives was an event where traditional Ghanaian rulers offered apologies for the roles that Africans played in the transatlantic slave trade" (Asare, "Ghanaian National Reconciliation Commission," 35).

20. Holsey, *Routes of Remembrance*, 168–69. For a close reading of the popular preference for a heroic narrative about this homecoming, see Richards, "Landscapes of Memory," 296–98.

21. That afternoon, I actually went so far as to ask a tourist at an arts market in downtown Accra if her group was from Brooklyn. It turns out that she and her fellow travelers were from Kingston, Jamaica. To be honest, I knew connecting with the Mo-CADA travelers was a long shot, but given the fact that I ended up seeing the Kingston tour group two more times on my four-day trip suggests I might just have been unlucky.

22. Porter, *Problem of the Future World*, 135–38.

23. http://mocada.org/ghana/ (accessed 2012).

24. Wright, *Black Power*, 18.

25. Ibid., 19.

26. A fairly typical passage is as follows: "And suddenly I was self-conscious; I began to question myself, *my* assumptions. I was assuming that these people had to be pulled out of this life, out of these conditions of poverty, had to become literate, Western, disinherited, and industrialized and I felt each day the pain and anxiety of it. Why then must I advocate the dragging of these people into my trap? But suppose I didn't? What would happen then? They would remain in these slavelike conditions forever" (ibid., 184).

27. Phillips, *Atlantic Sound*, 116.

BIBLIOGRAPHY

AUTHOR INTERVIEWS

Benjamin, Richard. Liverpool, U.K., October 11, 2011.
Holloway, Wendell. Telephone interview, January 2010.
Methany, Zack. Greensboro, N.C., June 10, 2011.
Smith, Jacqueline. Memphis, Tenn., August 26, 2011.

ELECTRONIC CORRESPONDENCE WITH THE AUTHOR

Holloway, Brian. January 27, 28, 2010.
Holloway, Karen. January 28, 2010.
Holloway, Wendell. January 27, 2010.
Johnson, Chris. January 25, 2010.

FILMS

An Evening with Alvin Ailey American Dance Theater. Directed by Thomas Grimm, 1986.
The First World Festival of Negro Arts. Directed by William Greaves. USIA, 1966.
Greensboro: Closer to the Truth. Directed by Adam Zucker. 2007.
Shaft. Directed by Gordon Parks. Metro-Goldwyn-Mayer, 1971.
Still a Brother: Inside the Negro Middle Class. Directed by William Greaves. NET, 1968.
Take This Hammer. Directed by Richard Moore. KQED, 1963.
Watermelon Man. Directed by Melvin Van Peebles. Columbia Pictures, 1970.

UNPUBLISHED DOCUMENTS, CONFERENCE PROCEEDINGS, AND GOVERNMENT PUBLICATIONS

Benjamin, Richard. "Exhibiting Sensitive Histories." Federation of International Human Rights Museums Conference, September 15, 2010.
"A Day in the Life of a Slave." Magnolia Mound Plantation lesson plan, n.d.
"Interpretation of Plantation Slavery Conference, May 2–3." Internal memorandum, May 14, 2008.
"Louisiana African American Heritage Trail." Louisiana Department of Culture, Recreation, and Tourism. Planning document, n.d.
Magnolia Mound Plantation Tour Script. July 22, 2009.

"What Are We Saying? Discovering How People of African Descent Are Interpreted at Louisiana Plantation Sites." LSU Rural Life Museum Conference, 2008.

ARTICLES AND ESSAYS

Adamic, Louis. "There Are Whites and Whites." *Negro Digest*, March 1946, 47–50.

Alexander, Jeffrey. "Toward a Theory of Cultural Trauma." In *Cultural Trauma and Collective Identity*, edited by Jeffrey Alexander, Ron Eyerman, Bernhard Giesen, Neil Smelser, and Piotr Sztompka, 1–30. Berkeley: University of California Press, 2004.

Asare, Abena. "The Ghanaian National Reconciliation Commission: Reparation in a Global Age." *Global South* 2, no. 2 (Fall 2008): 31–53.

"Backstage." *Ebony*, November 1945, 2.

Bailey, Charles W. "How Washington Insiders Ambushed Mickey Mouse—Fight against the Building of a Theme Park in Virginia by Walt Disney Co." *Washington Monthly* 26, no. 12 (December 1994): 10–14.

Balfour, Thelma. "Woman Evicted from Site of King Slaying." *USA Today*, March 3, 1988, A3.

Banks, James. "Teaching Black Studies for Social Change." *Journal of Afro-American Issues* 1, no. 2 (Fall 1972): 141–64.

Baraka, Ameer. "The Black Aesthetic." *Negro Digest*, September 1969, 5–6.

Bell, Derrick. "The Price and Pain of Racial Perspective." *Stanford Law School Journal*, May 9, 1986.

Berry, Faith. "Introduction." In *A Scholar's Conscience: Selected Writings of J. Saunders Redding, 1942–1977*, 1–14. Lexington: University Press of Kentucky, 1992.

"Black Student Demands." Northwestern University, April 22, 1968. In *The University Crisis Reader*, edited by Immanuel Wallerstein and Paul Starr. Vol. 1, *The Liberal University under Attack*, 297–98. New York: Random House, 1971.

Blassingame, John. "Black Autobiographies as History and Literature." *Black Scholar* 5, no. 4 (December 1973–January 1974): 2–9.

"Bonanza for Dixie Libraries." *Negro Digest*, August 1946, back cover.

Borgese, G. A. "A Bedroom Approach to Racism." *Negro Digest*, December 1944, 31–35.

Bourne, St. Clair. "Interview." In *Struggles for Representation: African American Documentary Film and Video*, edited by Phyllis R. Klotman and Janet K. Cutler, 334–37. Bloomington: Indiana University Press, 1999.

Bowser, Pearl. "Pioneers of Black Documentary Film." In *Struggles for Representation: African American Documentary Film and Video*, edited by Phyllis R. Klotman and Janet K. Cutler, 8–30. Bloomington: Indiana University Press, 1999.

Brundage, W. Fitzhugh. "No Deed but Memory." In *Where These Memories Grow: History, Memory, and Southern Identity*, edited by W. Fitzhugh Brundage, 1–28. Chapel Hill: University of North Carolina Press, 2000.

Bruner, Edward L. "Tourism in Ghana: The Representation of Slavery and the Return of the Black Diaspora." *American Anthropologist* 98, no. 2 (June 1996): 290–304.

Bundy, McGeorge. "Some Thoughts on Afro-American Studies." In *Black Studies in the University: A Symposium*, edited by Armstead Robinson, Craig Foster, and Donald Ogilvie, 174–75. New Haven: Yale University Press, 1968.

Carson, Cary. "Colonial Williamsburg and the Practice of Interpretive Planning in American History Museums." *Public Historian* 20, no. 3 (Summer 1998): 11–51.

Carson, Clayborne. "A Scholar in Struggle." *Souls* 4, no. 2 (2002): 28–37.

Cass, James. "Can the University Survive the Black Challenge?" In *Basic Black: A Look at the Black Presence in the University Community*, edited by John Buerk et al., 45–56. Melrose, Mass.: Keating & Joyce, 1970.

Clark, Cedric. "On Racism and Racist Systems." *Negro Digest*, August 1969, 4–8.

Clark, Kenneth. "Letter of Resignation from Board of Directors of Antioch College." In *Black Studies: Myths & Realities*, by Kilson Martin, C. Vann Woodward, Kenneth B. Clark, Thomas Sowell, Roy Wilkins, Andrew F. Brimmer, and Norman Hill, 33–34. New York: A. Philip Randolph Educational Fund, 1969.

Couch, W. T. "Publisher's Introduction." In *What the Negro Wants*, edited by Rayford Logan, ix–xxiii. Chapel Hill: University of North Carolina Press, 1944.

Craig, Bruce. "Historical Advocacy: The Past, Present, and Future." *Public Historian* 22, no. 2 (Spring 2000): 71–74.

Crespi, Muriel. "A Brief Ethnography of Magnolia Plantation: Planning for Cane River Creole National Historical Park." National Park Service, 2004.

Cruse, Harold. "Black Studies: Interpretation, Methodology, and the Relationship to Social Movements." *Afro-American Studies* 2, no. 1 (June 1971): 15–51.

Cutler, Janet K. "Rewritten on Film: Documenting the Artist." In *Struggles for Representation: African American Documentary Film and Video*, edited by Phyllis R. Klotman and Janet K. Cutler, 151–210. Bloomington: Indiana University Press, 1999.

Dailey, Jane. "The Limits of Liberalism in the New South: The Politics of Race, Sex, and Patronage in Virginia, 1879–1883." In *Jumpin' Jim Crow: Southern Politics from Civil War to Civil Rights*, edited by Jane Dailey, Glenda Elizabeth Gilmore, and Bryant Simon, 88–114. Princeton: Princeton University Press, 2000.

Daveson, Kathleen. "Letters and Pictures to the Editor." *Ebony*, May 1946, 50.

Davis, Arthur P. "My Most Humiliating Jim Crow Experience." *Negro Digest*, May 1944, 61–62.

Davis, David Brion. "Reflections." In *Black Studies in the University: A Symposium*, edited by Armstead Robinson, Craig Foster, and Donald Ogilvie, 215–24. New Haven: Yale University Press, 1968.

Davis, Frank Marshall. "My Most Humiliating Jim Crow Experience." *Negro Digest*, September 1944, 57–58.

Dwyer, Owen J. "Interpreting the Civil Rights Movement: Contradiction, Confirmation, and the Cultural Landscape." In *The Civil Rights Movement in American Memory*, edited by Renee C. Romano and Leigh Raiford, 5–27. Athens: University of Georgia Press, 2006.

Earley, Tony. "Introduction." In *Somehow Form a Family: Stories That Are Mostly True*, xv–xvi. Chapel Hill: Algonquin Books, 2001.

"Editorial Statement." *Afro-American Studies* 1, no. 1 (May 1970): inside front cover.

Ellison, Ralph. "*An American Dilemma*: A Review." In *Shadow and Act*, 303–17. 1964. Reprint, New York: Vintage, 1972.

———. "Richard Wright's Blues." In *Shadow and Act*, 77–94. 1964. Reprint, New York: Vintage, 1972.

Embree, Edwin R. "Basic Steps toward Democracy." *Pittsburgh Courier*, December 12, 1943, 3.

Eskew, Glenn T. "Selling the Civil Rights Movement: Montgomery, Alabama, since the 1960s." In *Dixie Emporium: Tourism, Foodways, and Consumer Culture in the American South*, edited by Anthony J. Stanonis, 175–202. Athens: University of Georgia Press, 2008.

"Evict Negro Soldier Even from Jim-Crow Seat in Bus." *Pittsburgh Courier*, November 21, 1942, 2.

Eyerman, Ron. "Cultural Trauma: Slavery and the Formation of African American Identity." In *Cultural Trauma and Collective Identity*, edited by Jeffrey Alexander, Ron Eyerman, Bernhard Giesen, Neil Smelser, and Piotr Sztompka, 60–111. Berkeley: University of California Press, 2004.

Fabre, Geneviève. "African-American Commemorative Celebrations in the Nineteenth Century." In *History & Memory in African-American Culture*, edited by Geneviève Fabre and Robert O'Meally, 72–91. New York: Oxford University Press, 1994.

Feather, Leonard. "Wanted: A White Mammy." *Negro Digest*, November 1945, 45–47.

Field, Marshall. "The Color of Injustice." *Negro Digest*, June 1945, 31–32.

Fleming, G. James. "My Most Humiliating Jim Crow Experience." *Negro Digest*, June 1945, 67–68.

Foley, Barbara. "History, Fiction, and the Ground Between: The Uses of the Documentary Mode in Black Literature." *PMLA* 95, no. 3 (May 1980): 389–403.

Franklin, John Hope. "The Dilemma of the American Negro Scholar." In *Race and History: Selected Essays, 1938–1988*, 295–308. Baton Rouge: Louisiana State University Press, 1989.

Gable, Eric, Richard Handler, and Anna Lawson. "On the Uses of Relativism: Fact, Conjecture, and Black and White Histories at Colonial Williamsburg." *American Ethnologist* 19, no. 4 (November 1992): 791–805.

Genovese, Eugene. "Black Studies: Trouble Ahead." In *Basic Black: A Look at the Black Presence in the University Community*, edited by John Buerk et al., 35–43. Melrose, Mass.: Keating & Joyce, 1970.

Greaves, William. "Interview." In *Struggles for Representation: African American Documentary Film and Video*, edited by Phyllis R. Klotman and Janet K. Cutler, 354–57. Bloomington: Indiana University Press, 1999.

Green, William. "Woman Won't Vacate Motel Where Rev. King Was Slain." *USA Today*, January 14, 1988, A3.

Hall, Jacqueline Dowd. "The Long Civil Rights Movement and the Political Uses of the Past." *Journal of American History* 91, no. 4 (2005): 1233–63.

Harding, Vincent. "Black Students and the Impossible Revolution." *Journal of Black Studies* 1, no. 1 (September 1970): 75–100.

————. "The Vocation of the Black Scholar and the Struggle of the Black Community." In *Education and Black Struggle: Notes from the Colonized World*, 3–29. Cambridge: Harvard Educational Review, 1974.

Hare, Nathan. "The Battle for Black Studies." In *Black Scholars on Higher Education in the '70s*, edited by Roosevelt Johnson, 65–87. Columbus, Ohio: ECCA Publications, 1974.

————. "What Should Be the Role of Afro-American Education in the Undergraduate Curriculum?" In *Basic Black: A Look at the Black Presence in the University Community*, edited by John Buerk et al., 15–24. Melrose, Mass.: Keating & Joyce, 1970.

Harris, Robert L., Jr. "We Can Best Honor the Past . . . by Facing It Squarely, Honestly, and Above All, Openly." *Journal of African American History* 94, no. 3 (Summer 2009): 391–97.

Heningburg, Alphonse, and Edwin Embree. "Letters and Pictures to the Editor." *Ebony*, December 1945, 51.

————. "Letters and Pictures to the Editor." *Ebony*, January 1946, 51.

Holloway, Jonathan Scott. "The Black Intellectual and the 'Crisis Canon' in the Twentieth Century." *Black Scholar*, Spring 2001, 2–13.

————. "Editor's Introduction." In *A Brief and Tentative Analysis of Negro Leadership*, by Ralph J. Bunche, 1–28. New York: New York University Press, 2005.

Hull, Gloria T., and Barbara Smith. "Introduction: The Politics of Black Women's Studies." In *All the Women Are White, All the Blacks Are Men, but Some of Us Are Brave: Black Women's Studies*, edited by Gloria T. Hull, Patricia Bell Scott, and Barbara Smith, xvii–xxxii. Old Westbury, N.Y.: Feminist Press. 1982.

Hurst, Fannie. "The Sure Way to Equality." *Negro Digest*, June 1946, 27–28.

Hurston, Zora Neale. "My Most Humiliating Jim Crow Experience." *Negro Digest*, June 1944, 25–26.

"Insult to Captain Mulzac." *Washington Afro-American*, October 9, 1943, 4.

Introduction to *Greensboro Truth and Reconciliation Commission Final Report*, 9–26. May 2006.

"An Investment in Understanding." *Negro Digest*, April 1946, back cover.

Jet, November 1, 1951, cover.

Jet, November 8, 1951, cover.

Johnson, Guy. "Whites Are Individuals Too." *Negro Digest*, December 1945, 34.

Johnson, Walter. "Building a Brave New World." *Negro Digest*, January 1944, 64.

Johnson, Roosevelt, "Urban Teachers as Change Agents: Implications for a Legitimate Curriculum." *Journal of Afro-American Issues* 1, no. 1 (Summer 1972): 93–98.

Kennedy, Randall L. "Racial Critiques of Legal Academia." *Harvard Law Review* 102, no. 8 (June 1989): 1745–1819.

Knee, Adam, and Charles Musser. "William Greaves, Documentary Film-Making, and the African-American Experience." *Film Quarterly* 45, no. 3 (Spring 1992): 13–25.

Lee, Felicia R. "Bench of Memory at Slavery's Gateway." *New York Times*, July 28, 2008.

————. "New Topic for Black Studies Debate, Latinos." *New York Times*, February 1, 2003, A1.

Lewis, John. "Foreword." In *A Traveler's Guide to the Civil Rights Movement*, by Jim Carrier, vii–ix. Orlando, Fla.: Harcourt Books, 2004.

Lewis, W. Arthur. "The Road to the Top Is Through Higher Education—Not Black Studies." *New York Times*, May 11, 1969. In *The University Crisis Reader*, edited by Immanuel Wallerstein and Paul Starr. Vol. 1, *The Liberal University under Attack*, 343–47. New York: Random House, 1971.

Little, Jimmy. "Letters and Pictures to the Editor." *Ebony*, August 1946, 50.

Logan, Rayford. "My Most Humiliating Jim Crow Experience." *Negro Digest*, March 1945, 49–50.

Lott, Tommy Lee. "Documenting Social Issues: 'Black Journal,' 1968–1970." In *Struggles for Representation: African American Documentary Film and Video*, edited by Phyllis R. Klotman and Janet K. Cutler, 71–98. Bloomington: Indiana University Press, 1999.

Mabry, Marcus. "Many Blacks in Largely White Frats Feel at Home." *Stanford Daily*, April 25, 1988, 6.

Mackey, Nathaniel. "The Changing Same: Black Music in the Poetry of Amiri Barak." *Boundary 2* 6, no. 2 (Winter 1978): 355–86.

Matthews, Christy S. "Where Do We Go from Here? Researching and Interpreting the African-American Experience." *Historical Archaeology* (1997): 107–13.

Matthews, Ralph. "My Most Humiliating Jim Crow Experience." *Negro Digest*, November 1944, 61–62.

McBride, Dwight A. "Can the Queen Speak? Racial Essentialism, Sexuality, and the Problem of Authority." *Callaloo* 21, no. 2 (1998): 363–79.

McWilliams, Carey. "The Economic Roots of Race Hate." *Negro Digest*, August 1944, 53–55.

Mills, Gary B., and Elizabeth Shown Mills. "'Roots' and the New 'Faction': A New Tool for Clio?" *Virginia Magazine of History and Biography* 89, no. 1 (1981): 3–26.

Minow, Martha. "Memory and Hate." *Greensboro Truth and Reconciliation Final Report*, 9. May 2006.

Mintz, Sidney. "Introduction." In *The Myth of the Negro Past*, by Melville Herskovits, ix–xxi. Boston: Beacon, 1990.

"Mitchell's Greatest Victory Doomed Jim-Crow Cars." *Pittsburgh Courier*, November 21, 1942, 5.

Mkalimoto, Ernie. "The Cultural Arm of Revolutionary Black Nationalism." *Negro Digest*, December 1969, 11–17.

Moon, Bucklin. "Dixie Bottleneck." *Negro Digest*, July 1945, 59–60.

Morrissey, Charles T. "Oral History and Boundaries of Fiction." *Public Historian* 7, no. 2 (Spring 1985): 41–46.

Moss, James Allen. "In Defense of Black Studies: Some Additional Notes." *Afro-American Studies* 1, no. 3 (January 1971): 217–22.

"Mulzac Back Home: Booker T.'s Skipper Evade Submarines, but Meets Jim Crow." *Washington Afro-American*, October 2, 1943, 1, 3.

"Nation Horrified by Murder of Kidnapped Chicago Youth." *Jet*, September 15, 1955, 5–9.

Negro Digest, November 1942, back cover.

Negro Digest, June 1945, back cover.

Negro Digest, October 1946, back cover.

"A Negro Magazine for Whites Also." *Negro Digest*, May 1946, back cover.

Nelson, Alondra. "The Factness of Diaspora: The Social Sources of Genetic Genealogy." In *Revisiting Race in a Genomic Age*, edited by Barbara A. Koenig, Sandra Soo-Jin Lee, and Sarah S. Richardson, 253–68. New Brunswick, N.J.: Rutgers University Press, 2008.

Nobile, Philip. "Uncovering *Roots*." *Village Voice*, February 23, 1993, 31–38.

Nora, Pierre. "Between Memory and History: *Les Lieux de Mémoire*." In *History & Memory in African American Culture*, edited by Geneviève Fabre and Robert O'Meally, 284–300. New York: Oxford University Press, 1994.

"Nursery Rhyme for Captain Hugh Mulzac, Commander of the USS Booker T. Washington, in Richmond." *Washington Afro-American*, October 9, 1943, 4.

Obichere, Boniface. "The Significance and Challenge of Afro-American Studies." *Journal of Black Studies* 1, no. 2 (December 1970): 161–77.

O'Meally, Robert. "On Burke and the Vernacular: Ralph Ellison's Boomerang of History." In *History & Memory in African-American Culture*, edited by Geneviève Fabre and Robert O'Meally, 244–60. New York: Oxford University Press, 1994.

"On Being Black at Yale." *Yale Alumni Magazine*, May 1969. In *The University Crisis Reader*, edited by Immanuel Wallerstein and Paul Starr. Vol. 1, *The Liberal University under Attack*, 378–91. New York: Random House, 1971.

"Our White Folks." *Negro Digest*, September 1944, back cover.

"Parlez-vous Francais? Da, Da, Tovarich." *Negro Digest*, December 1944, back cover.

Pollock, Channing. "Demonstrate Not Demand." *Negro Digest*, April 1945, 55–56.

Portelli, Alessandro. "History-Telling and Time: An Example from Kentucky." In *History & Memory in African-American Culture*, edited by Geneviève Fabre and Robert O'Meally, 164–77. New York: Oxford University Press, 1994.

Powell, Adam Clayton, Jr. "My Most Humiliating Jim Crow Experience." *Negro Digest*, August 1944, 75–76.

Rahn, Muriel. "My Most Humiliating Jim Crow Experience." *Negro Digest*, September 1945, 63–64.

Redding, J. Saunders. "My Most Humiliating Jim Crow Experience." *Negro Digest*, December 1944, 43–44.

Renan, Ernest. "What Is a Nation?" In *Nation and Narration*, edited by Homi Bhabha, 8–22. London: Routledge, 1990.

Richards, Sandra L. "Landscapes of Memory: Representing the African Diaspora's Return 'Home.'" In *Africa and Trans-Atlantic Memories: Literary and Aesthetic Manifestations of Diaspora and History*, edited by Naana Opoku-Agyemang, Paul E. Lovejoy, and David V. Trotman, 291–301. Trenton, N.J.: Africa World Press, 2008.

———. "What Is to Be Remembered?: Tourism to Ghana's Slave Castle-Dungeons." In *Critical Theory and Performance*, edited by Janelle G. Reinelt and Joseph Roach, 85–107. Ann Arbor: University of Michigan Press, 2007.

———. "Who Is This Ancestor? Performing Memory in Ghana's Slave Castle-Dungeons (A Multimedia Performance Meditation)." in *The SAGE Handbook of Performance Studies*, edited by D. Soyini Madison and Judith Hamera, 489–501. Thousand Oaks, Calif.: Sage Publications, 2006.

Romano, Renee C. "Narratives of Redemption: The Birmingham Church Bombing Trials and the Construction of Civil Rights Memory." In *The Civil Rights Movement in American Memory*, edited by Renee C. Romano and Leigh Raiford, 96–134. Athens: University of Georgia Press, 2006.

Sancton, Thomas. "Minority to Majority." *Negro Digest*, April 1943, 49–50.

Schuyler, George. "My Most Humiliating Jim Crow Experience." *Negro Digest*, March 1944, 11–12.

Seiler, Cotten. "'So That We as a Race Might Have Something Authentic to Travel By': African American Automobility and Cold-War Liberalism." *American Quarterly* 58, no. 4 (December 2006): 1091–1117.

"Sequence of Events on November 3rd 1979." *Greensboro Truth and Reconciliation Commission Final Report*, 170–89. May 2006.

Silberman, Noah. "The Battle That Disney Should Have Won." *Lingua Franca* 5, no. 1 (1994): 1–29.

Smith, Arthur. "Editor's Message." *Journal of Black Studies* 1, no. 1 (September 1970): 3.

"Some of Our Best Friends Are White." *Negro Digest*, March 1946, back cover.

"Speaking of Christmas." *Negro Digest*, September 1944, back cover.

Spingarn, Arthur B. "The Time is NOW." *Negro Digest*, May 1943, back cover.

Stegner, Wallace. "The Common Cause of Color." *Negro Digest*, May 1946, 59–60.

Stepto, Robert B. "A Greyhound Kind of Mood." In *A Home Elsewhere: Reading African American Classics in the Age of Obama*, 77–99. Cambridge: Harvard University Press, 2010.

———. "Washington Park." In *History & Memory in African-American Culture*, edited by Geneviève Fabre and Robert O'Meally, 272–83. New York: Oxford University Press, 1994.

"Still Stronger Demands." Northwestern University, April 1968. In *The University Crisis Reader*, edited by Immanuel Wallerstein and Paul Starr. Vol. 1, *The Liberal University under Attack*, 302–6. New York: Random House, 1971.

Sutherland, Robert. "Preface." In *Growing Up in the Black Belt: Negro Youth in the Rural South*, by Charles S. Johnson, xi–xii. Washington, D.C.: American Council on Education, 1941.

Taylor, Helen. "'The Griot from Tennessee': The Saga of Alex Haley's *Roots*." *Critical Quarterly* 37, no. 2 (September 2007): 46–62.

Todd, Arthur, and Alvin Ailey. "Roots of the Blues." *Dance and Dancers*, November 1961, 24.

Thompson, Becky. "Reflections on Ethics in Research: *The Death of White Sociology* Twenty Years Later." Department of Sociology, Center for Research on Women. Memphis State University, Fall 1993.

Turner, James, and C. Steven McGann. "Black Studies as an Integral Tradition in African-American Intellectual History." *Journal of Negro History* 49, no. 1 (1980): 52–53.

Tyrell, R. Emmett. "Stinging Portrayal of Slavery." *Washington Times*, July 10, 1999.

Unsigned statement. *Black Scholar* 1, no. 1 (November 1969): inside front cover.

Villard, Oswald Garrison. "No Time for Pessimism." *Negro Digest*, March 1943, 11.

Walker, Dionne. "Southern Heritage Tourism Luring a Growing Market of Black Americans." *USA Today*, July 25, 2005. http://www.usatoday.com/travel/destinations/2005-07-25-black-tourism_x.htm.

Walters, Ronald. "Teaching Afro-American History: An Interpretive Essay." *Afro-American Studies* 1, no. 4 (April 1971): 315–22.

Ward, Stephen. "'Scholarship in the Context of Struggle': Activist Intellectuals, the Institute of the Black World (IBW), and the Contours of Black Power Radicalism." *Black Scholar* 34, no. 3–4 (Fall/Winter 2001): 42–53.

Warren, Stacy. "Saying No to Disney: Disney's Demise in Four American Cities." In *Rethinking Disney: Private Control, Public Dimensions*, edited by Mike Budd and Max H. Kirsch, 231–60. Middletown, Conn.: Wesleyan University Press, 2005.

Wieseltier, Leon. "Scar Tissue." *New Republic*, June 5, 1989, 20.

Williams, Patricia J. "Alchemical Notes: Reconstructing Ideals from Deconstructed Rights." *Harvard Civil Rights–Civil Liberties Law Review* 22, no. 2 (Spring 1987): 401–34.

Wilson, Reginald. "Predominantly White Institutions." In *Encyclopedia of African American Education*, edited by Faustine Jones-Wilson et al., 361–66. Westport, Conn.: Greenwood Press, 1996.

Wright, Richard. "The Ethics of Living Jim Crow: An Autobiographical Sketch." In *Uncle Tom's Children*, 1–15. New York: HarperPerennial, 1993.

———. "How 'Bigger' Was Born." In *Native Son*, vii–xxxiv. New York: Harper & Row, 1940.

———. "Introduction." In *Black Metropolis: A Study of Negro Life in a Northern City*, by St. Clair Drake and Horace R. Cayton, xvii–xxxiv. 1945. Reprint, Chicago: University of Chicago Press, 1993.

Young, James E. "Between History and Memory: The Voice of the Eyewitness." In *Witness and Memory: The Discourse of Trauma*, edited by Ana Douglass and Thomas A. Volger, 275–84. New York: Routledge, 2003.

Zara, Louis. "Coming Days of Glory." *Negro Digest*, January 1946, 37–38.

BOOKS

Acham, Christine. *Revolution Televised: Prime Time and the Struggle for Black Power.* Minneapolis: University of Minnesota Press, 2004.

Adams, Jessica. *Wounds of Returning: Race, Memory, and Property on the Postslavery Plantation.* Chapel Hill: University of North Carolina Press, 2007.

Alexander, Elizabeth. *The Black Interior.* St. Paul: Graywolf Press, 2004.

Alexander, Jeffrey, Ron Eyerman, Bernhard Giesen, Neil Smelser, and Piotr Sztompka, eds. *Cultural Trauma and Collective Identity*. Berkeley: University of California Press, 2004.

Anquandah, Kwesi J. *Castles & Forts of Ghana*. Atalante: Ghana Museums & Monuments Board, 1999.

Arsenault, Raymond. *The Sound of Freedom: Marian Anderson, the Lincoln Memorial, and the Concert That Awakened America*. New York: Bloomsbury Press, 2009.

Baker, Houston, Jr. *Black Studies, Rap, and the Academy*. Chicago: University of Chicago Press, 1995.

Bass, Jack. *Widening the Mainstream of American Culture: A Ford Foundation Report on Ethnic Studies*. New York: Ford Foundation, 1978.

Bederman, Gail. *Manliness and Civilization: A Cultural History of Gender and Race in the United States, 1880–1917*. Chicago: University of Chicago Press, 1995.

Biondi, Martha. *The Black Revolution on Campus*. Berkeley: University of California Press, 2012.

———. *To Stand and Fight: The Struggle for Civil Rights in Postwar New York City*. Cambridge: Harvard University Press, 2003.

Blassingame, John. *Slave Community: Plantation Life in the Antebellum South*. New York: Oxford University Press, 1972.

Blight, David. *Race and Reunion: The Civil War in American Memory*. Cambridge: Belknap Press of Harvard University Press, 2001.

Bogle, Donald. *Prime Time Blues: African Americans on Network Television*. New York: Farrar, Straus and Giroux, 2001.

Brooks, Daphne. *Bodies in Dissent: Spectacular Performances of Race and Freedom, 1850–1910*. Durham: Duke University Press, 2006.

Brown, Sterling A., and Arthur P. Davis, eds. *Cavalcade: Negro American Writers from 1760 to the Present*. Boston: Houghton Mifflin, 1971.

———. *The Negro Caravan: Writings by American Negroes*. New York: Dryden Press, 1941.

Brown, William Wells. *Narrative of William W. Brown, A Fugitive Slave, Written by Himself*. Boston: Anti-Slavery Office, 1848.

Brown-Nagin, Tomiko. *Courage to Dissent: Atlanta and the Long History of the Civil Rights Movement*. New York: Oxford University Press, 2011.

Brundage, W. Fitzhugh, ed. *Beyond Blackface: African Americans and the Creation of American Popular Culture, 1890–1930*. Chapel Hill: University of North Carolina Press, 2011.

———. *Where These Memories Grow: History, Memory, and Southern Identity*. Chapel Hill: University of North Carolina Press, 2000.

Buerk, John, et al., eds. *Basic Black: A Look at the Black Presence in the University Community*. Melrose, Mass.: Keating & Joyce, 1970.

Burns, Ben. *Nitty Gritty: A White Editor in Black Journalism*. Jackson: University Press of Mississippi, 1996.

Cade, Toni. *The Black Woman: An Anthology*. New York: American Library, 1970.

Campbell, James. *Middle Passages: African American Journeys to Africa, 1787–2005*. New York: Penguin, 2006.

Carby, Hazel. *Race Men*. Cambridge: Harvard University Press, 1998.

Carrier, Jim. *A Traveler's Guide to the Civil Rights Movement*. Orlando, Fla.: Harcourt Books, 2004.

Chafe, William. *Civilities and Civil Rights: Greensboro, North Carolina, and the Black Struggle for Freedom*. New York: Oxford University Press, 1980.

———. *Civil Rights and Civil Liberties*. New York: Oxford University Press, 1981.

Cheseborough, Steve. *Blues Traveling: The Holy Sites of Delta Blues*. Jackson: University Press of Mississippi, 2009.

Clark, Kenneth. *Toward Humanity and Justice: The Writings of Kenneth B. Clark, Scholar of the 1954 Brown v. Board of Education Decision*. Edited by Woody Klein. Westport, Conn.: Praeger, 2004.

Cleaver, Eldridge. *Soul on Ice*. New York: Delta, 1991.

Cobb, Charles E., Jr. *On the Road to Freedom: A Guided Tour of the Civil Rights Trail*. Chapel Hill: Algonquin Books, 2008.

Conway, Jill Ker. *When Memory Speaks: Exploring the Art of Autobiography*. New York: Vintage, 1998.

Davis, Allison, and John Dollard. *Children of Bondage: The Personality Development of Negro Youth in the Urban South*. Washington, D.C.: American Council on Education, 1940.

Davis, Allison, Burleigh B. Gardner, and Mary R. Gardner. *Deep South: A Social Anthropological Study of Caste and Class*. Chicago: University of Chicago Press, 1941.

Davis, Angela Y. *Women, Race & Class*. New York: Vintage, 1981.

Davis, Townsend. *Weary Feet, Rested Souls: A Guided History of the Civil Rights Movement*. New York: Norton, 1998.

DeFrantz, Thomas. *Dancing Revelations: Alvin Ailey's Embodiment of African American Culture*. New York: Oxford University Press, 2004.

Diawara, Manthia. *In Search of Africa*. Cambridge: Harvard University Press, 2000.

Doreski, C. K. *Writing America Black: Race Rhetoric in the Public Sphere*. New York: Cambridge University Press, 1998.

Douglass, Frederick. *Narrative of the Life of Frederick Douglass, an American Slave, Written by Himself*. New York: Bedford/St. Martins, 2002.

Drake, St. Clair, and Horace R. Cayton. *Black Metropolis: A Study of Negro Life in a Northern City*. 1945. Reprint, Chicago: University of Chicago Press, 1993.

Dunning, Jennifer. *Alvin Ailey: A Life in Dance*. New York: Da Capo Press, 1996.

Edwards, Brent. *The Practice of Diaspora: Literature, Translation, and the Rise of Black Internationalism*. Cambridge: Harvard University Press, 2003.

Eltis, David. *Atlas of the Transatlantic Slave Trade*. New Haven: Yale University Press, 2010.

Eyerman, Ron. *Cultural Trauma: Slavery and the Formation of African American Identity*. New York: Cambridge University Press, 2001.

Fabre, Geneviève, and Robert O'Meally, eds. *History & Memory in African-American Culture*. New York: Oxford University Press, 1994.

Ferguson, Jeffrey. *Sage of Sugar Hill: George S. Schuyler and the Harlem Renaissance*. New Haven: Yale University Press, 2005.

Fogel, Robert, and Stanley Engerman. *Time on the Cross: The Economics of American Negro Slavery*. Boston: Little, Brown, 1974.

Frazier, E. Franklin. *The Negro Family in Chicago*. Chicago: University of Chicago Press, 1932.

———. *The Negro Family in the United States*. Chicago: University of Chicago Press, 1939.

———. *Negro Youth at the Crossways: Their Personality Development in the Middle States*. Washington, D.C.: American Council of Education, 1940.

Gaillard, Frye. *Alabama's Civil Rights Trail: An Illustrated Guide to the Cradle of Freedom*. Tuscaloosa: University of Alabama Press, 2010.

Gaines, Kevin K. *Uplifting the Race: Black Leadership, Politics, and Culture in the Twentieth Century*. Chapel Hill: University of North Carolina Press, 1996.

Genovese, Eugene. *Roll, Jordan, Roll: The World the Slaves Made*. New York: Pantheon, 1972.

Gilmore, Glenda. *Defying Dixie: The Radical Roots of Civil Rights, 1919–1950*. New York: Norton, 2008.

Gilroy, Paul. *The Black Atlantic: Modernity and Double Consciousness*. Cambridge: Harvard University Press, 1993.

Goldfield, David. *Still Fighting the Civil War: The American South and Southern History*. Baton Rouge: Louisiana State University Press, 2002.

Goldsby, Jacqueline. *A Spectacular Secret: Lynching in American Life and Literature*. Chicago: University of Chicago Press, 2006.

Grant, Colin. *Negro with a Hat: The Rise and Fall of Marcus Garvey*. New York: Oxford University Press, 2010.

Griffin, John Howard. *Black Like Me*. 1961. Reprint, New York: New American Library, 2010.

Gutman, Herbert. *The Black Family in Slavery and Freedom, 1750–1925*. New York: Pantheon, 1976.

Hairston, Otis, Jr. *Greensboro, North Carolina—Black America Series*. Charleston: Arcadia Publishing, 2003.

Halbwachs, Maurice. *On Collective Memory*. Edited and translated by Lewis Coser. Chicago: University of Chicago Press, 1992.

Halsell, Grace. *Soul Sister*. 1969. Reprint, Washington, D.C.: Crossroads International, 1990.

Hamilton, Charles V. *Adam Clayton Powell, Jr.: A Political Biography of an American Dilemma*. New York: Atheneum, 1991.

Hamlin, Françoise N. *Crossroads at Clarksdale: The Black Freedom Struggle in the Mississippi Delta after World War II*. Chapel Hill: University of North Carolina Press, 2012.

Hare, Nathan. *The Black Anglo-Saxons*. 2nd ed. Chicago: Third World Press, 1991.

Harms, Robert. *The Diligent: A Voyage through the Worlds of the Slave Trade*. New York: Basic Books, 2003.

Harris, Abram, Jr. *The Negro as Capitalist: A Study of Banking and Business among American Negroes*. New York: Haskell House Publishers, 1970.

Harris, Abram, Jr., and Sterling Spero. *The Black Worker: The Negro and the Labor Movement*. Port Washington, N.Y.: Kennikat Press, 1931.

Harris, Eddy L. *Native Stranger: A Black American's Journey into the Heart of Africa*. New York: Simon and Schuster, 1992.

Hartman, Saidiya. *Lose Your Mother: A Journey along the Atlantic Slave Route*. New York: Farrar, Straus and Giroux, 2007.

Herskovits, Melville. *The Myth of the Negro Past*. 1941. Reprint, Boston: Beacon, 1990.

Higginbotham, Evelyn Brooks. *Righteous Discontent*. Cambridge: Harvard University Press, 1993.

Hill, Robert, and R. Kent Rasmussen, eds. *Black Empire*. Boston: Northeastern University Press, 1991.

Holloway, Jonathan Scott. *Confronting the Veil: Abram Harris Jr., E. Franklin Frazier, and Ralph Bunche, 1919–1941*. Chapel Hill: University of North Carolina Press, 2002.

Holloway, Jonathan Scott, and Ben Keppel, eds. *Black Scholars on the Line: Race, Social Science, and American Thought in the Twentieth Century*. Notre Dame: University of Notre Dame Press, 2007.

Holsey, Bayo. *Routes of Remembrance: Refashioning the Slave Trade in Ghana*. Chicago: University of Chicago Press, 2008.

hooks, bell. *Talking Back: Thinking Feminist, Thinking Black*. Boston: South End Press, 1989.

Howlett, Peter, and Mary S. Morgan, eds. *How Well Do Facts Travel? The Dissemination of Reliable Knowledge*. New York: Cambridge University Press, 2011.

Huggins, Nathan. *Afro-American Studies: A Report to the Ford Foundation*. New York: Ford Foundation, 1985.

Hull, Gloria, Patricia Bell Scott, and Barbara Smith, eds. *All the Women Are White, All the Blacks Are Men, but Some of Us Are Brave: Black Women's Studies*. Old Westbury, N.Y.: Feminist Press, 1982.

Hunter, Tera. *To 'Joy My Freedom: Southern Black Women's Lives and Labor after the Civil War*. Cambridge: Harvard University Press, 1997.

Inscoe, John C. *Writing the South through the Self: Explorations in Southern Autobiography*. Athens: University of Georgia Press, 2011.

Jackson, Walter A. *Gunnar Myrdal and America's Conscience: Social Engineering and Racial Liberalism, 1938–1987*. Chapel Hill: University of North Carolina Press, 1990.

Jacobs, Harriet. *Incidents in the Life of a Slave Girl, Written by Herself*. New York: Simon and Brown, 2012.

Jacobson, Matthew. *Roots, Too: White Ethnic Revival in Post–Civil Rights America*. Cambridge: Harvard University Press, 2006.

———. *Whiteness of a Different Color: European Immigrants and the Alchemy of Race*. Cambridge: Harvard University Press, 1999.

Janken, Kenneth Robert. *Rayford W. Logan and the Dilemma of the African-American Intellectual*. Amherst: University of Massachusetts Press, 1993.

Johnson, Charles S. *Growing Up in the Black Belt: Negro Youth in the Rural South.* Washington, D.C.: American Council on Education, 1941.

———. *Patterns of Negro Segregation.* New York: Harper & Brothers, 1943.

———. *Shadow of the Plantation.* Chicago: University of Chicago Press, 1934.

Johnson, Charles S., Edwin R. Embree, and W. W. Alexander. *The Collapse of Cotton Tenancy: Summary of Field Studies and Statistical Surveys, 1933–1935.* Chapel Hill: University of North Carolina Press, 1935.

Johnson, John. *Succeeding against the Odds: The Autobiography of a Great American Businessman.* Chicago: Johnson Publishing, 1989.

Jones, LeRoi. *Blues People.* New York: Morrow, 1963.

Karagueuzian, Dikran. *Blow It Up! The Black Student Revolt at San Francisco State College and the Emergence of Dr. Hayakawa.* Boston: Gambit, 1971.

Kennedy, Stetson. *Jim Crow Guide: The Way It Was.* Boca Raton: University Press of Florida, 1990.

Kersten, Andrew. *A. Philip Randolph: A Life in the Vanguard.* New York: Rowman and Littlefield, 2006.

Klotman, Phyllis R., and Janet K. Cutler, eds. *Struggles for Representation: African American Documentary Film and Video.* Bloomington: Indiana University Press, 1999.

Kuklick, Bruce. *Black Philosopher, White Academy: The Career of William Fontaine.* Philadelphia: University of Pennsylvania Press, 2008.

LaCapra, Dominick. *Writing History, Writing Trauma.* Baltimore: Johns Hopkins University Press, 2001.

Ladner, Joyce, ed. *The Death of White Sociology: Essays on Race and Culture.* Baltimore: Black Classic Press, 1973.

Leak, Jeffrey B., ed. *Rac(e)ing to the Right: Selected Essays of George S. Schuyler.* Knoxville: University of Tennessee Press, 2001.

Lefever, Henry G., and Michael C. Page. *Sacred Places: A Guide to the Civil Rights Sites in Atlanta, Georgia.* Macon, Ga.: Mercer University Press, 2008.

Lerner, Gerda. *Black Women in White America: A Documentary History.* New York: Pantheon, 1972.

Levine, Lawrence W. *Black Culture and Black Consciousness: Afro-American Folk Thought from Slavery to Freedom.* New York: Oxford University Press, 1977.

Lewis, David Levering. *W. E. B. Du Bois, 1868–1918: Biography of a Race.* New York: Henry Holt, 1994.

———. *W. E. B. Du Bois, 1919–1963: The Fight for Equality and the American Century.* New York: Henry Holt, 2000.

Linenthal, Edward T. *Preserving Memory: The Struggle to Create America's Holocaust Museum.* New York: Columbia University Press, 2001.

Linn, Ruth. *Escaping Auschwitz: A Culture of Forgetting.* Ithaca: Cornell University Press, 2004.

Litwack, Leon. *Been in the Storm So Long: The Aftermath of Slavery.* New York: Random House, 1979.

Logan, Rayford W., ed. *What the Negro Wants.* Chapel Hill: University of North Carolina Press, 1944.

Mabry, Marcus. *White Bucks and Black-Eyed Peas.* New York: Scribner, 1967.

MacDonald, J. Fred. *Blacks and White TV: Afro-Americans in Television since 1948.* Chicago: Nelson-Hall Publishers, 1983.

Margalit, Gilad. *Guilt, Suffering, and Memory: Germany Remembers Its Dead of World War II.* Bloomington: Indiana University Press, 2010.

McKay, Claude, and William J. Maxwell. *Complete Poems.* Urbana: University of Illinois Press, 2008.

Morrison, Toni. *Beloved.* New York: Plume, 1988.

Miller, Eben. *Born along the Color Line: The 1933 Amenia Conference and the Rise of a National Civil Rights Movement.* New York: Oxford University Press, 2012.

Miller, Karl Hagstrom. *Segregating Sound: Inventing Folk and Pop Music in the Age of Jim Crow.* Durham: Duke University Press, 2010.

Moraga, Cherrie, and Gloria Anzaldua, eds. *This Bridge Called My Back: Writings by Radical Women of Color.* New York: Kitchen Table, Women of Color Press, 1983.

Murray, Florence, ed. *The Negro Handbook, 1944.* New York, 1944.

Myrdal, Gunnar. *An American Dilemma: The Negro Problem and Modern Democracy.* 1944. Reprint, Twentieth Anniversary Edition, New York: Harper & Row, 1962.

Novick, Peter. *The Holocaust in American Life.* Boston: Houghton Mifflin, 1999.

Ouellette, Laurie. *Viewers Like You? How Public TV Failed the People.* New York: Columbia University Press, 2002.

Park, Robert, and Ernest Burgess. *Introduction to the Science of Sociology.* Chicago: University of Chicago Press, 1924.

Pfeffer, Paula. *A. Philip Randolph: Pioneer of the Civil Rights Movement.* Baton Rouge: Louisiana State University Press, 1996.

Phillips, Caryl. *Atlantic Sound.* London: Faber and Faber, 2000.

Plunkett-Powell, Karen. *Remembering Woolworth's: A Nostalgic History of the World's Most Famous Five and Dime.* New York: St. Martin's Press, 2011.

Popkin, Jeremy. *History, Historians, & Autobiography.* Chicago: University of Chicago Press, 2005.

Porter, Eric. *The Problem of the Future World: W. E. B. Du Bois and the Race Concept at Midcentury.* Durham: Duke University Press, 2010.

Porter, Horace A. *The Making of a Black Scholar: From Georgia to the Ivy League.* Iowa City: University of Iowa Press, 2003.

Raiford, Leigh. *Imprisoned in a Luminous Glare: Photography and the African American Freedom Struggle.* Chapel Hill: University of North Carolina Press, 2011.

Redding, J. Saunders. *No Day of Triumph.* New York: Harper & Brothers, 1942.

———. *On Being Negro in America.* New York: Bobbs-Merrill, 1951.

———. *To Make a Poet Black.* Chapel Hill: University of North Carolina Press, 1939.

Rediker, Marcus. *The Slave Ship: A Human History.* New York: Viking, 2007.

Rice, Alan. *Creating Memorials, Building Identities: The Politics of Memory in the Black Atlantic.* Liverpool: Liverpool University Press, 2010.

Ritterhouse, Jennifer. *Growing Up Jim Crow: How Black and White Southern Children Learned Race.* Chapel Hill: University of North Carolina Press, 2006.

Robinson, Cedric J. *Forgeries of Memory and Meaning: Blacks and the Regimes of Race in American Theater and Film before World War II*. Chapel Hill: University of North Carolina Press, 2007.

Robinson, Jo Ann Gibson. *The Montgomery Bus Boycott and the Women Who Started It: The Memoir of Jo Ann Gibson Robinson*. Knoxville: University of Tennessee Press, 1987.

Rojas, Fabio. *From Black Power to Black Studies: How a Radical Social Movement Became an Academic Discipline*. Baltimore: Johns Hopkins University Press, 2007.

Romano, Renee, and Leigh Raiford, eds. *The Civil Rights Movement in American Memory*. Athens: University of Georgia Press, 2006.

St. Clair, William. *The Door of No Return: The History of Cape Coast Castle and the Atlantic Slave Trade*. New York: BlueBridge, 2007.

Schlosser, Jim. *Remembering Greensboro*. Charleston: History Press, 2009.

Schuyler, George S. *Black and Conservative: The Autobiography of George S. Schuyler*. New Rochelle, N.Y.: Arlington House, 1966.

———. *Black No More; being an account of the strange and wonderful workings of science in the land of the free*, A.D. *1933–1940*. New York: Macauley, 1931.

Singh, Nikhil. *Black Is a Country: Race and the Unfinished Struggle for Democracy*. Cambridge: Harvard University Press, 2005.

Smallwood, Stephanie. *Saltwater Slavery: A Middle Passage from Africa to American Diaspora*. Cambridge: Harvard University Press, 2008.

Sprigle, Ray. *In the Land of Jim Crow*. New York: Simon and Schuster, 1949.

Thompson, Daniel C. *A Black Elite: A Profile of Graduates of UNCF Colleges*. New York: Greenwood Press, 1986.

Trouillot, Michel-Rolph. *Silencing the Past: Power and the Production of History*. New York: Beacon, 1995.

Von Eschen, Penny. *Satchmo Blows Up the World: Jazz Ambassadors Play the Cold War*. Cambridge: Harvard University Press, 2004.

Walker, Margaret. *Richard Wright, Daemonic Genius: A Portrait of the Man, a Critical Look at His Work*. New York: Warner Books, 1988.

Wallach, Jennifer Jensen. *Closer to the Truth Than Any Fact: Memoir, Memory, and Jim Crow*. Athens: University of Georgia Press, 2008.

Wallerstein, Immanuel, and Paul Starr, eds. *The University Crisis Reader*. Vol. 1, *The Liberal University under Attack*. New York: Random House, 1971.

Warren, Robert Penn. *Who Speaks for the Negro?* New York: Random House, 1965.

Williams, Patricia J. *The Alchemy of Race and Rights: Diary of a Law Professor*. Cambridge: Harvard University Press, 1991.

Wright, Richard. *Black Power: A Record of Reactions in a Land of Pathos*. 1954. Reprint, New York: HarperPerennial, 2008.

———. *Native Son*. New York: Harper & Row, 1940.

———. *12 Million Black Voices: A Folk History of the Negro in the United States*. 1941. Reprint, New York: Thunder's Mouth Press, 1988.

Young, Harvey. *Embodying Black Experience: Stillness, Critical Memory, and the Black Body*. Ann Arbor: University of Michigan Press, 2010.

Young, James E. *The Texture of Memory.* New Haven: Yale University Press, 1993.

Ziegler, Philip. *Legacy: Cecil Rhodes, the Rhodes Trust, and the Rhodes Scholarships.* New Haven: Yale University Press, 2008.

WEBSITES

"A Bench by the Road." *World: Journal of the Unitarian Universalist Association* 3, no. 1 (January/February 1989): 4–5, 37–41. http://www.uuworld.org/ideas/articles/117810.shtml.

"Bench by the Road Project." *The Official Website of the Toni Morrison Society.* http://www.tonimorrisonsociety.org/bench.html.

Brown Alumni Magazine 101, no. 2 (November–December 2000). http://www.brown.edu/Administration/Brown_Alumni_Magazine/01/11-00/features/history.html.

Greensboro Sit-Ins: Launch of a Civil Rights Movement: Timeline. http://www.sitins.com/timeline.shtml.

"Mission & Facts." *National Civil Rights Museum.* http:www.civilrightsmuseum.org/?page_id=92.

"New Collaboration between Sit-In Movement, Inc., and North Carolina Agricultural and Technical State University." Press release (June 26, 2001). http://www.ncat.edu/Sit-In_News.pdf.

"Protester Is Removed from King Motel Site." *New York Times*, July 17, 1990. http://www.nytimes.com/1990/07/17/us/protester-is-removed-from-king-motel-site.html.

"Visitor FAQs." *National Civil Rights Museum.* http://www.civilrightsmuseum.org/?page_id=484.

"Why Boycott the Civil Rights Museum." http://www.fulfillthedream.net/pages/mlk.boycott1.html.

DISSERTATIONS

Rose, Julia. "Rethinking Representations of Slave Life at Historical Plantation Museums: Towards a Commemorative Museum Pedagogy." Louisiana State University, 2006.

Shaw, Patricia. "'Negro Digest,' 'Pulse,' and 'Headlines and Pictures': African American Periodicals as Informants, Morale Builders, and Articulators of Protest during World War II." University of Maryland, College Park, 1994.

INDEX

Note: As this work blends first- and third-person voices and family history and public history, I had to make a decision about how to cite family members and myself in the index. My family members (Holloway, Trent, and Matthews) are cited as they appear in the text. I have only cited myself in those very few instances where I refer to "Jonathan Holloway" in the third person.

African American studies. *See* Black studies

Afro-American studies. *See* Black studies

Afro-American Studies (journal), 126–28

Ailey, Alvin, 77–85, 91; references by to blood memory, 77–78. *See also* Alvin Ailey American Dance Theater

Alvin Ailey American Dance Theater, 76, 82–85, 98, 99; *Blues Suite*, 77, 78, 82; *Revelations*, 77–84, 80 (ill.), 91

American Dilemma, An (Myrdal), 22–28, 34, 233 (n. 21)

Armstrong, Louis, 157, 162

Baldwin, James, 87–89. See also *Take This Hammer*

Bell, Derrick, proponent of Critical Race Theory, 105. *See also* Stanford University: and controversy surrounding Derrick Bell

Black Journal, 85–86, 92, 99

Black Scholar, The, 126, 128, 130

Black studies, 105, 112–18, 122, 124, 125, 130, 132, 171, 241 (n. 29); questions of sexuality in, 132–33. *See also* White scholars' role in black studies; Women's role in black studies

Black World, 62

Blassingame, John, 4; and responsibility to the black community, 125

Brown University, 108–9, 111, 133, 240 (n. 10)

Cambridge, Godfrey, 92, 99–100

Cape Coast Castle, 214, 216–18, 220, 222–24, 227; Cape Coast Castle Museum Shop, 222

Carson, Clayborne, 124–25

Cayton, Horace, 33–38

Clark, Kenneth, 120–21

Colonial Williamsburg, 194, 213; struggles of with how to present the slave experience, 195–99

Cornell University, 112–13, 116

Couch, W. T., 30–32

Danforth Foundation, 133–34; Dorothy Danforth Compton Fellowship, 133–34

Davis, Allison P., 108

Davis, Arthur P., 44, 51–52

Davis, Charles T., 124

Davis, David Brion, 116. *See also* White scholars' role in black studies

Davis, Frank Marshall, 48–50

Dodson, Howard, 132

Door of Return, 222

Doors of No Return, 217, 221–22, 227, 247 (n. 1)

Drake, St. Claire, 33–37, 94–96

Du Bois, W. E. B., 2, 226; double-consciousness and, 60, 153; the racial veil and, 73, 157; and roots of black studies, 118. *See also* W. E. B. Du Bois Centre for Pan-African Studies

Ebony, 43, 63–65
Ellison, Ralph, 8, 11, 233 (n. 21)
Elmina Castle, 214, 216–18, 220–22, 227

First World Festival of Negro Arts, 85, 89–91
Fleming, G. James, 44
Ford Foundation, 85–86, 112, 115, 133, 241 (n. 29); Ford Foundation Minority Predoctoral Fellowship, 133
Franklin, John Hope, 107, 111
Frazier, E. Franklin, 17, 22, 32, 38

Genovese, Eugene, 117, 128. *See also* White scholars' role in black studies
Ghana: as a destination, 214–15; and changing sensibilities about tourism, 218–21, 226, 228, 229; Assin Manso, 221, 224; Joseph Project, 249 (n. 19). *See also* Cape Coast Castle; Door of Return; Doors of No Return; Elmina Castle; W. E. B. Du Bois Memorial Centre for Pan-African Culture
Gillespie, Dizzy: at Daughters of American Revolution Constitution Hall, 11–13; as cultural ambassador for State Department, 84
Greaves, William, 86–87, 89–95, 97–98; working for National Education Television, 93–94. See also *First World Festival of Negro Arts; Black Journal; Still a Brother: Inside the Black Middle Class*
Greensboro, N.C., 187–93; Woolworth's in, 187–90; Greensboro Truth and Reconciliation Commission, 192–93. *See also* International Civil Rights Center
Griffin, John Howard, 70–72, 74, 75

Haley, Alex, 174–76, 178
Halsell, Grace, 72–76
Harding, Vincent, and black scholars' obligations, 118–19
Hare, Nathan, 128, 131, 235 (n. 4); fired from Howard University, 114; and racial authority of black scholars, 116–18; coeditor of *Black Scholar*, 126
Harris, Eddy L., and tortured curiosity about Africa, 215–16
Hartman, Saidiya, 215
Holloway, Brian (my brother), 14–15, 67–69, 99, 148, 153, 159 (ill.), 161; pursuing family history, 14–15; e-mailing family history, 140–43
Holloway, Fannie (my paternal grandmother), 167 (ill.)
Holloway, John (my paternal grandfather), 166–68, 167 (ill.)
Holloway, Jonathan, 8, 195 (ill.); proximity of to civil rights movement, 141
Holloway, Karen (my sister), 141, 143, 159
Holloway, Kay (my mother), 28, 29 (ill.), 38, 83, 140, 144 (ill.), 156, 159, 196; social privilege and, 171, 173
Holloway, Wendell (my father), 27–29, 29 (ill.), 38–39, 83, 141, 143, 147 (ill.), 153, 159, 163–66, 169, 170–72, 176–77; and lessons about fighting, 6–7; avoiding family history, 136; career of in United States Air Force, 145–48
hooks, bell, 123, 131
Huggins, Nathan, 113, 116–17
Hughes, Langston, 30, 44; at First World Festival of Negro Arts, 90–91
Hull, Gloria, 129–31
Hurston, Zora Neale, 52–53, 55

Institute of the Black Word, 118, 132
International Civil Rights Center, 187, 190, 193, 213; Hall of Shame, 190–91, 193

International Slavery Museum, 218; Middle Passage Immersion, 218–19, 248 (n. 11)

Jet, 43, 63–66
Johnson, Charles S., 17–19, 22, 38
Johnson, Christopher, 137–38, 140, 149
Johnson, Guy, 30–31, 33, 58–59
Journal of Afro-American Issues, 126, 128
Journal of Black Studies, 126–28

Kennedy Center for the Performing Arts, 76, 82, 239 (n. 23). *See also* Alvin Ailey American Dance Theater
Kennedy, Stetson, 179–81, 183
Kerner Commission, 85–86, 239 (n. 26)
King, Martin Luther, Jr., 92, 180, 183, 185–87, 215; legacy of, 187. *See also* Lorraine Hotel; National Civil Rights Museum
Kinte, Kunta, 176
KQED, 87–88, 239 (n. 34)

Ladner, Joyce, 129, 130–31
Logan, Rayford, 48, 59; *What the Negro Wants* controversy, 30–32. *See also* Couch, W. T.; Johnson, Guy
Lorraine Hotel, 184–86, 188
Louisiana African American Heritage Trail, 200, 202, 209; "A Story Like No Other" (website and smartphone app), 200–201, 211; Oak Alley Plantation, 203; River Road Museum, 203; Evergreen Plantation, 204, 206; Cane River Creole National Historical Park, 206, 208; Magnolia Plantation, 206–8; Magnolia Mound Plantation, 208–9; New Orleans African American Museum, 210; St. Augustine Church and the Tomb of the Unknown Slave, 210–11, 211 (ill.)
Luster, Orville, 88–89. See also *Take This Hammer*

Matthews, Aunt Maggie (my grand-aunt), 14–16, 38
McBride, Dwight, 132–33
Montgomery Academy, 140; and determination to integrate, 145
Montgomery, Ala., 150, 168, 200, 243 (n. 4), 245 (n. 30); Air War College and Maxwell-Gunther Air Force Base, 137, 145, 149; my childhood in, 137–38, 139 (ill.), 140, 144 (ill.), 145; family reunion in, 158, 160–62
Morrison, Toni, 211–13
Mulzac, Hugh, 46–47, 57, 235–36 (nn. 9, 10)
Museum of Contemporary African Diasporic Art, 225, 227–29; "A Journey Home," 225
Museums. *See* Cape Coast Castle; Colonial Williamsburg; Elmina Castle; International Civil Rights Center; International Slavery Museum; Louisiana African American Heritage Trail; Museum of Contemporary African Diasporic Art; National Civil Rights Museum; Oxford University Museums
Myrdal, Gunnar, 22–28, 32, 38, 57. See also *American Dilemma, An*

National Association for the Advancement of Colored People, 2, 36, 44, 74, 108, 197
National Civil Rights Museum, 184–87, 213. *See also* King, Martin Luther, Jr.; Smith, Jacqueline
Negro Digest, 43, 47, 48, 51, 53, 62–65, 70, 234 (n. 2); "My Most Humiliating Jim Crow Experience," 42–43, 47, 58–59, 61–63; John Johnson at, 43, 57, 62, 234 (n. 2); final years of and as precursor to *Ebony* and *Jet*, 55–58; "If I Were a Negro," 57–59, 63, 70, 236–37 (nn. 34, 43). *See also* Davis, Arthur P.; Davis, Frank Marshall; Fleming, G. James; Hurston, Zora

Neale; Mulzac, Hugh; Powell, Adam
  Clayton, Jr.; Redding, J. Saunders;
  Schuyler, George; White, Walter
Negro Motorist Green Book, 70–71
Northwestern University, 121

Oxford University, 218; Rhodes House,
  218–19. *See also* Oxford University
  Museums
Oxford University Museums: Ashmolean
  Museum, 219; Bodleian Library
  ("Treasures of the Bodleian"), 219;
  Pitt Rivers Museum of Anthropology,
  219

Peebles, Melvin Van, 68–69, 99, 101, 240
  (n. 54). See also *Sweet Sweetback's
  Baadasssss Song*; *Watermelon Man*
Porter, Horace, 124–25
Powell, Adam Clayton, Jr., 44, 53–55
Pryor, Jonathan, 160, 162

Randolph, A. Philip, 2–3, 13, 16
Redding, J. Saunders, 55–56, 107–12
Robinson, Armstead, 122–23
Roots: The Next Generation (television
  miniseries), 176
Roots: The Saga of an American Family
  (novel), 174, 214
Roots: The Saga of an American Family
  (television miniseries), 175–76, 178
Rosenwald Fund, decision of to finance
  positions for black scholars, 108, 115.
  See also Davis, Allison P.

San Francisco State University, 113–14
Schomburg Center for Research in Black
  Culture, 132, 243 (n. 70)
Schuyler, George, 43–46
Scott, Patricia Bell, 129–31
Shaft, 67–69
Slave cabins, 204–5 (ill.)
Slave castles. *See* Cape Coast Castle;
  Door of Return; Doors of No Return;
  Elmina Castle

Smith, Jacqueline, 185–87. *See also* Lor-
  raine Hotel; National Civil Rights
  Museum
Sprigle, Ray, 74–75, 135
Stanford University, 42, 124, 164, 168–
  69, 172; and controversy surrounding
  Derrick Bell, 105–6; representational
  politics at, 152,
Stepto, Robert, 124
*Still a Brother: Inside the Black Middle
  Class*, 85, 87, 93–94
Sullivan, Henry Stack, 20–21
Sweet Sweetback's Baadasssss Song,
  68–69, 240 (n. 54)

Take This Hammer, 85, 87, 89. *See also*
  Baldwin, James; Luster, Orville
Till, Emmett, 66
Travelguide, 70–71
Trent, Viola (my maternal grandmother),
  154–57, 155 (ill.), 189
Trent, William J., Jr. (my grandfather),
  65 (ill.), 134, 141, 154–56, 237
  (n. 55)
Trouillot, Michel-Rolph, 10, 232 (n. 18)

United Nations Educational, Scien-
  tific, and Cultural Organization
  (UNESCO), 220–21, 248 (n. 10)
United Negro College Fund, 134, 141,
  156, 234 (n. 4), 237 (n. 55)
United States Air Force, 141, 146
United States Information Agency, 86,
  89–90
United States State Department, 84–85
University of California, San Diego, 102,
  104, 169–71

W. E. B. Du Bois Centre for Pan-African
  Studies, 225–27
Watermelon Man, 99–100 (ill.), 240
  (n. 54)
White, Walter, 2, 44, 74
White House Fellows Program, 169–70,
  172

White scholars' role in black studies, 119–20

Williams, Patricia J., 106, 131

Women's role in black studies, 129–31

Wright, Richard, 1–2, 21–22, 26, 37; *Native Son*, 1–2, 13; "How Bigger Was Born," 2, 15, 17; "Ethics of Living Jim Crow," 5; fighting and gems of Jim Crow wisdom, 5–8; disdain of for middle-class sensibilities, 15–18; *12 Million Black Voices*, 17, 21, 109; admiration of for *Black Metropolis*, 33–34; criticized by J. Saunders Redding, 109–10; travel to Gold Coast (Ghana), 228–29

Yale University, 42, 168–69; Black Student Alliance at Yale, 115, 122–23; debates about black studies, 115–16; *Yale Alumni Magazine* interviews, 122–24; transactional value of, 171–73

Made in the USA
Monee, IL
07 December 2019

18137321R00169